The Economics of a Disaster

THE ECONOMICS OF A DISASTER

The *Exxon Valdez* Oil Spill

Bruce M. Owen, David A. Argue,
Harold W. Furchtgott-Roth,
Gloria J. Hurdle, and Gale Mosteller

Q

QUORUM BOOKS
Westport, Connecticut • London

Library of Congress Cataloging-in-Publication Data

The economics of a disaster : the Exxon Valdez oil spill / Bruce M.
  Owen . . . [et al.].
     p. cm.
  Includes bibliographical references and index.
  ISBN 0–89930–987–9
    1. Water—Pollution—Economic aspects—Alaska—Prince William
Sound. 2. Oil spills—Economic aspects—Alaska—Prince William
Sound. 3. Tankers—Accidents. 4. Exxon Valdez (Ship). I. Owen,
Bruce M.
  HC107.A43W324   1995
  338.3—dc20   95–3782

British Library Cataloguing in Publication Data is available.

Library of Congress Catalog Card Number: 95–3782
ISBN: 0–89930–987–9

First published in 1995

Quorum Books, 88 Post Road West, Westport, CT 06881
An imprint of Greenwood Publishing Group, Inc.

Printed in the United States of America

The paper used in this book complies with the
Permanent Paper Standard issued by the National
Information Standards Organization (Z39.48–1984).

10 9 8 7 6 5 4 3 2 1

Contents

Figures and Tables   *ix*

Acknowledgments   *xiii*

Introduction   1

1. The Effect of Disasters on Prices of Goods and Services: An
   Economic Framework   7

2. Measuring the Effect of the *Exxon Valdez* Oil Spill on Alaskan
   Seafood Prices   19

3. Industry Background   29

4. Qualitative Evidence Concerning Price Effects   65

5. Japanese Consumer Demand   85

6. Salmon Benchmark Studies   91

7. Salmon Reduced Form Study   101

8. Salmon Processor Prices   111

9. Non-Salmon Species Studies   125

10. Supply Effects   145

11. Fishing Permit Values   153

12. Summary of Results   163

13. Conclusion   181

Appendix 1. A Brief Description of Statistical Terminology   183

Appendix 2. Modeling Japanese Consumer Demand   187

Appendix 3. Reduced Form Model for Alaskan Salmon   191

Appendix 4. Supply Effects   193

Selected Bibliography   195

Index   197

Figures and Tables

FIGURES

Figure 1.1   Decline in Demand   9

Figure 1.2   Price Increase as a Result of Producer Response   10

Figure 1.3   Price Decrease as a Result of Producer Response   11

Figure 1.4   Reduction in Supply   13

Figure 1.5   Decreased Stock of Housing   14

Figure 2.1   Difficulty in Identifying Shift in Demand   21

Figure 2.2   Possible Effect of Perceived Contamination of Alaskan Seafood   24

Figure 3.1   Alaska Salmon and Herring Fisheries   31

Figure 3.2   Salmon Landings by Species and Region, Annual Average 1980–1989   32

Figure 3.3   Alaska Share of World Harvest, 1989   33

Figure 3.4   World Salmon Catch: Farmed and Wild, 1985–1989   42

Figure 3.5   Largest World Producers of Farmed Salmon, 1985–1991   45

Figure 3.6   Consumption of Fresh and Frozen Salmon, 1988   49

Figure 9.1   Roe Herring Prices at 10 Percent Roe Content:
              Ratio of Kodiak to Prince William Sound   131

TABLES

Table 3.1   Summary Information: Salmon   36

Table 3.2   Summary Information: Non-Salmon Species   37

Table 3.3   Salmon Catch by Species and Country, 1985–1990   39

Table 3.4   Alaska Salmon Production by Product and Species,
             1980–1989   40

Table 3.5   Norwegian Salmon Exports for 1989   44

Table 3.6   U.S. Exports of Salmon to Japan as a Percentage
             of U.S. Salmon Exports to All Countries, by
             Species, 1987–1990   48

Table 4.1   ASMI Survey Results   69

Table 4.2   U.S. Retail Labeling of Canned Alaskan Salmon   74

Table 5.1   Salmon Purchases by Japanese Households,
             1988 and 1989   87

Table 6.1   British Columbia Benchmark Model, 1989 Price
             Effects for Salmon   95

Table 6.2   Bristol Bay Benchmark Model, 1989 Price Effects
             in Oil-Touched Regions   97

Table 7.1   Pooled Species Model, 1989 Price Effects
             (1978–1990 Data)   106

Table 7.2   Individual Species Model, 1989 Price Effects
             (1978–1990 Data)   107

Table 8.1   Alaska Statewide Nominal Margin: Data from
             The Alaska Seafood Industry   112

Table 8.2   Alaska Statewide Nominal Margin: CFEC Data   113

Table 8.3   Alaska Statewide Real Margin: CFEC Data   114

Table 8.4   1989 Processor Price Effects by Species   116

Table 8.5   1989 Processor Price Effects by Region   117

Table 8.6   1989 Processor Price Effects for Fresh and Frozen
             Salmon: British Columbia Benchmark Model   118

Table 8.7   1989 Processor Price Effects for Canned Salmon:
             British Columbia Benchmark Model   119

Table 9.1   1989 Ex-Vessel Prices for Non-Salmon Species in
             Fisheries Open for at Least Part of the 1989 Season   128

Table 9.2   1989 Price Effects for Sac Roe Herring in Oil-
             Touched Areas: Benchmark Model   130

Table 9.3   Roe Herring Prices at 10 Percent Roe Content:
             Ratio of Kodiak to Prince William Sound   132

Table 9.4   1989 Price Effects for Halibut: Benchmark Model   134

Table 9.5   Regression Analysis Results from Halibut Demand
             Model   136

Table 9.6   1989 Price Effects for Sablefish: Benchmark
             Model   137

Table 9.7   1989 Processor Price Effects for Frozen Roe
             Herring   139

Table 10.1   Regional Salmon Fisheries for which 1989 Price
             Data Are Missing from Official State of Alaska
             Publications   146

Table 10.2   Estimated 1989 Ex-Vessel Prices for Salmon
             Fisheries for which Data Are Missing from
             Official State of Alaska Publications   147

Table 10.3   Estimated 1989 Ex-Vessel Prices for Non-Salmon
                Fisheries Closed for the 1989 Season   149

Table 10.4   Price Effects from Forgone Salmon Harvests in
                Regions Touched by the Oil Spill   150

Table 11.1   Average Prices for Fishing Permits: Salmon,
                Herring, and Herring Roe, 1988–1991   156

Table 11.2   Total Values for Fishing Permits: Salmon,
                Herring, and Herring Roe, 1988–1990   158

Table 12.1   Statistical Evidence Consistent with Significantly
                Lower 1989 Alaskan Seafood Prices   165

Table 12.2   Economic Evidence Consistent with 1989 Price
                Suppression from Oil Spill   166

Table 12.3   Statistical Evidence Consistent with Significantly
                Higher 1989 Alaskan Seafood Prices   168

Table 12.4   Economic Evidence Consistent with 1989 Price
                Elevation from Oil Spill   170

Table 12.5   Statistical Evidence Consistent with the Absence
                of a 1989 Effect on Alaskan Seafood Prices   172

Table 12.6   Economic Evidence Consistent with the Absence
                of 1989 Price Effects from Oil Spill   177

Table 12.7   Average Ex-Vessel Prices for Alaskan Seafood
                in 1989   178

Table 12.8   Processor Prices for Salmon in 1989 in Regions
                Touched by the Oil Spill   180

Table A4.1   Forgone Salmon Catch, 1989   194

Acknowledgments

This book is based on research conducted by Economists Incorporated on behalf of the Trans-Alaska Pipeline Liability Fund. The research was reported in "An Economic Analysis of the Effect of the *Exxon Valdez* Oil Spill on Alaskan Seafood Prices," released in 1991 by the Fund. The authors of the report include Michael G. Baumann and Jeffrey W. Smith, in addition to those listed as authors of this book. We benefited from the advice of Professor James E. Wilen of the University of California, Davis, whose model of Japanese consumer demand appears in Appendix 2 and is discussed in Chapter 5. We are grateful to the many other individuals who assisted in this research.

The Economics of a Disaster

Introduction

If the consequences of one's actions are felt only by one's self, one will take optimal precautions to avoid accidents. Economists predict that a rational person will invest in accident avoidance just enough resources so that the marginal cost of accident avoidance equals the marginal benefit of accident avoidance. This minimizes the total of the two costs: the cost of accidents plus the cost of precautions.

In the case of accidents that affect others, the individual's incentive to take precautions is not optimal, unless the liability system acts to "internalize" the costs of accidents. Various liability rules (such as strict liability, negligence, and no fault) affect people's incentives to take economically appropriate precautions. If people know that they can be held responsible for some or all of the costs or damages sustained in an accident, they will change their behavior to make the accident less likely to occur or to reduce the damages should it occur.

Some liability systems produce too much precaution; others produce too little. An excessively cautious individual may reduce the chances of an accident to zero by staying home in bed all day, but the cost in lost income would be very high. Similarly, a liability system that yields too much precaution may lead manufacturers to produce the only perfectly safe airplane—one that never leaves the ground. Conversely, if the liability system did not allow people involved in automobile accidents to sue the responsible party for damages, drivers would have less incentive to be careful. The actions people take every day indicate that individuals and society accept the riskiness of some activities. Eliminating all risks, if possible, would be overly cautious.

Any liability system that seeks to optimize the trade-off between the costs of accidents and the costs of preventing them must take into account, among other things, *all* the costs associated with accidents. If some important category of costs is ignored by the system, individuals will tend to take too little precautionary action. By the same token, if the system exaggerates the costs, there will be a tendency to take too much precaution.

The common sense observation that all costs associated with accidents should be taken into account raises the question of why the tort law liability system in the United States ignores some of the commercial losses caused by accidents that affect market prices.[1] Consider the following example. A single toll bridge provides the only link between a tomato farming community and a nearby town. Farmers produce large crops of tomatoes but can sell only a small portion to the local population. The farmers rely on shipments to the town, their only other market, for most of their sales. The town receives agricultural products from other areas, but it purchases all of its tomatoes from the farms across the bridge. As a result of an accident, the bridge is closed in the middle of harvest season. Direct damages from the accident include the damage to the bridge and the loss of the toll revenue. In addition, the price of tomatoes will be affected. Presumably, tomatoes will be in abundant supply in the farm community and prices there will go down, while tomatoes will be unavailable at any price in the town.

Generally speaking, the owner of the bridge can sue the individual responsible for the accident, claiming monetary damages equal to the value of the repairs necessary and the lost toll revenue. (We suppose the individual responsible for the accident had already taken precautions to avoid accidents appropriate under the prevailing liability rules and that the accident occurred despite these precautions.)

Several groups of individuals without a proprietary interest in the bridge are also affected by its loss. The tomato farmers, for example, suffer losses from the lower price of tomatoes caused by the accident. Nevertheless, under tort law they cannot sue to recover their damages resulting from lower prices because neither they nor their property was physically injured.[2] Likewise, the townspeople are forced to purchase substitute goods to replace the missing tomatoes. They, too, cannot sue for their loss of well-being. On the other hand, farmers in other areas who sell substitute foods in the town benefit from the loss of the tomatoes, and the farm community consumers benefit from the lower price of tomatoes there. Neither of these groups can be sued for their gains.

Limiting standing to just those directly injured in the accident may be the socially optimal policy if the losses of some individuals as a result of the accident are offset by the gains of others. Suppose the losses of the tomato farmers and the townspeople are *exactly* offset by the gains of the farmers in the other areas and the farm community consumers. (We leave aside for now the vexing problem of determining this balance.) A transfer of wealth takes place from the former group to the latter. But the net social cost is confined to the losses of the bridge owner. Because the bridge owner is the only party allowed to sue for damages, the socially optimal amount of accident avoidance is undertaken.

If the losses of the tomato farmers and the townspeople are *not* fully offset by the gains of the other farmers and the farm community consumers, then the net social cost extends beyond the damage sustained by the bridge owner. In that case, under existing tort law the investment in precaution by the party responsible for the accident would be less than optimal. He would consider only the losses to the bridge owner, not the additional social loss. If all affected persons were allowed to seek restitution of both losses incurred and gains bestowed (ignoring transaction costs and the obvious measurement difficulties), the resulting accident prevention would again be optimal.[3] In addition, the pre-existing distribution of income would be restored.

The existence of liability insurance also affects the incentives to invest in accident avoidance because the cost to the injurer equals the present value of the increase in premiums rather than the victim's loss. This does not necessarily result in a nonoptimal allocation of resources, however. To the extent that insurance companies are imperfect monitors of insureds' behavior, there will be more accidents than under a liability system alone. Yet if the victims are fully compensated, liability insurance is efficient. If government regulation and the cost of information result in groups of individuals with variable likelihood of accidents paying the same premium, some individuals may be overdeterred and others underdeterred.[4]

The tomato example may seem contrived because the town has no other source of tomatoes and the farmers have no other markets. This contrivance is necessary in order to make plausible the notion of price changes due to the accident. There would be no price changes if the town had many other sources of tomatoes and the farmers could freely ship tomatoes to many different markets. Most accidents do not cause significant price changes because they do not affect the trade of large enough quantities of goods or resources in the market. Accidents that can cause broad price changes are rare, and they are often called "disasters."

While it may not be sensible to attempt to measure the price effects of small accidents, disasters are a different story. The resources required to measure the price effects of disasters may be relatively small compared with the potential consequences being measured. Taking account of all the costs of disasters is an important objective of any system in which decentralized decision-makers take actions that can lead to great disasters.

Of course, reaching this objective requires a determination of the magnitude of costs, including price effects. Individuals are held liable for the damages measured by the liability system, but these damages are not necessarily the same as the damages actually incurred. If the damages of a disaster are overestimated or underestimated, nonoptimal investment in accident avoidance will result. As important as it is to account for price changes, it is nonetheless difficult to measure them. This is examined at great length in the chapters that follow.

There is one important exception to the rule that only individuals who suffer personal or property injury can recover damages under tort law. The exception involves fishermen. Fishermen can recover damages resulting from accident-induced price changes regardless of whether they or their property suffered any physical harm.[5] There are two rationales for allowing fishermen to recover damages. One is that property rights are not established for the fish; thus the fishermen are chosen as surrogate plaintiffs.[6] The other is that the fishermen are claimaints in their own right rather than surrogates.[7] Under either theory, the courts give them a legal avenue for seeking redress.

While the fishermen are allowed to sue for damages resulting from price changes, the party responsible for the accident is not allowed a claim on the gains made by others (e.g., fishermen from other areas) as a result of the accident. This has implications for investment in actions to prevent accidents. The net social cost may be less than the full change in price, but the responsible party may be forced to compensate fishermen for it anyway. As a result, the responsible party may choose to invest more in accident avoidance than is socially optimal.

One might argue, however, that overavoidance by potentially responsible parties may be necessary to offset the insufficient accident prevention taken by the fishermen. The fishermen tend to underprotect the fish supply because it is a commonly owned resource. Each fisherman has an incentive to let other fishermen take precautions (e.g., lobbying government for tight restrictions on oil tanker traffic) because he would benefit from their actions without having to make any expenditures of his own.

Many interesting economic issues that pertain to disasters are associated with the liability system. For example, the method by which natural resource damages are evaluated is hotly debated. This book, however, is concerned only with the following question: How does one actually measure the price effects of great disasters? The answer to this question raises an important larger question: In all disasters, not just maritime ones, should liability be extended beyond physical injury to cover individuals whose only losses are due to price changes?

The *Exxon Valdez* oil spill is the case that prompted this study. On March 24, 1989, the oil tanker *Exxon Valdez* hit a reef and spilled more than 11 million gallons of oil into Prince William Sound, a major fishing area in Alaska for salmon, shrimp, roe herring, herring roe on kelp, and other seafood. Because some Alaskan fisheries were closed for various periods, the oil spill came within the "fisherman" exception to the physical impact rule. Alaskan fishermen alleged they were damaged by the oil spill, claiming that they could not catch as much seafood as they would otherwise have caught and that seafood prices were suppressed by the disaster.

In the trial that followed the spill, a jury was asked to determine whether the oil spill reduced the harvests or caused price declines for herring and salmon in various locations in Alaska from 1989 to 1995.[8] The fishermen had asked for $895 million, including $550 million for depressed salmon prices in the years following the spill based on the argument that the market's fear of tainted salmon drove prices down.[9] Exxon had offered $113 million in addition to the $130 million it had already paid to fishermen.[10] Exxon argued that record salmon harvests, an increase in the availability of farmed salmon, and high inventories in Japan had led to low prices.[11] The jury awarded the fishermen $287 million, including $130 million for reduced salmon and herring prices in 1989, but did not find price declines in 1990 and 1991.[12] The jury had difficulty making sense out of the widely divergent damage estimates by Exxon and the fishermen.[13] Consequently, they reviewed Alaska Department of Fish and Game records and developed their own mathematical formula for computing damages.[14]

Although our study is focused narrowly on the question whether and to what extent the price of seafood was affected by the *Exxon Valdez* oil spill, it has wider relevance. Our methods are applicable to evaluating the price effects of other disasters. In addition, the difficulties we encounter provide some insight into the wisdom of broadening the exception to the physical injury rule to include price changes from disasters affecting goods other than seafood.

NOTES

1. *See* Robins Dry Dock & Repair Co. v. Flint, 275 U.S. 303 (1927).
2. Restatement (Second) of Torts, Section 766c.
3. R. POSNER, ECONOMIC ANALYSIS OF LAW 169 (3d ed. 1986) for a discussion of these issues.
4. *See Id.* at 186-191 and Shavell, *On Liability and Insurance*, 13 BELL J. ECON. 120-122 (1982) for a discussion of these issues.
5. Carbone v. Ursich, The Del Rio, 209 F. 2d 178 (9th Cir. 1953) and Union Oil Co. v. Oppen, 501 F. 2d 558 (9th Cir. 1974). *See also*, State of La. Ex. Rel. Guste v. M/V Testbank, 752 F. 2d 1019 (1985). See Goldberg, *Recovery for Economic Loss Following the* Exxon Valdez *Oil Spill*, 23 J. LEGAL STUD. 1, 8–14 (Jan. 1994) for a discussion of these issues.
6. W. LANDES & R. POSNER, THE ECONOMIC STRUCTURE OF TORT LAW 253 (1987).
7. *See Oppen, supra* note 5.
8. In re the *Exxon Valdez*, Special Verdict for Phase II-A of Trial, U.S. District Court for the District of Alaska, No. A89-0095-CV (HRH) (Consolidated). The verdict form asked about price declines in 1989, 1990, and 1991. The jury also determined whether the value of fishing permits had declined and, if so, how much.
9. Phillips, *Damage: $287 Million, Fishermen Unhappy; Exxon Says It's Pleased*, Anchorage Daily News, Aug. 12, 1994 [hereinafter Fishermen Unhappy] at A1.
10. Phillips, *Exxon Spill Payment Sets Record $287 Million State's Largest*, Anchorage Daily News, Aug. 13, 1994, at B1.
11. Pagano, *Judge Decides Jury Will Make Decisions on Spill Damages*, Anchorage Daily News, July 9, 1994, at B2.
12. Fishermen Unhappy, *supra* note 9.
13. Phillips, *The Exxon Decision 'We Did the Right Thing' Jury Foreman Recounts Long Haul to Judgment*, Anchorage Daily News, Sept. 18, 1994, at A1.
14. *Id.*, Fishermen Unhappy, *supra* note 9.

1

The Effect of Disasters on Prices of Goods and Services: An Economic Framework

By definition, disasters are uncommon occurrences. Some of them, like natural disasters, might be considered unavoidable, while others, like industrial accidents, are probably avoidable at the price of costly precautions. Some inflict enormous suffering and loss of human life, while others cause relatively few injuries or deaths. Invariably, disasters have an economic impact. Economic losses can take many forms, such as loss of wages, property damage, and closed business operations. We denote losses associated with business operations as commercial losses. Commercial losses are frequently covered by insurance or are recoverable through legal action.

The commercial losses that arise from a disaster are determined by changes in the demand for and supply of the goods and services affected by the disaster. Changes in demand and supply may cause the price of a good or service to fall, producing commercial losses even if the quantity purchased remains the same. Similarly, changes in demand and supply may cause the quantity of the good or service to fall, resulting in commercial losses even if the price remained unaffected. This book is primarily devoted to examining the price effects of disasters, but the same forces that change price will likely change quantity demanded as well. The total loss to society of a disaster may extend well beyond commercial losses, but those aspects are not within the scope of this book.

In this chapter we build a conceptual framework for understanding how disasters affect supply and demand and, consequently, price. Several disasters are briefly described. Despite tremendous differences in each event, the underlying economic consequences (shifts in supply and demand) allow us to classify them in three simple categories: demand-side disasters, supply-side disasters, and mixed-effects disasters. Although this is a useful framework to classify and describe the price effects of disasters, it is very difficult to measure precisely the price effects of a specific disaster, as later chapters on the *Exxon Valdez* oil spill make clear.

THE ECONOMIC FRAMEWORK

Virtually all disasters affect supply or demand for some goods and services. As a result of the shifts in supply and demand, the market price for these goods and services can change. Careful analysis of supply and demand changes is needed to distinguish price changes resulting from a disaster from price changes resulting from other factors. A disaster may affect the supply and demand of products so that the price changes in one direction—either up or down. A disaster also may affect demand and supply so that price effects in both directions offset one another, and the direction of the net price change is uncertain.

The analysis of price changes from a disaster often involves a two-step process. First, one must determine whether there is a sound basis to conclude that the disaster significantly affected prices in one direction as opposed to another. Second, if price were significantly affected in one direction, one must determine the best estimate of the magnitude of the price shift. The estimated price change attributable to a disaster can then be used to determine the commercial losses caused by it.

The economic effects of disasters on prices involve two basic stages: the initial event and the responses that follow. Measuring the overall effect can be very complex, but each of the stages can be examined on a conceptual basis in relatively straightforward terms. In the first stage of a disaster, supply and/or demand for a good or service may be affected. The responses to the disaster that occur in the second stage cover a broad range of possibilities. If the disaster involved product quality, producers may cease production or try to improve quality control. Producers or other entities (such as the government) may try to influence demand through advertising or press releases. Other aspects also must be accounted for in the second stage. For example, the length of the interval over which the events occur may vary, and disasters may affect markets for several goods and services. Isolating these effects is fundamental to determining the direction of a change in price. The framework we establish allows us to consider each effect separately.

Our economic framework classifies three types of disasters: those that initially affect demand primarily, those that initially affect supply primarily, and those that initially affect demand and supply (mixed-effects disasters). A demand-side disaster usually occurs when customers believe the quality or safety of the product has declined, and they become unwilling to pay as much for the product as they did before. Supply-side disasters occur when the supply of a product is sharply reduced. Mixed-effects disasters simultaneously affect the demand and the supply of the product. Because most disasters ultimately affect both supply and demand, the classification system is used to separate the effects that happen immediately after the event from those that take place subsequently in response to the disaster. Alternatively, we can think of the classification as separating the initial effects that occur without any response to the disaster from the effects after mitigation. This classification is useful because the response to a disaster can vary a great deal, from no response at all to demand-side and supply-side responses.

DEMAND-SIDE DISASTERS

Demand-side disasters involve a decline in demand due to a decline in customers' perceptions of quality or safety of the product. As a result of the change in perceptions, customers are willing to purchase less of the good or service at any given price, shifting the demand curve inward and thereby reducing price in the first stage. (See Figure 1.1.)

When a disaster shifts demand for a particular good or service, it also generally shifts demand for substitutes or complements. For example, a decrease in demand for a product causes an increase in demand for substitutes and a decrease in demand for complements. This occurs even though the quality of the substitutes or complements is not affected.

Many of the disasters that have befallen companies due to customers' perceptions of lower quality or safety of their products have resulted in demand shifts. For example, after seven people died late in 1982 from taking Extra-Strength Tylenol capsules tainted with cyanide, Tylenol sales decreased by 25 percent within two weeks. The market share of Ford's Pintos fell 20 percent in the first month after the public began to learn about the car's rear-end collision fires. An association between toxic shock syndrome and Rely tampons reported by the Center for Disease Control four months after Rely tampons were introduced led to a significant decline in the percentage of adult women using tampons.[1]

The shift of the demand curve is caused essentially by the spread of negative information stemming from the disaster. If information about the quality or safety of a good or service is uniformly negative and is disseminated quickly, customers' responses will likely be rapid, leading to a rapid price change. If customers' awareness of the problem develops gradually because of a slow trickle of information, or if the information about quality is mixed, customers' responses will be slow, caus-

Figure 1.1
Decline in Demand

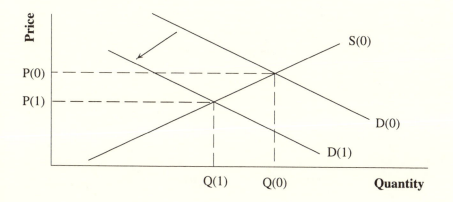

ing a gradual change in price.

Timing is important in determining the price effect of all disasters. In the Ford Pinto example, information was received by customers over a long period of time. Ford introduced the Pinto in 1970, and during the next six years more than 2 million Pintos were sold. The Pinto was criticized for being poorly designed and dangerous because its gas tank was located just seven inches from the rear bumper. Negative publicity mounted as fiery accidents resulted in deaths and individuals brought lawsuits against Ford. In August 1977, an article in *Mother Jones* raised public awareness further. In February 1978, a California jury granted a $128 million award in a Pinto accident case. In May and June 1978, two more Pinto accidents occurred, and "60 Minutes" vividly depicted the problems with the car. In June 1978, in an agreement with the National Highway Traffic Safety Administration, Ford recalled 2 million Pintos built between 1971 and 1976. Another fatal crash occurred in August 1978, and Ford was charged with reckless homicide. From July 1977 to July 1980, Pinto's market share fell by nearly two-thirds.[2]

The Ford Pinto case exemplifies the gradual change in customers' perceptions of the safety of the product. For two reasons, gradual changes in perceptions may make it harder to distinguish price changes resulting from the disaster from price changes resulting from other factors. First, it may not be obvious when each negative publicity event occurs. Second, many other factors may change over a period of time.

Demand-side disasters differ not only in the timing of the effect, but also in breadth of the effect. Some demand-side disasters affect a specific brand, some result in a decrease in demand for a narrow group of nearly identical products (albeit with different brand names), and some result in a decrease in demand for a broad group of products. For example, problems with the Pinto probably reduced demand for only the branded product. In the toxic shock disaster, the demand for

Figure 1.2
Price Increase as a Result of Producer Response

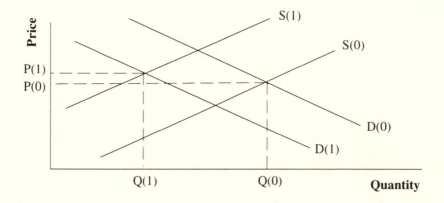

all tampons, not just the Rely brand, declined. The Tylenol poisonings may have reduced demand for an even broader group of products, including all over-the-counter medications, especially those in capsule form.

Responses to Demand-side Disasters

Because demand-side disasters are usually caused by changes in customers' perceptions about the safety or quality of the product, firms often respond by trying to restore customers' confidence. This can take the form of a recall of the product, redesign of the product to improve quality and safety, increased advertising, or, more likely, some combination of these actions. Recalls of the product sharply reduce supply. Similarly, design changes to ensure the safety or quality of the product in the future and promotional campaigns may increase costs and thereby also reduce supply.

The net effect on price of a reduction in supply varies with the magnitude of the supply shift. Figures 1.2 and 1.3 depict the same initial demand shift and alternative supply shifts. The relatively large decrease in supply in Figure 1.2 (attributable to a relatively large increase in costs) results in an increase in the post-disaster price over the pre-disaster price. The relatively small decrease in supply in Figure 1.3 produces a decline in price from the pre-disaster level.

The firm's responses described above may also shift the demand curve. A promotional campaign may offset some of the disaster-induced decline in demand and thus raise the price. Likewise, demand would increase and the price would rise if the product's recall and redesign restored customers' confidence in the product. These effects are not illustrated in Figures 1.2 and 1.3.

Ford's response to the Pinto disaster fits well within this framework. Ford en-

Figure 1.3
Price Decrease as a Result of Producer Response

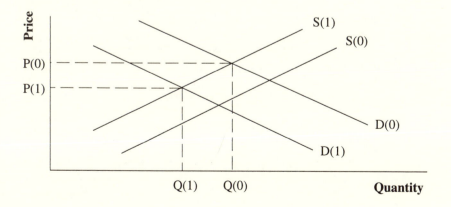

gaged in a promotional effort that included advertisements and the inclusion of additional options at no extra charge (an implicit decrease in price) to try to forestall buyers from substituting other cars or modes of transportation for the Pinto. Throughout this period, however, Ford did not modify the design of the Pinto or effectively counter the negative publicity.

The 1982 Tylenol poisonings are a classic example of corrective actions that actually reestablish the product's safety and quality but probably at an increased cost. Within a few days of the deaths from the tainted Tylenol in late September, Johnson & Johnson halted all advertising of Tylenol and production in one of its two plants. On October 8, Johnson & Johnson recalled 22 million bottles of Tylenol. The company also began a massive promotional campaign, began packaging the medicine in tamper-proof containers, and introduced tamper-proof caplet forms. Sales dropped precipitously in the first few weeks, but they recovered substantially within a year and almost completely within four years.[3]

The demand for Tylenol decreased dramatically after the media revealed the poisonings. Customers stopped using Tylenol capsules, and to some extent they probably shifted away from purchasing other brands of analgesics in capsule form. Johnson & Johnson reduced the supply of Tylenol capsules with the recall and plant closure. When it reintroduced Tylenol in a different form (caplets) and with modifications in packaging and additional advertising, costs probably increased.[4] In this disaster the impact fell primarily on one firm, but the entire industry was affected because other drug manufacturers were vulnerable to similar terrorism and were compelled to introduce more tamper-resistant packaging. Price effects were probably felt by other manufacturers, distributors, and retailers.

Summary

The first stage of a demand-side disaster, the reduction in demand stemming from the initial event, has an unambiguously negative effect on the price of the directly affected product. However, the price effect of the disaster is complicated by the responses in later stages. Restoring demand by dispelling negative perceptions of product quality or safety helps to mitigate the decline in price. Whether or not there are interactions, the price effect due to the disaster must be separated from that attributable to other factors. Furthermore, the scope of products affected by the decline in demand will vary among disasters, and there will likely be increased demand, and consequently increased price, for unaffected substitutes.

SUPPLY-SIDE DISASTERS

In supply-side disasters, supply is restricted, but demand initially remains unaffected. As Figure 1.4 shows, the reduction in supply raises the price. As with demand-side disasters, the full reduction in supply following a disaster may come

Figure 1.4
Reduction in Supply

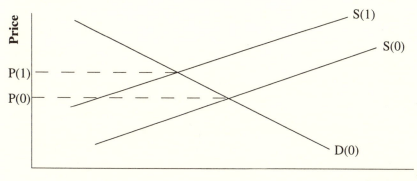

Quantity

about quickly or over a period of time following the initial event. The more rapidly the supply reduction occurs, the more quickly the price increase will be evident. In some disasters, like crop failures, the shortfall in supply can be forecast, which tends to cause an increase in price before the shortfall actually occurs.

Agricultural markets are prone to supply-side disasters because weather extremes affect the supply of crops without affecting demand. For example, during the first half of 1988, the midwestern states began to suffer the effects of a damaging drought. The severity of the drought varied throughout the Midwest (for example, central Nebraska received more than normal rainfall, while Iowa faced extreme drought conditions), but a large swath of the crop-growing areas was affected. The U.S. Department of Agriculture (USDA) estimated that because of the drought, grain production in 1988 would be 24 percent lower than in 1987. Soybean production would be down 13 percent. The winter wheat crop was harvested before the drought, but the smaller spring wheat crop was predicted to be less than half the normal size, leaving total wheat output 13 percent lower than in 1987. The corn crop was estimated to be 26 percent smaller. In early August, USDA raised its estimate of the corn production shortfall to 37 percent. Prices of futures contracts for these crops surged upward after the USDA announcements. Retail price increases were expected to be moderate and short lived, unless the drought persisted beyond one growing season.[5]

The supply of corn, soybeans, and wheat decreased as a result of the drought. The magnitude of the price increase was mitigated by the availability of inventories. A net reduction in the supply (harvest and inventory) of these crops would tend to increase market prices. The sharp increase in the price of futures contracts reflected the realization that a supply disaster was pending in these markets.

In addition to agricultural disasters, other disasters can restrict the supply of some goods and services without reducing demand. For example, a devastating

Figure 1.5
Decreased Stock of Housing

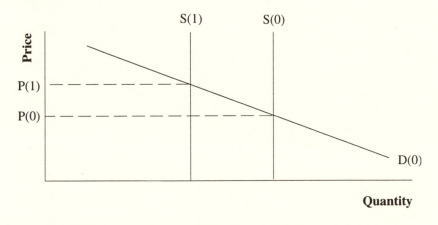

fire obliterated entire residential neighborhoods in Oakland, California, in October 1991. The loss of more than 3,000 residences reduced the supply of housing in that area.[6]

The supply curve in Figure 1.5 represents all Oakland-area housing units, whether or not the units were actually on the market. Similarly, the demand curve represents the individuals who want housing, whether they own a unit, rent a unit, or are looking to purchase or rent. If the entire housing stock were for sale and all individuals were "in the market," the equilibrium price would be P(0). If individuals believed the fire to be a random event (as opposed to an event, such as an earthquake, that is likely to be repeated in the same area), demand for housing in Oakland would not be expected to fall.[7] As shown in Figure 1.5, the model predicts that the initial fall in the stock of housing in Oakland would lead to an increase in the price of housing. The same number of individuals wanted housing, but the supply had been restricted. This disaster unambiguously put upward pressure on the price of housing in the Oakland area.

Responses to Supply-side Disasters

Responses to supply-side disasters include the use of inventories to offset supply losses, methods of increasing production, and alternative production sources, or a combination. The response of individual farmers to a drought depends on the particular growing practices and ownership of inventories of each farmer. Farmers with substantial inventories might release them to the market, shifting the supply curve to the right and thereby mitigating the price increase. Additional supply may also come from farmers located outside the drought area. The demand side does not appear likely to be affected, but if quality of the products declines, then demand might decline as well, reducing upward pressure on prices. Response to the Oakland fires could take the form of reconstruction of housing in the burned-out area as well as new construction in nearby areas.

Summary

The direction of the initial price change stemming from a supply-side disaster is clear: price increases. Like demand-side disasters, however, the price increase may be offset by responses such as sales of inventories that increase supply. In some supply-side disasters, supply responses come slowly as the supply of the product (e.g., housing) is reestablished.

MIXED-EFFECTS DISASTERS

Disasters that initially affect both supply and demand are conceptually more complicated than supply-side disasters or demand-side disasters. A disaster may change customers' perceptions of the quality or safety of a good while simultaneously affecting the supply. If both demand and supply decline, the price effects will tend to offset each other, as was shown in Figures 1.2 and 1.3. Such a disaster could result in an increase, decrease, or no change in price.

An oil spill that affects commercial fishing grounds is an example of a mixed-effects disaster. If the news of the oil spill changed buyers' perceptions of the quality or safety of seafood harvested in the spill-affected area, then demand would decrease. A decline in demand, with everything else unchanged, would lead to a fall in price, as depicted in Figure 1.1. If the spill also resulted in a smaller harvest (because fishermen had less access to the fish because of the oil or because fish were damaged or killed), supply would also decline, thereby raising price above the level in Figure 1.1. Whether the ultimate price is above or below the original price depends, as Figures 1.2 and 1.3 show, on the magnitude of the supply shift relative to the demand shift.

Now consider the *Exxon Valdez* disaster on March 24, 1989, when the oil tanker hit a reef and spilled more than 11 million gallons of oil into Prince William Sound, affecting fisheries there and in nearby areas. The previous analysis would predict a decrease in the price of Alaskan seafood to the extent that demand fell because customers perceived that the quality or safety of Alaskan seafood declined after the accident. For example, customers might fear contamination of the seafood from the oil. In addition, supply might be affected if fishermen were forced to harvest closer to the spawning grounds, where the quality of the fish is lower. If changed fishing patterns resulted in increased harvests of lower-quality seafood and decreased harvest of normal-quality seafood, the overall price of seafood would decline.

Responses to Mixed-effects Disasters

As in other types of disasters, the responses of parties involved in an oil spill can affect supply and demand of seafood. The supply effect would be exacerbated by government closure of fishing grounds as a reaction to the spill. Such a supply effect may be largely overcome when the fishing grounds are reopened. Similarly, responses such as the closure of the fishing grounds itself, clean-up of the spill, and public reassurance regarding the quality of the seafood may restore consumer confidence, as was hoped following the *Exxon Valdez* spill.

Because commercial fish harvesting is seasonal, the effect of an oil spill on fisheries is dependent on the timing of the spill. If closure of the fishing grounds takes place entirely before the fishing season starts, the supply of seafood might be unaffected. To the extent customers are confident that the seafood is not contaminated, there may be no effect on demand and thus the spill might have no effect on price. If, however, the prohibition on commercial fishing extends into the fishing season, the total supply of seafood—which includes seafood harvested in the oil-touched areas as well as harvests from oil-free areas and inventories—would decline, putting upward pressure on prices. If this is combined with a decrease in demand during the season and the accompanying downward pressure on prices, the net effect on price can be determined only through the kind of empirical analysis we discuss in later chapters.

In addition, the clean-up effort associated with a spill the size of the *Exxon Valdez* may affect supply and demand. The clean-up in Alaska occupied many fishermen and their equipment. As a result of the reduced resources available, the harvest suffered delays and damage that may have reduced the quality of the seafood. Moreover, competition from Exxon for fishermen and equipment forced seafood processors to offer higher prices for seafood to induce the fishermen to harvest seafood rather than work for Exxon on the clean-up. This raised the processors' costs and thereby reduced supply.

Summary

Initial price changes in mixed-effects disasters are considerably more complicated than in demand- or supply-side disasters. The direction and relative magnitudes of the demand and supply shifts determine whether prices change, the direction of the change, and the amount of the change.

CONCLUSION

The process of organizing disasters based on their fundamental economic effect—changes in supply and demand—provides a means for determining the qualitative nature of the price change. In some of the less complicated disasters, the direction of change is obvious. In those that involve post-disaster reactions by the affected individuals, even the direction of change in price may be difficult to determine a priori, however.

NOTES

1. Weinberger & Romeo, *The Impact of Negative Product News*, BUSINESS HORIZONS, Jan.-Feb. 1989.

2. *Id.*

3. *Id.*

4. Although costs probably increased, they could have declined due to the redesign and different packaging and advertising. Before the poisoning, caplets may have been less costly than capsules, but because demand for caplets was lower than for capsules, it was more profitable to produce capsules. After the poisoning, demand for capsules fell, while demand for caplets increased, increasing the profitability of the latter.

5. Smith, *Drought 1988: Farmers and the Macroeconomy*, ECONOMIC REVIEW, Federal Reserve Bank of Dallas, September 1988, at 16, 21; and Hillenbrand, *What the Drought Hath Wrought*, TIME, July 25, 1988, at 60.

6. Yoachum, *Comparing Quake, Fire is Difficult, Numbers Alone Don't Reveal Impact on the East Bay*, SAN FRANCISCO CHRONICLE, October 28, 1991, at A13.

7. The demand for housing in the affected area, however, could be reduced by the destruction of the foliage and scenic beauty of the area. Also, some people may elect to leave the area because of the psychological trauma associated with remaining.

2

Measuring the Effect of the *Exxon Valdez* Oil Spill on Alaskan Seafood Prices

For some disasters, one can determine the expected qualitative nature of any price effects. For example, a reduction in demand with no change in supply will reduce price. Changes in other factors, however, could lead to distortions in the size of the price effect and even reversals in its direction. In some cases even the direction of the price change cannot be predicted from the simple diagrammatic models of supply and demand. This may occur when the initial impact of the disaster and all of the subsequent reactions by firms, individuals, and governments are taken into account. Qualitative changes in price may also be ambiguous for mixed-effects disasters if the changes in supply and demand tend to have offsetting effects on price (for example, a reduction in demand coupled with a decrease in supply).

The initial impact of the *Exxon Valdez* oil spill on Alaskan seafood prices could have been on both the demand side and the supply side. Consequently, the disaster is placed in the mixed-effects category (see chapter 1). Reactions by government authorities, Exxon, the fishermen, and purchasers of Alaskan seafood could have affected supply and/or demand. Other factors unrelated to the oil spill also must be taken into account to determine the net effect on price.

The oil spill may have had little, if any, effect on Alaskan seafood prices for at least three reasons. First, demand and supply conditions for Alaskan seafood may have been unchanged as a result of the oil spill. Second, even if some of the demand and supply conditions for Alaskan seafood changed, global market conditions that determine Alaskan seafood prices may have been largely unchanged as a result of the oil spill, thereby leaving Alaskan prices unaffected. Finally, prices may have been unchanged because the supply factors that tend to elevate prices were offset by demand factors that tend to depress prices.

PRICE-RELATED ISSUES

In our study of the *Exxon Valdez* oil spill, we examine three types of price-related issues. First, no 1989 prices are observed for the few Alaskan fisheries that were closed for the entire season. We estimate what prices would have been if these fisheries had been open and if the oil spill had not happened.

Second, prices may have been affected by the oil spill in fisheries that were open. We examine whether the various participants in the Alaskan seafood industry received different prices because of the spill than they would have received otherwise. In evaluating what Alaskan seafood prices would have been absent the oil spill, we examine the following possibilities: prices were suppressed by the oil spill, prices were elevated by the oil spill, and prices were unaffected by the oil spill. Third, we consider whether prices for Alaskan seafood after 1989 were affected by the spill.

Our approach to all three issues is grounded in economics. For each issue, we seek answers that conform to both (1) the historical record about Alaskan seafood prices and factors that affected them before and after the *Exxon Valdez* oil spill and (2) the economics of seafood markets and market forces that might have plausible linkage to a price effect attributable to the oil spill.

FACTORS AFFECTING ALASKAN SEAFOOD PRICES

In theory, if all of the many supply and demand factors that affect the prices of Alaskan seafood in its various markets could be fully described absent the *Exxon Valdez* oil spill, the prices that would have prevailed could be measured exactly. It is difficult, however, to characterize in complete detail the actual conditions underlying observed prices in a given year. It is even more difficult to determine what those conditions would have been under a hypothetical situation (no oil spill in 1989).

Supply conditions have not been predictable over time. By far the most important species in the Alaskan seafood harvest are sockeye salmon and pink salmon. Both species are harvested in very large quantities, and sockeye, in particular, accounts for a large portion of total revenue. The Alaska Department of Fish and Game (ADF&G) forecasts harvests for these and other seafood species. Between 1975 and 1990, ADF&G statewide forecasts have deviated from actual harvest by an average of 32 percent per year for pink salmon and 39 percent per year for sockeye salmon. Local differences in the quality of seafood may also vary from year to year in an unpredictable manner.

Similarly, many factors on the demand side change each year. For most of its major seafood products, Alaska supplies a world market rather than a local market. As a result, demand for Alaskan seafood is affected by changes in world demand and by competing supplies of seafood. Competition comes from wild harvests or farmed harvests in other regions and from inventories of seafood. All of these sources affect demand for, and consequently prices of, Alaskan seafood. Of course, changes in consumer demand for seafood generally, and for Alaskan seafood in particular, will also affect prices for Alaskan seafood.

Even attributing all demand-side price effects to the oil spill would not necessarily allow for a direct measure of the effect of the oil spill on price. For example, consider the price decline for Alaskan salmon from 1988 to 1989. The 1989 Alaskan salmon harvest was much larger than the 1988 harvest; indeed, it was a record catch. Determining whether a price change such as occurred from 1988 to 1989 was the result of a movement only in the supply curve not affected by the oil spill, as opposed to movements in supply and demand, is difficult. Both the left-hand and right-hand sides of Figure 2.1 present hypothetical situations in which prices change by the same amount, from P_{1988} to P_{1989}. The supply shift is hypothesized to be independent of the oil spill, while the demand shift is hypothesized to be induced by the spill. On the left-hand side of Figure 2.1, this price decline reflects entirely an increase in supply (outward shift of the supply curve). On the right-hand side of Figure 2.1, the price decline reflects a combination of the increase in supply (not related to the spill) and a decrease in demand (related to the oil spill).

Constant demand and supply conditions over time would simplify the calculation of Alaskan seafood prices in 1989 absent the oil spill. As noted above, however, demand and supply conditions for Alaskan seafood have not been constant even in years without unusual events such as the oil spill. These changes in demand and supply conditions have created volatility of prices. For example, average Alaskan ex-vessel prices for at least one salmon species changed—up or down—by more than 25 percent in each year from 1981 through 1989. Consequently, prices in either 1988 or 1990 are not likely to be good indicators of what prices would have been absent the oil spill in 1989.

Figure 2.1
Difficulty in Identifying Shift in Demand

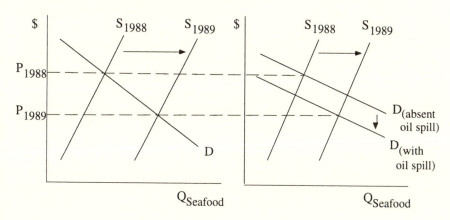

Under normal circumstances, Alaskan seafood prices would certainly have changed in 1989 relative to 1988—or any other year—to reflect many changes in demand and supply conditions. For example, seafood prices in 1988 were unusually high—particularly for salmon, Alaska's primary seafood export—relative to prior or succeeding years. These high prices were partly the result of low harvests in Alaska and worldwide, low inventories in the United States and Japan, and a strong yen relative to the dollar.

Several factors affecting both demand and supply, independent of the oil spill, probably would have reduced the 1989 ex-vessel and processor prices of salmon in Alaska relative to the 1988 prices. The 1989 season started with higher inventories of frozen salmon than in 1988 in the Japanese market, where much Alaskan salmon is sold. Inventories may also have been affected by ADF&G's low forecast relative to actual catch, to the extent that traders relied on the forecasts and held higher inventories than they would have otherwise. Moreover, fishermen around the world had record-setting harvests of several species of salmon in 1989. Japan imported increasing amounts of farm-bred salmon from Norway, Chile, and elsewhere in 1989. Finally, the U.S. dollar increased in strength relative to the Japanese yen in 1989, making Alaskan salmon more expensive in Japan and reducing the quantity demanded there.

STATISTICAL ESTIMATES OF ALASKAN SEAFOOD PRICES IN 1989

Based on statistical techniques and observations of many years of market data, we can estimate what Alaskan ex-vessel and processor prices would have been in 1989 for several species of seafood. Our estimates of 1989 prices are based on the assumption that the same relationship between prices and the observed market data would have held in 1989 as held in other years in our sample period.

Like all statistical models, ours is unlikely to forecast a 1989 price for a species that is identical to the actual 1989 price. Of more importance for statistical interpretation is whether the 1989 price lies inside or outside the 1989 forecast range determined by the variability of the statistical model. If inside, the forecast is not "significantly" different from the actual value; if outside, the forecast value is "significantly" different from the actual value. In statistical parlance "significant" refers to the relationship between the price and the forecast range, not to the absolute size of the price. (Statistical methods are discussed further in Appendix 1.)

Applying statistical techniques, we estimate Alaskan seafood prices using two types of models. One type relates the Alaskan prices (spill-area prices) to British Columbian prices (nonspill-area prices). This approach explores whether there was a 1989 price effect specific to Alaska or to the oil-touched regions of Alaska. The other type of model measures the effect of several nonprice variables on Alaskan ex-vessel prices. These approaches are complementary. We also estimate Alaskan salmon processor prices based on ex-vessel prices and on British Columbian processor prices.

IDENTIFYING THE EFFECT OF THE OIL SPILL

We begin our examination of whether prices were affected by the oil spill by exploring plausible suppositions about how the oil spill might have affected prices through changes in either supply or demand for seafood. With these theories, we structure our analysis to isolate and examine specific linkages between the oil spill and price determination in Alaskan seafood markets.

Our statistical models provide an estimate of Alaskan seafood prices in 1989, but they do not indicate whether any differences between the predicted values and the actual prices are attributable to the *Exxon Valdez* oil spill. Consequently, they do not indicate exactly what prices would have been without the oil spill. Many factors, including the oil spill, that are not explicitly included in our models may have contributed to any difference between observed and predicted prices.

Although evidence can be "consistent" or "inconsistent" with the claims of price effects from the oil spill, no single piece of evidence will likely provide a complete and exact test of how much, if at all, the oil spill affected Alaskan seafood prices. It is therefore necessary to seek alternative methods to determine the underlying supply and demand changes that resulted in any observed price differences.

POSSIBLE DEMAND EFFECTS OF THE OIL SPILL ON 1989 PRICES

There may have been a "psychological" effect on consumer demand for Alaskan seafood, especially in Japan. Some consumers may have avoided purchasing seafood of a certain type or from a certain location if they believed that there was some risk of it being contaminated by oil from the spill or that its quality was lower than usual. Similarly, if processors and traders thought there was a substantial risk that some consumers might view Alaskan seafood as being contaminated by oil from the spill or that its quality was lower than usual, the processors and traders might have insisted on paying less for any given quantity of seafood to cover risks associated with its resale to other buyers. If so, these purchasers' demand for Alaskan seafood would be less than what it would have been without the spill.

Figure 2.2 illustrates how a decline in consumer demand could lead to a decline in the price of Alaskan seafood. It shows the observed price in 1988, P_{1988}, where the prespill supply and demand curves intersect, and the observed price in 1989, P_{1989}, where the postspill supply and demand curves intersect. Had the spill not affected demand, the price would be P* rather than P_{1989}. Figure 2.2 also shows that only a portion of the difference between the 1988 and 1989 prices is attributable to the oil spill. The remaining difference is attributable to the increased supply of seafood between 1988 and 1989.

In order to examine whether price was suppressed due to a downward shift in demand induced by the oil spill, we consider four hypotheses related to changes in demand:

•   Was world consumer demand for a species of seafood, or group of species of seafood, regardless of source of supply, affected by the oil spill?

•   Was world consumer demand for Alaskan seafood affected by the oil spill?

•   Was world consumer demand for seafood from regions of Alaska affected by the oil spill?

•   Were processor prices affected by the oil spill?

The first three hypotheses pertain to changes in consumer demand for seafood. If such changes in consumer demand occurred, they could have resulted in reduced ex-vessel prices. Even if consumer demand remained unchanged, perhaps because no contaminated fish were ever reported to have reached consumer markets, the uncertainty surrounding demand could have led to lower prices relative to costs for processors, as suggested in the fourth hypothesis. We will now examine these questions in more detail.

Figure 2.2
Possible Effect of Perceived Contamination of Alaskan Seafood

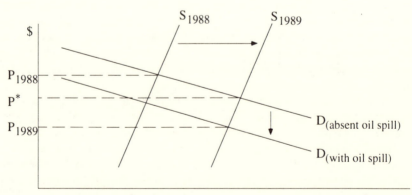

P_{1988} = Observed price in 1988
P^* = 1989 price absent the oil spill
P_{1989} = Observed price in 1989

Changes in Consumer Demand

The first three hypotheses rest on the premise that consumers avoided seafood potentially tainted by the oil spill. Rather than risk purchasing potentially tainted seafood, some consumers may have avoided purchasing all seafood commonly harvested in Alaska or all seafood from oil-touched regions of Alaska. Depending on the extent of consumer knowledge of the source of seafood, the net effect of such consumer reaction would be to suppress demand for seafood from (1) all regions of the world, (2) Alaska, or (3) regions of Alaska. The plausibility of each of these theories rests on the degree of consumer certainty about the source of seafood within the group. Extensive labeling of seafood by source provides consumers with a high degree of certainty. In addition, sellers from both the oil-touched and oil-free areas may have been able to develop other signals to buyers indicating source.

Insofar as consumers' certainty about the source of seafood (either from labeling or other signals developed by seafood sellers) extended to specific regions in Alaska, demand for seafood from oil-touched regions might have fallen, thereby tending to lower the prices of that seafood. If consumers were able to distinguish only between seafood from Alaska and non-Alaskan sources (as opposed to different regions within Alaska), they might have responded to the oil spill by consuming less seafood from all regions of Alaska, resulting in downward pressure on all Alaskan seafood prices. Finally, if consumers possessed little certainty about the source of seafood (as the absence of source labels in many retail markets like Japan suggests), then the demand for seafood worldwide might have fallen in response to the oil spill, suppressing the price of seafood generally.

We marshal several types of evidence to examine the plausibility of changes in consumer demand. We review economic studies of world seafood prices and demand, studies of consumer reaction to the oil spill, and reports in the trade press. We look at seafood labeling in different markets to determine whether buyers could have selectively avoided Alaskan seafood. We review trade reports and other accounts to determine whether consumers switched from one group of seafood to another that they might have considered to be safer. Finally, we examine whether there was an unexplained decline in seafood prices after the oil spill in 1989 relative to supply and demand factors in that year.

Changes in Processor Prices

Even if consumer demand were unaffected by the oil spill, demand faced by processors might have been affected because of uncertainty and fear of future reactions by consumers. This theory would be plausible if seafood traders and distributors treated Alaskan seafood (or seafood from oil-touched regions of Alaska) as risky to hold and sell in the market. At all levels of trade, seafood of the same species and quality that are otherwise undifferentiated tend to sell for the same price in a single market. Yet traders may have perceived that there was some additional risk in selling Alaskan seafood (or seafood from oil-touched regions of Alaska) after the oil spill. In order to bear this risk, these traders may have paid a lower price to processors for Alaskan seafood. Retail prices could have remained unaffected, but prices at other levels of trade may have been lower.

POSSIBLE SUPPLY EFFECTS OF THE OIL SPILL ON 1989 PRICES

The oil spill may have affected the supply of certain Alaskan seafood by (1) limiting the harvest, (2) altering the quality and composition of seafood actually harvested, or (3) changing the costs incurred by fishermen and processors. In general, supply effects are likely to have been local, perhaps affecting different fishermen and processors within the same region differently, and quite likely affecting regions differently.

In theory, some of these supply factors, such as a possible reduction in the quality of seafood caused by the oil spill, could have reduced Alaskan seafood prices. Many supply factors, however, were likely to have increased 1989 prices of Alaskan seafood.

Less seafood may have been caught in some localities because fisheries were closed for parts of the season. We use biologists' estimates to calculate the lost seafood harvest attributable to the oil spill. Other things being equal, if less seafood were caught, one would expect the prices that fishermen and processors received to be higher. This effect taken by itself would tend to benefit those fishermen who were able to harvest and sell seafood.

The Exxon cleanup activities may have led to higher Alaskan seafood prices in 1989. To compete with Exxon for the services of fishing boats and crew who were offered substantial inducements to work on the cleanup operation, processors may have raised ex-vessel prices. Similarly, processors may have been forced to offer higher wages to employees who could have worked on the cleanup operations. Higher wages and higher ex-vessel prices would have resulted in higher processor prices.

The Exxon claims program itself may have led to higher Alaskan seafood prices. During the summer of 1989, Exxon paid some fishermen for claims for forgone catches in fisheries that were closed by the oil spill.[1] Processors may have felt compelled by concerns of equity to pay ex-vessel prices that were at least as high as those paid by Exxon for forgone harvests in closed fisheries.[2] In some instances, processors may have been willing to pay higher ex-vessel prices than they would have ordinarily in the belief that Exxon might ultimately compensate them for lost profits in 1989. Given the uncertainty of future compensation, however, it is unlikely that processors would have been willing to pay substantially higher ex-vessel prices.

POSSIBLE EFFECTS OF THE SPILL ON FUTURE PRICES

We also examine trends in the prices at which fishing permits were bought and sold. A decline in the value of permits in 1989 might be attributable to the adverse effect of the oil spill on the anticipated future profits from Alaskan fisheries. Although changes in permit values might not reflect short-run (single season) effects of the oil spill, they should capture the long-term monetary and nonmonetary effects of the oil spill on fishermen.

NOTES

1. *See* Alaska State Legislature, Legislative Research Agency, Memorandum from Sheila Fay Helgath to Representative Mike Navarre, Re: Fishermen's Exxon Oil Spill Claims, Research Request 90.079, October 9, 1989. As of September 17, 1989, Exxon had made payments to commercial fishing permit holders and crew members totaling $86,000,000.

2. Processors did not face direct price competition from Exxon for fish that were harvested in 1989. The Exxon claims program during 1989 did not compensate fishermen for seafood that was harvested and sold. However, processors purchased seafood from fishermen in the same fishery, or in a fishery adjacent to one that may have been closed earlier in the season and for which Exxon may have been compensating fishermen for lost harvests.

3

Industry Background

This chapter examines the principal aspects of supply, demand, and market structure that affect the pricing of Alaskan seafood. After a brief description of the fishing industry in Alaska, the chapter discusses the supply of seafood, factors affecting demand for seafood, sources of demand for Alaskan seafood, and the importance of substitute products. Following the sections on supply and demand is a discussion of the linkages between regional and global markets. Market structure as it can affect price is covered in the final part.

As the chapter will show, "many different factors may affect fisheries prices, including harvests in Alaska and elsewhere, inventories, exchange rates, and changes in technology and consumer tastes. Also, the determinants of fisheries prices vary widely between different species."[1]

ALASKAN FISHING INDUSTRY

The seafood industry is the largest private employer in the state of Alaska. It accounted for 16 percent of basic industry employment and payroll in 1987.[2] Employment in the harvesting industry can be calculated in different ways. The broadest measure is the number of participants, including both permit holders and crews, whether full-time or not. The total number of permit holders ranged between 18,000 and 19,000 for most of the 1980s. In 1990, 18,105 individuals held 32,215 permits. More than 14,000 of these permits are for limited entry fisheries, and the remainder are for open-to-entry fisheries. In addition, more than 32,000 crew licenses were issued, bringing the total number of participants to about 50,000.[3]

The ex-vessel value of total Alaska harvests increased from $696 million in 1983 ($573 million for domestic harvests) to $1.6 billion (all domestic) in 1988, before declining to $1.3 billion in 1989 due to a sharp drop in salmon prices. Even with this decline, the total value of harvests from Alaska waters (all nations) increased by 88 percent in just six years, while the total value of harvests by U.S. vessels increased by 128 percent.[4]

Production Stages

Production of Alaskan seafood involves three primary stages: harvesting, processing, and distribution. Fishermen begin the process by harvesting the seafood and selling it to processors at the "ex-vessel" price.[5] Throughout this book the term "harvest" refers to the volume of fish caught by the fishermen. Tender boats often transport the harvest from the fishing boats to the processors; alternatively, the fishermen may bring it directly to the processors.[6]

Sometimes fishermen conduct the first few processing steps (heading and gutting) on the fishing vessel before delivering the catch to the processors. Processing may take place on board a vessel or at a land-based facility. For most fish, processors remove and discard the heads and entrails and freeze or can the remainder.[7] Sac roe herring are most often frozen whole by Alaskan processors.[8] We will refer to the output of this initial processing stage as "production." Production is almost always smaller than harvest in volume, but it is higher in dollar sales due to the value added by processing.

After the first level of processing, the seafood may exchange hands several times before final purchase by consumers. Processors sell the seafood to wholesalers, brokers, or other processors at the "processor price." Depending on the final product desired, the output of the first processing stage may be used as an input to additional processing stages. For example, *surimi,* a minced fish meat produced at the first stage, may be used by processors to make other seafood products, such as imitation crab legs. On the other hand, the canning process yields a product directly salable to the consumer. Virtually all of the processing in Alaska is limited to the primary stages; most secondary (and beyond) processing is done out of state.[9] After all processing is complete, the seafood is sold to wholesalers in a distribution chain and ultimately to consumers at the retail level.

Regional Differences

The Alaskan seafood industry is spread throughout the state (see Figure 3.1), but the harvest, processing, and employment are concentrated in four regions—Southeast, Prince William Sound, Bristol Bay, and Peninsula-Aleutians.[10] These four regions accounted for 79 percent of Alaska's salmon harvest in 1989. The Cook Inlet and Kodiak Island fisheries are also important, together contributing another 16 percent of the salmon harvest.[11]

As Figure 3.2 shows, different salmon species are concentrated in different areas. For example, Southeast and Prince William Sound have the greatest concentrations of pink, while Bristol Bay is by far the largest source of sockeye. Southeast

Figure 3.1
Alaska Salmon and Herring Fisheries

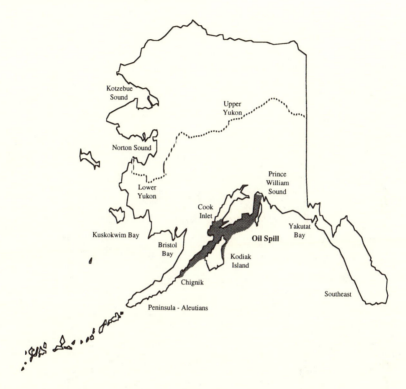

accounts for more than 41 percent of the comparatively small coho salmon harvest. Chum is the most evenly distributed species; no region has more than one-quarter of the total chum harvest.

Species under Consideration

Although many species of seafood are harvested in the areas that the oil spill reached, the economic value of harvest and processing is concentrated in a few species. We estimate prices for five species of salmon: sockeye (red), coho (silver), chinook (king), chum (dog), and pink (humpy). We also estimate prices for herring, halibut, sablefish, and two species each of shrimp and crab.

Salmon

Alaska is a major world supplier of salmon, especially pink and sockeye (Figure 3.3). The species vary widely in physical characteristics such as average weight

Figure 3.2
Salmon Landings by Species and Region, Annual Average
1980–1989

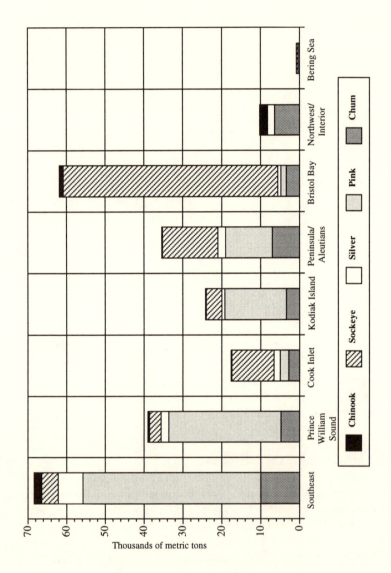

Figure 3.3
Alaska Share of World Harvest, 1989

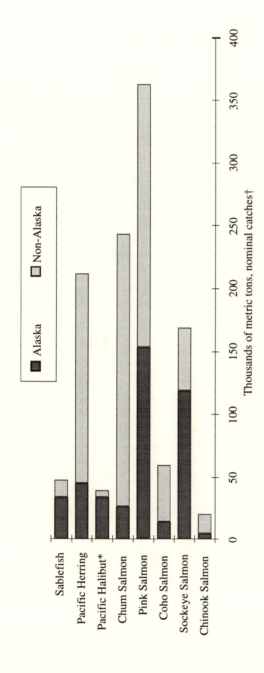

Thousands of metric tons, nominal catches†

†Landings converted to a live weight basis.
*Landed weight in source; nominal catch is estimated assuming landed weight ≈ 0.75 x live weight.

Sources:
  Alaska Harvest: Sablefish: PacFIN Reports. Herring and Salmon: Alaska Department of Fish and Game (AD&G), *Preliminary Alaska Fisheries Harvests and Values, 1989*. All preceding data as reported in Knapp and Smith, 1991. The source for the halibut data is the International Pacific Halibut Commission.
  World Harvest: All Species: *FAO Yearbook, Fishery Statistics, Catches and Landings, 1989*.

and age at maturity (Table 3.1). Most of the salmon harvest in Alaska occurs during July (peak sockeye season) and August (peak pink season). The size of the harvest and its value vary from the large sockeye harvest (118.7 thousand metric tons valued at $321 million in 1989) to the small chinook harvest (4.8 thousand metric tons, $15.8 million in 1989).[12]

Herring Roe

Herring fisheries include the food and bait fishery, the fishery for sac roe herring (during the peak spawning period), the wild roe-on-kelp fishery, and the pound roe-on-kelp fishery.[13] In the sac roe herring fishery, fishermen catch roe herring before spawning and sell the entire fish. In the wild roe-on-kelp fishery, divers gather roe-laden kelp after the herring have spawned. The pound roe-on-kelp fishery differs slightly in that pre-spawning roe herring are seined, placed in floating net cages (pounds) that are partially filled with kelp, and left to spawn. The herring season is in the spring, concluding for the most part before the salmon runs begin (Table 3.2).

The sac roe herring harvest accounts for a large portion of the total harvest, averaging 86 percent of volume and 90 percent of value during the 1980s. The fishery for roe on kelp in Prince William Sound and Bristol Bay (Togiak) is relatively small in volume (0.6 percent of total harvest), but relatively high in value (2.4 percent of total value).[14]

Halibut

Halibut runs from May to September. The number of fishing permits is not restricted. The fishery is managed by opening the season for brief (24 hour) derbies, usually three or four times a year in the Gulf of Alaska. In addition, the regulations require longline gear. The result has been an increase in the size and efficiency of the boats used to catch halibut as each boat tries to maximize fish caught per hour. Halibut is processed into strips, steaks, or other forms.[15]

Kodiak and the Central Gulf region of Alaska account for more than half of the total Alaska harvest of halibut (an average of 12.3 thousand metric tons out of 22.4 thousand metric tons in the 1980s). Southeast Alaska and the Alaska Peninsula together contribute most of the remainder.[16]

Sablefish

Most of the sablefish (black cod) run occurs between March and July. Harvesting is primarily by longline. The Eastern Gulf region of Alaska accounted for nearly 40 percent (13.5 thousand metric tons) of Alaska's 1989 harvest of 34.2 thousand metric tons. The Central Gulf region contributed an additional 12.2 thousand metric tons.[17]

Shrimp

The two species of shrimp under consideration are spot, which are comparatively large, and the smaller-sized pink. They are usually caught by bottom trawl, but pot gear is also used.[18] One of the most striking changes in the Alaskan shrimp fisheries in the 1980s was the sharp decline in the size of the harvests, most of which occurred in the first half of the decade. Both the volume of the shrimp catch and its value in 1989 were a small fraction of the 1980 level.[19]

Crab

The two species of crab we are considering are brown king crab and Dungeness crab. Both species are caught in pot gear. The crab fisheries are managed in three ways. Crab smaller than a minimum size may not be harvested, female crab may not be harvested, and the duration of the season is limited.[20]

SUPPLY OF SEAFOOD: WORLD AND ALASKA

The price of seafood depends, in part, on supply factors such as the quantity and quality available in the market. All else equal, as the world supply of salmon increases, the price will decline. The greater the share of total world production attributable to Alaska, the greater the likelihood that a reduction in Alaskan production will lead to increased prices. For the species potentially affected by the *Exxon Valdez* oil spill, Alaska provides a significant share of the world's catch. The price of seafood also depends on its quality. Lower-quality fish, such as those that are damaged or bruised during harvest, tend to fetch a lower price than higher-quality ones.

The amount of wild seafood harvested in Alaska is governed by regulation. Salmon and herring are managed by the Alaska Department of Fish and Game (ADF&G). Halibut is managed by the International Pacific Halibut Commission, a joint commission with Canada. Sablefish is managed by the Alaska Department of Fish and Game in Alaskan waters and the North Pacific Fishery Management Council in the remaining areas. The North Pacific Council sets fixed limits for groundfish.[21]

Quotas limit the amount of seafood that may be harvested, while permits govern who is allowed to fish. In addition, some fisheries (such as salmon, herring, and sablefish) are regulated by a limit on the number of permits available. More than 14,000 permits had been issued for these limited entry fisheries (most are for salmon) as of 1990. Permits are issued for specific combinations of species, gear type, and fishery. A market exists for permits; 549 were involved in monetary transfers in 1990, trading at an average value of $89,160.[22] Other fisheries are controlled by limiting the periods one can fish and limiting the size and quantity of fish taken.[23]

These regulations are not price-based, thus making the supply of seafood insensi-

Table 3.1
Summary Information: Salmon

Species	Average Weight	Age at Maturity	Harvest Alaska, 1989 (metric tons)	Ex-Vessel Value Alaska, 1989	Largest World Producers, 1989 (by volume)	Largest Importers of U.S. Production, 1990 (by volume)
Sockeye (Red)	6 lbs.	4-6 yrs.	118,690	$321,844,000	U.S. 74% Canada 20%	Japan 86% United Kingdom 8%
Coho (Silver)	6 lbs.	3-4 yrs.	13,890	$20,519,000	Japan 34% U.S. 33%	Japan 61% France 22%
Chinook (King)	12-20 lbs.	3-7 yrs.	4,750	$15,799,000	U.S. 68% Canada 24%	Japan 80% France 9%
Chum (Dog)	11 lbs.	3-5 yrs.	26,170	$21,920,000	Japan 75% U.S. 13%	Japan 39% France 22%
Pink (Humpy)	4 lbs.	2 yrs.	153,660	$121,955,000	U.S. 46% U.S.S.R. 40%	Japan 28% United Kingdom 20%

Sources:

Average Weight and Age at Maturity: Netboy. 1980 [Netboy, Anthony. *Salmon: The World's Most Harassed Fish* (Tulsa: Winchester Press, 1980)] as reported in Wessells, 1990 at 12.

Alaska Harvest and Ex-Vessel Value: Knapp and Smith, 1991 at 16.

Largest World Producers: *FAO Yearbook, Fishery Statistics, Catches and Landings, 1989* (Table II-4).

Largest Importers of U.S. Production: U.S. Department of Commerce, Bureau of the Census, FT-446: U.S. Exports (7-digit, Schedule B, Commodity Number by Country), 1990.

Table 3.2
Summary Information: Non-Salmon Species

Species	Average Weight	Age at Maturity	Run/ Season Length	Harvest Alaska, 1989 (metric tons)	Ex-Vessel Value Alaska, 1989	Largest World Producers, 1989 (by volume)
Pacific Herring			March-June	45,256	$18,804,000	U.S.S.R. 47% U.S. 26%
Halibut	29.1 lbs.†	8 yrs.	April-October ††	33,895	$85,750,000	U.S. 87% Canada 13%
Sablefish (Black Cod)	3-7 lbs.	4 yrs.	March-July	34,239	$62,865,000	U.S. 88% Canada 7%
Shrimp		2 yrs.	March-April•	887	$1,343,000	U.S. 100%*
Crab**			Spring, Fall•	15,322	$113,127,000	

† This is the landed weight.
†† Openings given by the International Pacific Halibut Commission (IPHC) for Area 3A, 1981-1990.
* The United States is responsible for the entire world catch of "pacific" shrimps.
** Dungeness and king crab only.
• Season length for Prince William Sound area, 1988-1990.

Sources:
Halibut average weight, age at maturity, season length: Correspondence with Gordon Peltonen, IPHC (May-June 1991).
Herring season length: *Preliminary Forecasts of Catch and Stock Abundance for Alaska Herring Fisheries*, Alaska Department of Fish and Game (ADF&G), 1989-1991.
Sablefish season length: *Federal Groundfish Fisheries Off Alaska, Domestic and Joint Venture Closings, Hook and Line Openings*, National Marine Fisheries Service (NMFS), 1988-1991.
Shellfish season length: Correspondence with Jay Johnson, AFD&G, Cordova.
Alaska harvest and ex-vessel value: Knapp and Smith, *The Alaska Seafood Industry*, 1991.
World producers: *FAO Yearbook, Fishery Statistics, Catches and Landings*, 1989.

tive to price changes in the short run. If prices increase, fishermen cannot increase wild seafood production much, and if prices fall, they will not cut production much. Fishermen try to maximize the quantity of fish harvested under existing regulations.[24] They seldom reduce their efforts except under unusual circumstances, such as those leading to the 1991 Bristol Bay strike when processors were offering ex-vessel prices substantially below those of the previous year.[25]

Supply of Salmon

Changes in the worldwide supply of salmon, like other types of seafood, are important determinants of changes in price. The worldwide supply of salmon contracted sharply between 1985 and 1987 and rose only slightly in 1988. However, supply increased 20 percent in 1989 and another 13 percent in 1990. The rapid increase in world supply of salmon led to record levels of inventories and lower salmon prices.[26] In markets around the world, salmon of different species and from different sources compete against one another.

Salmon from the United States

The United States is the world's largest producer of sockeye, pink, and chinook salmon. Until recently, it also was the largest producer of coho salmon (Table 3.3). Alaska is the world's largest source of Pacific salmon, which accounted for over 94 percent of the U.S. production of salmon in 1990.[27] Alaska's major competitors vary by species. Washington, Oregon, and Canada rival Alaska in chinook, sockeye, and coho salmon, while Japan and the former Soviet Union compete in pink and chum salmon.[28] British Columbia harvests about one-quarter as much salmon as Alaska.[29] Table 3.4 details Alaska's salmon production figures for each species. Atlantic salmon, which is not produced in Alaska, is also an important part of the world salmon supply, though the United States is not a significant producer.

Supply of Alaskan salmon is largely determined by biological decisions about the size of a sustainable fish population. Enhancement programs, number of permits issued, and opening and closing of fisheries are the instruments that the state uses to implement its plans. These factors generally are not price based, thus reducing the effect of price on supply. However, farmed salmon, from other countries as well as other regions of the United States, is becoming an increasingly important part of total supply.

Salmon from Canada

Salmon harvests in British Columbia are similar in many ways to those in Alaska. On average in the late 1980s, pink salmon accounted for 35 percent of the salmon harvest by volume in Canada and 39 percent in the United States. Chinook made

Table 3.3
Salmon Catch by Species and Country, 1985–1990
(live weight in thousands of metric tons)

Species and Country	1985	1986	1987	1988	1989	1990 *
Atlantic						
Norway	31.2	46.5	48.9	81.7	116.6	150.0
UK Scotland	7.5	10.3	12.7	18.0	29.0	35.0
Denmark**	2.5	2.8	4.2	4.4	8.8	0.9
Ireland	2.2	2.9	3.5	4.2	5.5	8.2
Canada	1.3	2.0	2.9	3.9	3.9	—
Other	5.5	5.8	6.1	6.3	11.0 †	2.0
Species Total	50.3	70.3	78.3	118.4	174.7 †	196.1
Pink						
USA	144.8	121.9	76.8	80.1	166.9	120.0
USSR	90.9	40.4	97.7	37.8	145.6	—
Canada	37.7	29.3	26.5	31.4	30.6	26.0
Japan	27.6	20.2	17.1	15.2	19.9	—
Species Total	301.0	211.7	218.1	164.4	363.1	—
Chum						
Japan	178.7	151.5	144.1	159.3	181.6	—
USA	42.0	39.2	39.2	66.4	31.2	32.0
USSR	23.5	23.4	23.7	30.5	21.7	—
Canada	23.6	24.9	10.2	30.0	9.2	17.0
Species Total	267.8	239.1	217.1	286.3	243.6	—
Cherry						
Japan (Species Total)	3.9	3.6	3.4	2.5	2.8	—
Sockeye						
USA	107.1	96.3	103.2	86.2	124.3	146.0
Canada	31.6	29.8	14.8	11.8	33.9	37.0
USSR	9.6	8.1	11.5	8.5	9.9	—
Japan	2.6	2.3	1.7	0.8	0.9	—
Species Total	150.9	136.5	131.1	107.2	168.9	—
Chinook						
USA	12.3	14.0	18.1	20.7	14.3	10.0
Canada	5.5	4.4	5.2	5.1	5.1	5.0
USSR	1.8	2.2	1.7	1.6	1.2	—
Japan	0.7	0.6	0.7	0.4	0.4	—
Species Total	20.3	21.2	25.6	27.8	21.0	—
Coho						
Japan	8.8	7.5	3.2	17.2	20.5	—
USA	23.6	27.4	17.7	21.5	19.9	20.0
Canada	9.0	11.7	8.3	6.1	8.6	11.0
Chile	0.5	1.1	1.8	4.1	7.0	—
USSR	6.0	4.9	3.7	2.7	3.0 †	—
France	0.2	0.2	0.3	0.3	1.1 †	—
Species Total	48.0	52.9	35.0	52.0	60.0 †	—
Grand Total	842.1	735.1	708.7	758.5	1,034.2	—

* Preliminary; missing data not available.
** Includes Faeroe Islands.
† FAO estimate.

Sources:
   1985: *FAO Yearbook, Fishery Statistics, Catches and Landings, 1988.*
   1986-1989: *FAO Yearbook, Fishery Statistics, Catches and Landings, 1989.*
   1990: GLOBEFISH (FISHDAB - 19910731).

Table 3.4
Alaska Salmon Production by Product and Species, 1980–1989
(thousands of metric tons)

Year	Chinook	Sockeye	Coho	Pink	Chum	Total
1980	4.29	55.30	6.75	58.20	21.07	145.61
1981	5.38	69.95	8.49	66.27	28.10	178.19
1982	6.46	63.37	15.61	62.11	27.61	175.16
1983	6.54	100.29	10.27	53.81	23.72	194.63
1984	4.31	74.31	14.59	75.20	30.33	198.74
1985	4.63	77.31	16.40	81.08	28.38	207.80
1986	3.94	62.75	16.60	66.19	27.49	176.97
1987	4.75	72.17	8.45	45.56	24.40	155.33
1988	5.36	57.90	11.01	45.93	37.56	157.75
1989	4.19	91.43	11.21	83.30	19.42	209.56[†]
1980	96%	45%	85%	16%	55%	38%
1981	98%	65%	90%	16%	55%	47%
1982	99%	90%	96%	39%	85%	72%
1983	97%	70%	90%	17%	75%	58%
1984	99%	70%	92%	26%	76%	56%
1985	99%	87%	98%	32%	88%	67%
1986	100%	87%	93%	27%	90%	66%
1987	99%	80%	94%	35%	84%	69%
1988	99%	92%	94%	45%	92%	79%
1989	95%	82%	94%	25%	78%	60%

† Includes production listed as "other" in the CFEC source. "Other" production in 1989 was (in thousands of metric tons): Chinook: 0.027, Sockeye: 0.055, Coho: 0.013, Pink: 0.579, Chum: 0.068, Total: 0.743. Total may not add correctly due to rounding.

Sources:
    1980-1983: Alaska Department of Fish and Game (ADF&G), *Catch and Production*, 1980-1983, as reported in G. Knapp and T. Smith, 1991, at 70. Report prepared for Alaska Department of Commerce and Economic Development and Alaska Industrial Development and Export Authority.
    1984-1988: Commercial Fisheries Entry Commission (CFEC), reported in Boyce, 1990, Tables A-11 and A-12, as reported in G. Knapp and T. Smith, 1991, at 70. Report prepared for Alaska Department of Commerce and Economic Development and Alaska Industrial Development and Export Authority.
    1989: Summary of wholesale pricing information, Alaska Commercial Operator's Annual Reports, 1989, Reports 3A and 3B. Prepared by CFEC.

up 6 percent of Canada's salmon harvest, nearly the same portion as in the United States. Canada's salmon harvest was 10 percent coho and 22 percent chum. For the United States, coho accounted for 7 percent of the harvest and chum accounted for 14 percent. The American harvest had a higher portion of sockeye (34 percent) than did the Canadian harvest (27 percent).[30]

Salmon landings in British Columbia in 1989 were 88,700 metric tons, up slightly from 87,500 metric tons in 1988. This compares with Alaskan harvests of 317,200 metric tons in 1989 and 238,800 metric tons in 1988.[31]

Salmon from Japan

Because of Japan's importance as an export market for Alaskan salmon, the supply of salmon in Japan can have a large impact on purchases from Alaska. All sources of domestic supply increased significantly between 1988 and 1989. Japanese pink and farmed coho harvests increased by 27.4 percent and 26.8 percent, respectively. The harvest of fall chum, typically the largest source of supply, rose by 13.7 percent. Although high-seas catch and Japanese pink harvests declined in 1990, fall chum increased by 25.9 percent over 1989. Imports, which account for more than one-third of total Japanese supply, remained essentially flat between 1988 and 1989, but they increased 16.4 percent in 1990.[32]

Inventories are also a potentially important source of supply in Japan. They are used primarily to spread seasonal production over the year. When high inventories are being drawn down, less additional supply is needed to meet consumer demand. Japanese salmon inventories stood at nearly 60,000 metric tons in 1989 and 1990 or between 14 percent and 16 percent of consumption. They were substantially smaller in 1988 at 35,900 metric tons or 11.2 percent of consumption. Inventories reached unusually high levels in 1989 and 1990—only once in the 1980s were they this high (1986 inventories were slightly more than 60,000 tons). Otherwise, they were usually lower than 40,000 metric tons.[33]

World Supply of Farmed Salmon

A major factor influencing price in the salmon industry is the dramatic increase in farmed salmon production in recent years. Farmed salmon represented about 1 percent of the world salmon supply in 1980, and about 30 percent in 1990. Farmed salmon production nearly doubled between 1988 and 1990. The growth in farmed salmon, wild salmon, and total world production of salmon is shown in Figure 3.4.

Farmed salmon are raised in pens, or large nets, anchored in bays or inlets of the ocean. (Ranch salmon, in contrast, are hatched in hatcheries, spend their lives in the wild, and return to the hatchery.) Salmon farming involves several production stages ranging from collecting salmon eggs and raising smolt (juvenile salmon) to harvesting adult salmon. Farmed production of Atlantic salmon (which accounts for the vast majority of all farmed production) takes three years. Thus, capacity decisions must be made three years prior to actual production. While the supply

Figure 3.4
World Salmon Catch: Farmed and Wild, 1985–1989

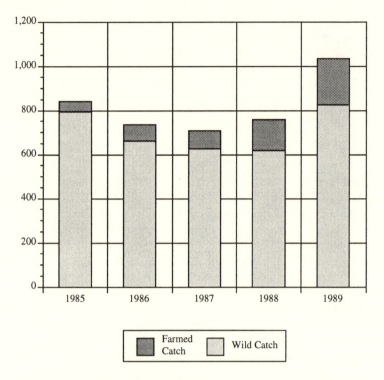

Sources: World total: *FAO Yearbook, Fishery Statistics, Catches and Landings*, 1988 and 1989.
             Farmed catch: GLOBEFISH.
             Wild catch: World total catch minus farmed catch.

can be increased only with a three-year lag, it need not all be harvested.[34] Atlantic
salmon can be held for as long as four years if they undergo a costly reconditioning
(fattening) process after spawning.[35]

Laws in both Norway and the United States prohibit the commercial harvest of
wild Atlantic salmon, although both countries allow recreational fishing of the
species. A relatively small amount of Atlantic salmon farming occurs in the United
States in Maine, New Hampshire, and Washington (the only West Coast state that
permits it). Oregon allows farming only of native species, and Alaska has a mora-
torium on all farming.[36]

Norway produces well over half of all farmed salmon. The total Norwegian
fresh and frozen harvest in 1990 was 150,000 metric tons, up from 117,000 metric
tons in 1989 and 80,000 metric tons in 1988 (Figure 3.5). It was estimated to fall to
120,000 metric tons in 1991 under a government program in which surplus fish
are purchased and frozen by the government.[37] As Norwegian production has risen,

the price has fallen, as shown in Table 3.5 for 1988 and 1989.

The United Kingdom is the second-largest producer of farmed salmon. All of the United Kingdom's production, which grew rapidly in the late 1980s, takes place in farming operations in Scotland. The most important market for Scottish farmed salmon is the United Kingdom itself. About 60 percent of Scottish production was consumed domestically in the late 1980s, and this represents the bulk of the domestic fresh and frozen market.[38]

Japanese salmon farming consists mostly of coho. Japan's farmed production increased nearly fourfold between 1985 and 1990. It is the largest producer of farmed Pacific salmon and the third-largest producer of all farmed salmon. The declining trend in coho prices in Japan may be due in part to the increase in farmed coho production.

British Columbia's farmed salmon production has increased greatly since 1980. The industry's production of 13,000 metric tons in 1990 was the second-largest Pacific salmon production, following Japan. New Brunswick's production of 5,000 metric tons of Atlantic salmon in 1990 brings Canada's total to 18,000 metric tons, the fourth-highest in the world.

Supply of Non-Salmon Species

Herring Roe

In the 1988–1989 fishing year, the herring harvest was valued at $18.8 million, down sharply from the 1987–1988 value of $61.0 million (Table 3.2).[39] The size of the sac roe herring catch, which accounts for most of the total herring harvest, did not vary substantially between those two periods, but the statewide average ex-vessel price fell from $0.49 per pound in 1988 (nearly twice the average for the decade) to about $0.30 per pound in 1989.[40] Alaska's 1988 herring production of more than 41,500 metric tons represented 88 percent of the U.S. total.[41]

Other major sources of Pacific roe herring include Canada, with a 1989 catch comparable to that of the United States. The former Soviet Union is the largest harvester of Pacific herring. It gathered nearly 100,000 metric tons in 1989, but this harvest did not appear to be destined for the roe market.[42]

Halibut

Alaskan waters yielded a halibut harvest of 33,900 metric tons worth $85.8 million in 1989 (Table 3.2). Both harvest and price have been relatively stable since 1986 after rising substantially during the early 1980s. Consequently, the total value of the harvest remained comparatively stable in the latter part of the decade. In 1989, Alaska's harvest represented a large majority of the world harvest of Pacific halibut (Figure 3.3).

The length of the halibut season has changed dramatically over time: 93 days in

Table 3.5
Norwegian Salmon Exports for 1989
(metric tons)

Country	Fresh	Frozen	Total	Percentage of Total Exports	Change in Tons 1988-1989	Change in Price 1988-1989
France	20,102	7,318	27,420	28%	+47%	-25%
Denmark	13,663	2,683	16,346	17%	+15%	-21%
USA	12,843	116	12,959	13%	+30%	-22%
West Germany	9,601	446	10,047	10%	+34%	-21%
Spain	7,068	120	7,188	7%	+89%	-23%
Japan	4,678	1,023	5,701	6%	+93%	-18%
Others	15,563	3,764	19,327	20%	+75%	
TOTAL	83,518	15,470	98,988	100%	+46%	-22%
FOB value† (Million US$)	435.7	79.7	515.3		0.1	

† Dollar value calculated using exchange rate of 6.9045 Norwegian Kroners/U.S. Dollar (Source: Midpoint rate on which the calculation of other rates is based at the fixing at the Oslo Boers at 11:00 a.m. each business day, as reported in International Financial Statistics, Sept. 1991, at 402).

Source:

The Fresh Fish Export Organization Statistics 31.12.88 and 31.12.89; as reported in *Salmon Market Newsletter*, Volume 2, No. 1, International Institute of Fisheries Economics and Trade, March 1990 at 10.

Figure 3.5
Largest World Producers of Farmed Salmon, 1985–1991

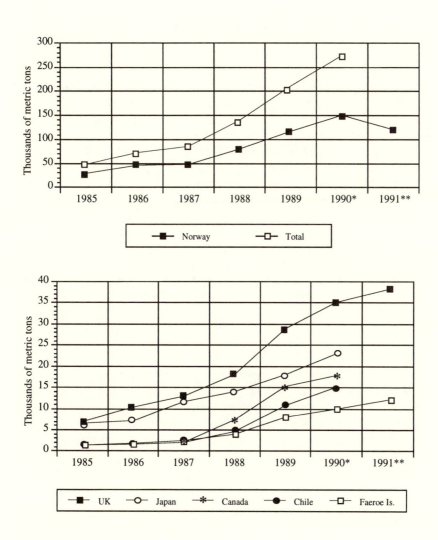

*Preliminary
**Estimates
Source: FAO, GLOBEFISH, 1991.

1955, 178 days in 1971, and 3 days in 1990.[43] The number of fishing permits, which is not restricted, has increased dramatically, leading the International Pacific Halibut Commission (IPHC) to offset increased participation by shortening the season. The IPHC also imposes catch limits on halibut. Technological improvements have allowed fishermen to harvest more quickly and efficiently, but the increased catch per derby may result in poorer quality fish as fishermen and processors have difficulty handling large harvests.[44]

Sablefish

Sablefish catches increased steadily from 1985 to 1988, before dropping to 34,200 metric tons valued at $62.9 million in 1989 (Table 3.2). The average price fell from $0.946 per pound in 1988 to $0.833 per pound in 1989.[45] Alaska was a major world source of sablefish in 1989 (Figure 3.3).

The largest exploitable populations of sablefish are found off the western coast of the United States and Canada. During the 1970s, Japanese fishermen who harvested sablefish in these waters met the Japanese demand for sablefish, while U.S. and Canadian fishermen met the North American demand. However, the Magnuson Fishery Conservation and Management Act of 1977 changed the traditional separation of the markets by phasing out the foreign harvest of sablefish in U.S. waters. The Japanese catch, which averaged 35,000 metric tons per year in the seven years prior to the Magnuson Act, has fallen to almost nothing. During the 1980s, though regulated by quotas, sablefish harvesting by U.S. fishermen expanded rapidly, as did U.S. sablefish exports to Japan, in a process known as Americanization of the fishery.[46]

Shrimp

The size of the Alaskan shrimp harvest declined steeply during the 1980s. The 1981 Alaskan shrimp harvest of 11,500 metric tons was less than half of the previous year's 23,700 metric tons. By 1989, the harvest reached only 900 metric tons (Table 3.2). The value of the Alaskan shrimp harvest has declined almost continuously from its $16.8 million level in 1980 to less than one-tenth that in 1989.[47]

Crab

The Alaskan harvest of Dungeness crab fluctuated between 2,700 metric tons and 7,200 metric tons during the 1980s, averaging 4,600 metric tons for the decade. The value of the harvest has shown similar fluctuation and averaged $10.1 million for the 1980s. Canada is the only other significant producer of Dungeness crab.[48] The king crab harvest fell steeply in the first half of the 1980s, from 84,200 metric tons in 1980 to 7,300 metric tons in 1985. In the latter part of the decade, the king crab harvest appears to have stabilized. The value of the king crab harvest ($104.9 million in 1989) did not fall as sharply because the harvest prices rose from just over $1.00 per pound in 1980 to about $4.00 per pound in 1988 and 1989.[49] The former Soviet Union is the largest king crab producer (41,900 metric tons in 1989) and the only significant alternate source of supply.[50]

DEMAND FOR WORLD AND ALASKAN SEAFOOD

The price of seafood depends not only on the quantity available, but also on the amount demanded by consumers around the world. If world demand for seafood increases, the price of seafood will rise, all else equal. The sources of demand for U.S. seafood can be divided into exports, domestic consumption, and changes in inventories. For example, 49 percent of the U.S. salmon harvest was exported in 1990. Japan, Canada, France, and the United Kingdom were all significant export markets.[51] Exports of fresh and frozen salmon are largest for sockeye, followed at some distance by pink, chum, and coho. Chinook exports are relatively small (Table 3.6). Since most U.S. production of salmon comes from Alaska, these figures mirror the exports of Alaskan salmon.

Consumers in different countries have preferences for different species of salmon, processed into different products. For example, a large amount of canned pink salmon is exported to the United Kingdom, but Japan's imports of pink salmon are almost exclusively fresh or frozen. Consumers' preferences for seafood relative to other goods can shift. News reports on the benefits of eating seafood for overall health or on the risks of eating contaminated seafood can cause such a shift.[52] The likelihood of this type of shift affecting seafood from a particular area depends on whether consumers can identify the source. If the specific location of the seafood is on the label, consumers can change their consumption pattern of seafood among different sources as their preferences change. Without source labeling, most consumers could not identify the particular harvest location of seafood and would be unable to alter their consumption pattern according to source.

Consumers' tastes are only one of many different variables that affect demand, and consequently price. Other factors include income, inflation and exchange rates, and prices of substitute products. Both population and real income per capita have generally been growing since the early 1980s in major seafood-consuming nations and would therefore have a positive effect on the price of seafood.

Exchange rates affect the demand for Alaskan seafood abroad, because a change in the exchange rate changes the price of local seafood (and other local substitutes) in a foreign country relative to the price of imported Alaskan seafood. Alaskan seafood is sold in many countries around the world, but exchange rates between the dollar and yen have the greatest effect on demand for Alaskan seafood because most direct exports of Alaskan seafood go to Japan.[53] The yen generally strengthened against the dollar between 1982 and 1988, with the greatest change taking place between 1985 and 1988. However, in 1989 and 1990, the dollar gained on the yen. The strengthening yen increased the purchasing power of Japanese consumers, thus increasing their demand for Alaskan seafood. This contributed to a

Table 3.6

U.S. Exports of Salmon to Japan as a Percentage of U.S. Salmon Exports to All Countries, by Species, 1987–1990
(thousands of metric tons)

Year and Category	Chinook	Chum	Pink	Coho	Sockeye
1987					
U.S. Exports to Japan	3.3	8.2	9.6	4.3	58.8
U.S. Exports to All Countries	4.5	18.8	16.1	9.6	62.7
Percentage to Japan	73.6 %	43.6 %	59.4 %	44.6 %	93.7 %
1988					
U.S. Exports to Japan	3.6	16.6	17.5	5.9	61.0
U.S. Exports to All Countries	4.8	25.9	23.8	9.0	62.7
Percentage to Japan	74.7 %	64.2 %	73.5 %	65.2 %	97.2 %
1989					
U.S. Exports to Japan	3.8	11.3	9.2	11.2	81.0
U.S. Exports to All Countries	4.5	17.5	21.9	16.0	85.4
Percentage to Japan	85.1 %	64.6 %	42.1 %	69.8 %	94.8 %
1990					
U.S. Exports to Japan	2.2	4.7	7.4	8.2	87.7
U.S. Exports to All Countries	2.8	11.4	17.0	13.4	92.0
Percentage to Japan	79.3 %	41.1 %	43.6 %	61.0 %	95.4 %

Note: Exports include fresh, frozen, and chilled salmon.

Source: U.S. Department of Commerce, Bureau of the Census, FT-446: U.S. Exports (7-digit, Schedule B, Commodity Number by Country), 1987-1990.

Figure 3.6
Consumption of Fresh and Frozen Salmon, 1988
(metric tons)

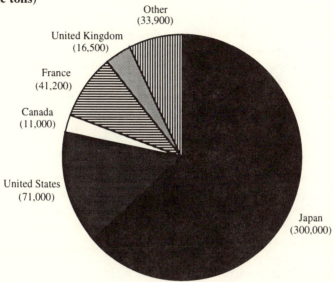

Sources: *World Markets in Salmon: Pen-reared Salmon Impacts,* The Sea Fare Group, 1988. British Columbia Salmon Farmers Association/The DPA Group, Inc. Susan Shaw, University of Stirling. As reported in *Current Developments in World Salmon Markets, Economic and Commercial Analysis,* Report no 46, Canadian Department of Fisheries and Oceans, January 1990.

sharp increase in Alaskan salmon and herring prices between 1985 and 1988.[54] Wholesale prices in Japan rose 29 percent between 1986 and 1988. In addition, the yen appreciated against the dollar, yielding a combined price increase of 71 percent.[55]

Demand for Salmon

We will examine the demand for salmon from several different perspectives: the form of the product (canned, fresh, or frozen); the country of consumption (Figure 3.6); the species of salmon; and the manner in which the salmon population is managed (wild or farmed).

The Japanese market, by virtue of its sheer size, heavily influences world demand for salmon and deserves special attention. Throughout the 1980s, most of the sockeye caught in Alaska was exported to Japan, arriving during the late summer months. Significant portions of the harvest of other Alaskan salmon species also were exported to Japan. The fish either immediately enter the retail sector or are frozen for later distribution. Salted salmon is the most popular salmon product in Japan. However, unsalted salmon is also commonly purchased. These products are staples in the Japanese diet.[56]

Alaskan salmon faces a number of substitutes in Japan that change throughout the season and in different regions. In the fall, Japan's coastal fisheries land large quantities of chum salmon, most of which originates in a highly productive salmon ranching system. The chum catch is especially important and leads to a coinciding seasonal increase in the consumption of fresh salmon. Pink salmon, which runs in the spring in Japan, is a relatively close substitute for Alaskan sockeye. Yellowtail substitutes for salmon in the southern part of Japan.[57]

Demand for Alaskan Salmon

The relative importance of domestic and foreign markets for Alaskan salmon depends on the species and product form. During the 1980s, fresh and frozen salmon became an increasingly large percentage of Alaskan salmon production. By 1989 it accounted for 60 percent of total production. Pink salmon production varies substantially from that of other species. Fresh and frozen pink salmon accounted for only 25 percent of total production in 1989 (Table 3.4).

Domestic markets are particularly important for pink, chum, and chinook. A comparison of data for U.S. catch with U.S. exports reveals that U.S. exports of fresh, frozen, and canned pink amounted to only 22 percent of the U.S. harvest in 1990.[58] This is consistent with the fact that most of Alaska's pink harvest is canned, and most of Alaska's canned salmon is consumed in the United States.[59] U.S. exports of chinook and chum (almost exclusively fresh or frozen) were 28 percent and 38 percent of the species' U.S. harvests, respectively.

Overall, the United States exports nearly one-half of its salmon harvest. Alaska's figures are likely to mirror those of the entire United States, given its importance for U.S. production.[60] In 1988, 89 percent of fresh and frozen U.S. production was exported, compared with only 38 percent of canned production.[61] Export markets are important for all salmon species, but especially so for sockeye and coho. Following is a breakdown of export destinations by species and form of processing:

- *Sockeye.* Of the vast majority of the Alaskan sockeye harvest that is fresh and frozen (82 percent in 1989), most is exported to Japan, though some goes to Europe. The United Kingdom is the leading export market for canned Alaskan sockeye production, 40 percent of which is exported.

- *Coho.* Most Alaskan coho is sold in fresh or frozen form. Japan is the leading export market despite heavy marketing in Europe.

- *Pink.* Most Alaskan pink salmon is canned (75 percent in 1989), and most is sold domestically. Significant export markets include the

United Kingdom, Australia, and Canada. Little of the canned Alaskan pink is exported to Japan, though most fresh or frozen pink exports go there. Other countries in Europe, as well as Canada and Korea, buy fresh or frozen pink.

- *Chum.* Both domestic and foreign markets are important destinations for the chum harvest. The largest export market for fresh and frozen chum from Alaska is Japan. Canada, the United Kingdom, and the rest of Europe are other markets.

- *Chinook.* Virtually all Alaskan chinook is sold fresh or frozen. Most exports go to Japan and France.[62]

Table 3.6 shows the percentages of U.S. exports of fresh, frozen, or chilled salmon to Japan. Japan received practically all U.S. exports of sockeye in 1990, as well as most U.S. exports of chinook and coho. Between 1987 and 1990, exports to Japan never accounted for less than 41 percent of total U.S. exports of any salmon species.

Demand for Canadian Salmon

Domestic and export markets are important destinations for Canadian salmon—approximately 39 percent was consumed domestically in 1989, with the remainder exported.[63] Domestic sales of fresh and frozen salmon amounted to 11 thousand metric tons in 1989; 7 thousand metric tons of that came from harvests of wild Pacific salmon in British Columbia and the remainder from farming operations on both coasts.[64] More than half of the Canadian salmon harvest was canned in 1989, and roughly half of that was consumed domestically.[65]

Most Canadian exports of fresh and frozen salmon go to Japan, European Economic Community members, and the United States. The United Kingdom and Australia receive most canned exports, primarily pink and sockeye. Canada also imports a relatively large amount of fresh pink and chum salmon, but it is likely that these imports are destined for processing plants whose demand is not satisfied by Canadian sources.[66]

The British Columbian salmon industry merits particular attention because of its proximity and similarity to the Alaskan industry. The contribution of the different species to the total salmon catch is comparable for the two areas. Both British Columbia and Alaska export a large majority of their sockeye and coho catches in fresh or frozen form. Almost all of both areas' sockeye exports (95 percent in 1989) go to Japan, as do most of their coho exports (about 60 percent in 1989). In addition, the United Kingdom is the largest export market for canned sockeye from both areas.[67]

The primary market for Alaskan chinook, virtually all of which is fresh or frozen, appears to be the United States, based on the comparison of catch and export statistics discussed above. Likewise, two-thirds of British Columbia's fresh and frozen exports of chinook are destined for the United States. The next largest market for both Alaskan and British Columbian chinook is Japan. Pink salmon from both Alaska and British Columbia is most commonly canned. The United Kingdom is the largest export market for canned pink from both areas; however, again comparing catch and export statistics indicates that a large portion of the Alaskan canned pink production is consumed domestically.[68] Similarities are slightly weaker for chum salmon. Domestic consumption appears to account for a large part of fresh and frozen Alaskan chum, and Japan is the biggest export market. Japan, France, and Denmark are important destinations for British Columbian fresh and frozen chum, each accounting for 15 to 20 percent of exports.

Demand for Japanese Salmon

Salmon demand in Japan is met by several sources: domestic wild and ranched salmon (both coastal and high-seas catch), domestic farmed salmon, imports of both wild and farmed salmon, and inventories. Total Japanese salmon consumption reached 425,000 metric tons in 1990, up 12.4 percent from 1989 and over 100,000 metric tons more than 1988.[69] Japan exports very little salmon. It consumes virtually all of its wild catch and farmed harvest.[70] Japan's fall chum (by far its largest source of wild and ranched salmon) runs from August to January. During this period, Japanese consumers tend to switch from imported sockeye to fresh chum. Near the end of the season, they move back to frozen imported sockeye. This pattern of demand shows up as a seasonal peak of fresh salmon consumption in the fall months. Seasonal demand for salted chum peaks in December, when a whole salted chum makes a popular New Year's gift. The high seas catch is largely chum, but it differs from fall chum in that it is harvested in spring before spawning and is preferred by Japanese consumers for its higher fat content. Pink salmon caught on the high seas is primarily sold fresh; other pink is salted. Japanese pink represents only a small portion of total Japanese consumption.[71]

Demand for Farmed Salmon

In recent years the world supply of farmed salmon has increased dramatically as buying patterns have changed. Between 60 and 80 percent of fresh farmed Atlantic salmon is sold to restaurants. The remainder goes to supermarkets and retail fish markets.[72] Consumers increasingly prefer fresh salmon, which can be purchased from farms year-round.[73] Additionally, farmed salmon can be higher quality than wild salmon, due to less bruising in the harvesting process. The year-round availability of fresh farmed salmon affects the demand for Alaskan salmon because off-season supplies from Alaska are necessarily frozen or canned.

Prices of farmed salmon fell dramatically from 1988 to 1989. Industry sources report that the reasons for the decline in the 1989 price of salmon include high production of farmed Atlantic salmon, the large wild salmon catch, and increased inventories in Japan and North America, all of which served to depress price. Early marketing of Canadian farmed salmon before an expected December freeze also reportedly lowered price.[74]

Substitutability of Wild and Farmed Salmon. Several studies have examined the extent to which farmed salmon substitutes for wild salmon.[75] One found that substitutes for farmed Atlantic salmon include fresh coho, chinook, and sockeye.[76] Wholesalers in the United States were surveyed to determine the degree of substitutability between farmed Atlantic salmon and wild species.[77] Between one-half and two-thirds of them thought there was strong substitution between farmed Atlantic salmon and fresh chinook, sockeye, and coho. However, relatively few thought farmed Atlantic salmon was a substitute for chum or pink or any frozen salmon. Another study found that wholesalers generally considered frozen salmon to be a poor substitute for fresh salmon.[78] Despite perceptions of poor substitutability between fresh and frozen salmon, the year-round availability of fresh farmed salmon has cut into the traditional markets for frozen salmon.[79]

France is the world's third-largest purchaser of farmed salmon, after Japan and the United States. One study indicates that fresh and frozen wild chinook is a substitute for fresh and frozen Norwegian farmed salmon in the French market.[80] Norway sold 28 percent of its exported salmon to France in 1989 (Table 3.5). Norway increased its share of French imports from 4 percent to 47 percent between 1980 to 1990. The United States and Canada accounted for 93 percent of France's imports in 1980 but only 38 percent in 1990. "Atlantic salmon has become more competitive as the price has fallen and this has obviously resulted in substitution between Pacific and Atlantic salmon in the French smoking industry."[81] The price of frozen Atlantic salmon in France in 1980 was 140 percent higher than the price of Pacific salmon, but by 1989, prices of the two species had nearly equalized. As the price of wild salmon increased in 1988, more European buyers turned to farmed salmon.[82]

Effect of Farmed Salmon on Pacific Salmon Prices. Numerous articles in the press have attributed low prices for Pacific salmon in 1989 to the increased production and marketing of farmed salmon. One article states that "for the past two years, those of us in the wild salmon business have priced ourselves out of the market." They "not only lost sales because of the high price, but lost market share when the buyers went to farmers for their supply."[83] Another reports that a "series of good Alaska fishing years and price-cutting by competing Norwegian salmon farms have created a glut on the canned and frozen salmon markets."[84]

Many of the articles note the importance of increased Norwegian farmed salmon production, but they also reference salmon farming in Japan, Chile, Sweden, Ireland, British Columbia, and the Pacific Northwest.[85] For example, one article states: "Other depressing trends for 1989 were the increase in Japanese hatchery production of chum salmon and the rise in sales of internationally farm-raised salmon. Last year Norway sold about 150,000 metric tons of pen-reared salmon in markets that historically had purchased Alaska frozen fish. . . . It hurt us [Alaskan fishermen] on the fresh market, especially in the price for cohos."[86]

Sales of farmed salmon have increased significantly in many countries. French imports of Norwegian farmed salmon grew dramatically during the 1980s, with a corresponding reduction in imports from Alaska. Exports of Alaskan salmon to Japan also suffered from competition from pen-reared salmon from Europe and South America. The Japanese have been investing in Canadian salmon farming operations.[87]

This view of farmed salmon is not universal, however. One article downplays the importance of farmed salmon, noting that increases in wild salmon harvests in Alaska and British Columbia alone have matched increases from farm production during the 1985–1990 period.[88]

The advent of farmed salmon appears to have fundamentally altered world salmon markets. Variations in the wild harvest, among other factors, will likely continue to cause short-run fluctuations in prices. But over the long run, the world price of salmon will not be sustained above farmed salmon production cost because farmers will increase output, thereby lowering price. Similarly, price will not remain below production costs of farmers because they will decrease output, thereby increasing price.[89]

Demand for Non-Salmon Species

Herring Roe

Throughout the 1980s, exports of herring ranged from about 70 percent to 90 percent of U.S. production. One source estimates that exports of sac roe herring are even higher, approaching 100 percent. It is not possible to calculate exact figures because export statistics combine all fresh and frozen herring as well as Atlantic and Pacific herring. On average during the 1980s, the sac roe herring harvest accounted for 86 percent of the total herring harvest. Japan is by far the largest export market for U.S. herring. It received 78 percent of fresh and frozen exports by value in 1989. Korea was the second-largest market, with 11 percent by value in 1989. The former Soviet Union purchased a large volume of herring in 1989, but it was much lower valued than that exported to other countries.[90]

Japan is of obvious importance in any consideration of world herring demand. Most of the Alaskan herring harvest is exported as whole (round) fish to Japanese processors, who process virtually all Pacific herring roe for the salted roe market.[91] Although salted herring roe is consumed year-round, purchases traditionally peak in December, when the Japanese buy salted herring roe, a symbol of fertility and prosperity, to exchange during the New Year holidays.[92] Demand for this luxury item is relatively insensitive to price changes.[93] Because the North American harvest of roe herring occurs in the spring, suppliers must hold roe herring and salted roe in inventory for months. Consequently, speculation about December prices for salted roe plays a role in setting North American ex-vessel prices.[94] A newer product, flavored herring roe (lower quality roe mixed with various seasonings and sauces), has begun to play an increasingly large role in the market because it is priced low relative to other roe products and is less time-consuming to prepare. However, its lower quality appears to render flavored herring roe a distant substitute for salted herring roe.[95]

Halibut

In 1989, 59 percent of U.S. halibut production (virtually all of which came from Alaska) was consumed domestically. The portion of U.S. production exported rose sharply in 1989, mostly due to greater exports to Japan. In 1990, the United States exported 9.1 thousand metric tons, of which 5.4 thousand metric tons went to Japan and 2.7 thousand metric tons went to Canada.[96]

Sablefish

In 1989, U.S. exports of whole or dressed sablefish reached 21 thousand metric tons. Approximately half of U.S. production of sablefish is exported, and close to half of exports come from Alaska. The primary export market for sablefish is Japan. Before Americanization of the fishery, Japanese fishing vessels accounted for the bulk of the sablefish catch. As the Japanese catch dwindled in recent years, U.S. shipments to Japan rose dramatically, accounting for most of the increase in exports.[97]

Japanese demand for sablefish is highest in the late fall and winter months, which led Japanese fishermen to harvest most sablefish at that time. However, as American laws and regulations took effect in the late 1970s, the season moved to the spring. This change in season has forced the Japanese to store much of the sablefish imports for several months before demand increases in the fall.[98]

Shrimp

Spot shrimp, which are large and generally caught in pot gear, are primarily sold locally in Anchorage and Seward to the fresh market, such as restaurants.[99] Although shrimpers using pot gear focus on large shrimp, they sometimes harvest smaller pink shrimp in the process.[100] The relatively small shrimp harvests in Alaska do not compete with shrimp from the South Atlantic and Gulf Coast states.[101]

Crab

Alaska accounts for all U.S. production of king crab. Thus, export figures for the United States entirely reflect Alaska's exports. In 1988, more than half of U.S. king crab production was exported. The pattern of export volume in recent years follows the crash and slow recovery of the king crab harvests, falling from 13.7 thousand metric tons in 1980 to 0.5 thousand metric tons in 1983 and reaching 2.4

thousand metric tons in 1988. Japan is by far the largest importer of U.S. fresh and frozen crab. In both 1988 and 1989, Japanese imports accounted for more than 90 percent of the volume and value of crab exports.[102] Domestic sales of Dungeness crab account for almost all of Alaska's production.

MARKET LINKAGES

The forces of supply and demand link local markets for seafood in Alaska and elsewhere to global markets. Supply conditions are affected by the entry of out-of-region suppliers drawn by high price levels and the exit of regional suppliers pushed to other regions when prices are too low. Similarly, demand conditions are affected by the entry of out-of-region purchasers attracted by low price levels and the departure of regional purchasers to other regions when prices are too high.

Seafood of many species and product forms is traded on world markets, signifying that price differences across regions for seafood of identical quality should be no greater than transportation costs plus tariffs. Otherwise, if prices in one region of the world were substantially higher than in others, buyers from the high-priced region would purchase seafood from other regions and pay the transportation costs themselves. Likewise, if prices in one region of the world were substantially lower than in others, sellers from the low-priced region would sell seafood to other regions and pay the transportation costs themselves.

Nevertheless, regional markets for seafood are not entirely integrated, and a single world price for a particular species of seafood of identical quality does not exist. Relative prices may vary slightly from year to year across regions to reflect changes in local demand and supply conditions that are small relative to transportation costs. Yet the regional price differences for seafood of similar quality should be fairly stable over time and reflect differences in transportation costs of bringing the seafood to market. One would expect that the pattern of Alaskan seafood prices over time would be similar to that of comparable seafood from other regions.

MARKET STRUCTURE OF SEAFOOD INDUSTRY

The structure of an industry can be an important determinant of price. In addition to the influence of supply and demand, variables such as the number of buyers and sellers, their geographic distribution, the likelihood of collusion, and the nature of contracts can influence the price that prevails in the market. If, for example, an industry is characterized by a small number of sellers of a product in a certain geographic area, they may be able to sell their product at a higher price than would prevail with a large number of sellers. However, if it is relatively easy for new firms to enter this industry, any price rise by the existing sellers could be quickly undercut, thus forcing them to keep their prices at a competitive level.

Harvesting

The seafood harvesting industry is centered around the fleet of fishing boats that gather seafood in Alaskan waters. In 1990, more than 17,000 vessels were licensed to fish commercially in Alaska, a figure that varied little during the 1980s. The number of permit holders is approximately as large. The number of permits is considerably larger, however, because one individual can hold multiple permits.[103] The magnitude of the number of fishing vessels and individuals involved in harvesting fish suggests that the harvesting industry is highly competitive.

Processing

Industry Characteristics

The seafood processing industry in Alaska is characterized by a number of plants dispersed among the prime harvesting areas. According to Bureau of the Census data, there were 89 seafood processing plants in Alaska in 1988 with an average size of 94 employees; however, half of all plants employed fewer than 20 people. The plants are most heavily concentrated in four regions—Cook Inlet (17 plants), Southeast (14 plants), Kodiak Island (13 plants), and Bristol Bay (12 plants).[104] Some firms operate more than one plant. About half of all fresh and frozen salmon, 70 percent of canned salmon, and half of all Alaskan halibut processing are handled by seven of the top ten processors in Alaska.[105]

Fixed costs borne by processing operations, such as investment in plant and equipment, tend to be large compared with the cost of processing an extra pound of fish. Fixed costs are apparently becoming increasingly important as production shifts from labor-intensive canning to fresh and frozen forms, which require relatively more capital equipment per pound of fish processed. Despite some indications that year-round processing is growing, the need of processors to meet seasonal peaks in the harvest requires the maintenance of large facilities.[106] In some fisheries, like Cook Inlet, processors have added capacity to account for increased run sizes and the proximity to other fisheries such as Bristol Bay. This allocation of capacity confirms that the harvest can be readily transported among nearby fisheries. There are some indications that firms located in areas as far from Alaska as Seattle process excess harvest (and thus could be effective competitors to Alaska-based harvesters).[107]

Foreign Ownership of Seafood Processors

Japanese companies own a substantial portion of the Alaskan seafood processing industry. Concerns that Japanese-owned processors were working together to keep ex-vessel prices low surfaced in the Bristol Bay strike in 1991.[108] One study of the Alaskan seafood industry lists 16 Japanese parent firms among firms in

Alaska with some foreign ownership.[109] Some of these parents have stakes as small as 0.7 percent in the processing companies. Of the 33 processors with Japanese parents (accounting for 49 processing plants), 14 are wholly Japanese-owned, and another 5 are majority Japanese-owned. Seven companies have non-Japanese foreign parents.

In terms of shares of revenue, Japanese ownership is much less significant. The top 20 seafood processors headquartered in Puget Sound account for a total of 46 shore-based processing plants in Alaska. The two largest companies are American-owned and contributed 28 percent of the nearly $2 billion in total revenue of the top 20 companies in 1988. The third-largest processor, which accounts for an additional 10 percent, has recently been purchased by an Indonesian company. Overall, non-Japanese-owned firms accounted for more than two-thirds of the total revenue, leaving the remaining one-third for the five Japanese-controlled processors.[110] Collusion among the 16 Japanese parent firms would be problematic at best. It is highly unlikely that Japanese-owned firms are engaged in pricing behavior that systematically holds down the price that processors pay to fishermen.[111]

Moreover, even if these Japanese firms did possess the market power necessary to keep ex-vessel prices below competitive levels, market power would matter for the purposes of this report only if it *changed* between 1989 and earlier years. If market power existed throughout the 1980s, for example, it would not have caused the price to decline only in 1989—the price would have been low for the entire decade. If market power first arose in 1989, that might explain the decline in the price of salmon. But even it that were so, market power has nothing to do with the *Exxon Valdez* oil spill, and its existence actually would provide an independent explanation of changed prices.

Contracts and Vertical Relationships

Ex-Vessel

Fishermen sell their catch either directly to a processor or to a "cash buyer" who, in turn, sells to a processor. Ex-vessel prices are typically "posted" by a processor at the beginning of an opening. These posted prices tend to be low estimates of what the market price will be. Consequently, they often rise during the season because of short supply or competitive pressures. For example, an aggressive processor may bid up the price in order to increase market share or to attract enough fish to fulfill contract commitments. Posted prices occasionally decline over the season, usually in the event of very large harvests. Post-season adjustments are also made to account for factors such as the actual selling price of wholesale products made from the fish purchased by the processor and bonuses that are dependent on the volume of fish delivered by a fisherman to a specific processor.[112]

Ultimately, the variability of ex-vessel prices seems more characteristic of spot-market prices than long-term contract prices.

> Although price agreements between processing companies and fishermen often are reached before the season, the prices are subject to change throughout the season. In effect, processors and "cash buyers" compete for the available fish, which often causes prices to escalate.[113]

Processor

Sales agreements appear to be fairly common only for frozen sockeye. The terms of these agreements are typically set a month or less before the fishing season begins. Relatively little contracting exists for sales of the other species in fresh or frozen form or for canned salmon. Sales agreements between processors and wholesalers may be based on an ex-vessel price adjusted by a margin for the processor. These are still subject to post-season adjustments and bonuses that weaken the price-determining effect of the agreements. In addition, some agreements include adjustment factors that are negotiated to reflect changes in supply or demand conditions as the season progresses.[114]

Wholesale prices in Japan also appear to be spot market prices. Even some of the agreements between Alaskan processors and Japanese wholesalers provide for prices that vary with the ex-vessel spot-market prices.[115]

CONCLUSION

The pricing of Alaskan seafood—salmon, herring roe, halibut, sablefish, shrimp, and crab—is affected by many factors: the species of seafood, the product form (fresh, frozen, or canned), regional and global harvests, inventories, exchange rates, income, and consumers' tastes. Having examined in detail these many determinants of Alaskan seafood prices, we turn in chapter 4 to the *Exxon Valdez* oil spill and consider evidence concerning its effects on supply and demand and, ultimately, whether it affected the prices of Alaskan seafood.

NOTES

1. G. Knapp & T. Smith, The Alaska Seafood Industry (1991) at 115 (report prepared at the Institute of Social and Economic Research, University of Alaska, Anchorage, for Alaska Department of Commerce and Economic Development & the Alaska Industrial Development and Export Authority).

2. *Id.* at ii.

3. *Id.* at 161–162; Commercial Fisheries Entry Commission, State of Alaska, Annual Report at 12, 14 (1990) [hereinafter cited as CFEC Annual Report 1990].

4. G. Knapp and T. Smith, *supra* note 1 at 5.

5. The "ex-vessel price," as used later in this book, includes bonuses and other post-season adjustments.

6. G. Knapp & T. Smith, *supra* note 1 at 53.

7. The processing term "dressed" refers to headed and gutted fish; "semi-dressed" fish are gutted but not headed. C. Wessells, An Economic Analysis of the Japanese Salmon Market: Consumption Patterns, the Role of Inventories and Trade Implications 72 (1990) (unpublished Ph.D. Dissertation, Dept. of Agricultural Economics, University of California, Davis).

8. Fish that are frozen whole are said to be "round." Ultimately, the herring roe are stripped from the fish, but Alaska state law prohibits discarding the herring carcass. G. Knapp & T. Smith, *supra* note 1 at 96.

9. *Id.* at 53.

10. *Id.* at 24, 42, 169, 183, 191. The regulatory bodies that govern management and fishing of the different species have established different regional boundaries within the state. They usually call these regions by similar but slightly different names.

11. *Id.* at 22.

12. *See* Economists Incorporated, An Economic Analysis of the Effect of the *Exxon Valdez* Oil Spill on Alaskan Seafood Prices, Submitted to the Trans-Alaska Pipeline Liability Fund, Table II-2 (December 1991) [hereinafter cited as Economists Incorporated Report] .

13. Roe herring refers to egg-bearing herring; herring roe refers to the eggs themselves. The fishery for food and bait, conducted in the fall, is very small.

14. Roe are harvested in Prince William Sound both as wild roe-on-kelp and pound roe-on-kelp. Togiak has only wild roe-on-kelp. G. Knapp & T. Smith, *supra* note 1 at 34, 38.

15. A longline is a continuous length of line (up to several miles in length for sablefish though shorter for halibut) with a large number of shorter lines attached. Hooks are affixed to the shorter lines and baited. The longline is set along the bottom and later retrieved with the catch. *Id.* at 37 note 15 and at 82.

16. *Id.* at 44.

17. *Id.* at 50.

18. *Id.* at 31. A pot is an enclosed framework of wire, wood, or wicker for catching fish, lobster, crab, or shrimp. Pots are generally baited and left unattended for a period of time. The shrimp swim into the pot to get the bait but usually cannot find their way out.

19. *Id.* at 32.

20. *Id.* at 31.

21. *Id.* at 13.

22. CFEC, ANNUAL REPORT 1990, *supra* note 3 at 12.

23. *See for example* PACIFIC HALIBUT FISHERY REGULATIONS 6 (1989).

24. G. Knapp & T. Smith, *supra* note 1 at 132.

25. W. Wahpepah, *Salmon Showdown Divides Bristol Bay*, Oregonian, July 5, 1991, at C10.

26. G. Knapp, Alaska Salmon Markets and Prices 2 (October 1991) (prepared for a presentation to the Salmon Strategy Task Force) [hereinafter referred to as Alaska Salmon Markets].

27. NATIONAL MARINE FISHERIES SERVICE, NATIONAL OCEANIC AND ATMOSPHERIC ADMINISTRATION, U.S. DEPARTMENT OF COMMERCE, FISHERIES OF THE U.S. 15 (1990) [hereinafter cited as FISHERIES OF THE U.S. (1990)].

28. G. Knapp & T. Smith, *supra* note 1 at 93.

29. Economists Incorporated Report, *supra* note 12, Table II-2.

30. MARKET ANALYSIS GROUP, CANADIAN DEPARTMENT OF FISHERIES AND OCEANS, ECONOMIC AND COMMERCIAL ANALYSIS REPORT 81, SALMON MARKET OUTLOOK at xxix, xxxii (JANUARY 1991) [hereinafter cited as SALMON MARKET OUTLOOK].

31. CANADIAN DEPARTMENT OF FISHERIES AND OCEANS, ANNUAL SUMMARY OF BRITISH CO-LUMBIA COMMERCIAL CATCH STATISTICS, PACIFIC REGION 11 (1989) [hereinafter cited as Annual Summary (1989)]; and G. Knapp & T. Smith, *supra* note 1 at 16.

32. Economists Incorporated Report, *supra* note 12, Table II-6.

33. NATIONAL MARINE FISHERIES SERVICE, NATIONAL OCEANIC AND ATMOSPHERIC ADMINIS-TRATION, U.S. DEPARTMENT OF COMMERCE, FOREIGN FISHERY INFORMATION RELEASE (various numbers, 1981–1991). The only four years in which inventories exceeded 40,000 metric tons were 1986 (60,400), 1990 (60,000), 1989 (59,100), and 1987 (51,700).

34. UNITED STATES INTERNATIONAL TRADE COMMISSION, PUBLICATION NO. 2371, FRESH AND CHILLED ATLANTIC SALMON FROM NORWAY (April 1991) [hereinafter cited as ITC].

35. *Id.* at 28.

36. *Id.* at 5 note 13 and at A-15.

37. *Id.* at A-39.

38. *Id.* at 8 and 74.

39. In 1985 the reported fishing year was changed to span calendar years.

40. G. Knapp & T. Smith, *supra* note 1 at 39, and COMMERCIAL FISHERIES ENTRY COMMIS-SION, Basic Information Tables.

41. G. Knapp & T. Smith, *supra* note 1 at 109.

42. FOOD AND AGRICULTURE ORGANIZATION, FISHERY STATISTICS YEARBOOK, CATCHES AND LANDINGS, Vol. 68 (1989) at 221 [hereinafter cited as FAO (1989)].

43. These season lengths refer to District 3A, which includes the Gulf of Alaska in central Alaska where the majority of catch is taken. A few districts have quite different season lengths from District 3A, but they account for a small portion of the catch. *See* Fax from Gordon Peltonen, International Pacific Halibut Commission (May 21, 1991) (Sum-mary of the commercial Pacific halibut fishery by regulatory area and fishing period, vari-ous years); *id.* (June 26, 1991); *id.* (June 29, 1991).

44. INTERNATIONAL PACIFIC HALIBUT COMMISSION, SCIENTIFIC REPORT NO. 72, METHODS OF POPULATION ASSESSMENT OF PACIFIC HALIBUT; H. Bernton, *Halibut Fleet Caught Up in Short Fishing Frenzy*, Washington Post, May 18, 1991; The McDowell Group, Alaska Seafood Industry Study: An Economic Profile of the Seafood Industry in Alaska (May, 1989) (pre-pared for the Alaska Seafood Industry Study Commission).

45. G. Knapp & T. Smith, *supra* note 1 at 46.

46. The Japanese harvest off the coast of Canada and in the northwestern Pacific also dropped to low levels during the 1980s. See J. HASTIE, AN ECONOMIC ANALYSIS OF MARKETS FOR U.S. SABLEFISH 1 (National Marine Fisheries Service, NOAA Technical Memorandum F/NWC-171, September, 1989) at 1–2; and J. Hastie, D. Squires, and S. Herrick, *Integra-tion of Japanese and United States Sablefish Markets*, 87 FISHERY BULLETIN No. 2 at 341–351 (1989).

47. G. Knapp & T. Smith, *supra* note 1 at 32.

48. FAO (1989), *supra* note 42 at 258.

49. G. Knapp & T. Smith, *supra* note 1 at 32 and 34.

50. FAO (1989), *supra* note 42 at 259.

51. Economists Incorporated Report, *supra* note 12, Tables II-9 and II-10.

52. K. Wellman, Chicken of the Sea? The U.S. Consumer Retail Demand for Fish Prod-ucts (1990) (unpublished Ph.D. dissertation, Dept. of Economics, University of Washing-

ington).

53. G. Knapp & T. Smith, *supra* note 1 at 99. *See also* Tables II-9 and II-10 for U.S. salmon exports to Japan.

54. FAO (1989), *supra* note 42; *Id.* at 130.

55. Alaska Salmon Markets, *supra* note 26 at 2.

56. J.L. ANDERSON & Y. KUSAKABE, THE JAPANESE SEAFOOD MARKET: SALMON, 23–25 (Market Analysis Group, Canadian Department of Fisheries and Oceans, Economic and Commercial Analysis Report No. 21, April 1989) [hereinafter cited as THE JAPANESE SEAFOOD MARKET: SALMON].

57. C. Wessells, *supra* note 7 at Ch. IV.

58. *See* Economists Incorporated Report , *supra* note 12, Tables II-4 and II-11. Exports of canned salmon are not included in Table II-11, but are also derived from U.S. Bureau of the Census data. This comparison of U.S. catch with U.S. exports is necessarily imprecise. Even if all the fish caught in a particular year are exported, harvest figures will likely be larger than export figures because harvest is measured in live weight (before any processing), while exports are in terms of production (after processing). Some fish such as sac roe herring are frozen whole before being exported, resulting in little reduction in weight, but others undergo some processing first. *Id.* at 71.

59. G. Knapp & T. Smith, *supra* note 1 at 103.

60. FISHERIES OF THE U.S. (1990), *supra* note 27 at 15.

61. G. Knapp & T. Smith, *supra* note 1 at 103.

62. The McDowell Group, *supra* note 44 at 87–88. Economists Incorporated Report, *supra* note 12, Table II-5 and Table II-11.

63. SALMON MARKET OUTLOOK, *supra* note 30 at 14.

64. B.C. SALMON FARMERS ASSOCIATION, CURRENT DEVELOPMENTS IN WORLD SALMON MARKETS: IMPLICATIONS FOR THE CANADIAN SALMON FARMING INDUSTRY 80 (Canadian Department of Fisheries and Oceans, Economic and Commercial Analysis Report No. 46, January 1990). Nearly three-quarters of farmed Canadian salmon are Pacific salmon from farms in British Columbia.

65. SALMON MARKET OUTLOOK, *supra* note 30 at Chart 1.

66. C. Wessells, *supra* note 7 at 29.

67. Economists Incorporated Report, *supra* note 12, Table II-12, CANADIAN DEPARTMENT OF FISHERIES AND OCEANS, FISH PRODUCT EXPORTS OF BRITISH COLUMBIA 4 (1989) [hereinafter cited as FISH PRODUCT EXPORTS] at 6–14; The McDowell Group, *supra* note 44 at 87–88.

68. *Id.;* shows no fresh or frozen pink salmon exports from British Columbia in 1989.

69. Economists Incorporated Report, *supra* note 12, Table II-6.

70. NATIONAL MARINE FISHERIES SERVICE, NATIONAL OCEANIC AND ATMOSPHERIC ADMINISTRATION, U.S. DEPARTMENT OF COMMERCE, WORLD SALMON TRADE: EXPORT/IMPORT STATISTICS 108–09 (April 1990); C. Wessells, *supra* note 7 at 33 indicates that Japan consumes all of its domestic chum catch.

71. C. Wessells, *supra* note 7 at 60, 69, and 80.

72. ITC, *supra* note 34 at A-20.

73. Alaska Seafood Marketing Institute, Salmon 2000, at 41 [hereinafter cited as Salmon 2000].

74. ITC, *supra* note 34 at A-55.

75. *Id.* Increased imports of Norwegian salmon at low prices into the United States led to a complaint before the International Trade Commission (ITC) that "dumping" was occurring. That investigation considered, among other things, products that were similar to Norwegian salmon. In its decision in the fresh and chilled Atlantic salmon investigation, the

International Trade Commission found that other species of salmon, and frozen salmon, were not "like products" of Atlantic salmon. However, the ITC definition of "like products" in such a proceeding is narrow and does not necessarily encompass all economic substitutes.

76. Mittelhammer, Herrmann & Lin, An Economic Analysis of the Pacific Salmon Industry: Effects of Salmon Farming (1990) (prepared for the National Marine Fisheries Service).

77. SALMON MARKET NEWSLETTER, July 1989 at 8.

78. Mittelhammer, Herrmann & Lin, U.S. Salmon Markets: A Survey of Seafood Wholesalers (1990).

79. Salmon 2000, *supra* note 73 at 46.

80. D. DeVoretz & K. Salvanes, Demand for Norwegian Farmed Salmon: A Market Penetration Model. (1988) (Working Paper No. 25, Centre for Applied Research, Norwegian School of Economics and Business Administration), summarized in THE SALMON MARKET NEWSLETTER, April 1989, at 6.

81. THE SALMON MARKET NEWSLETTER, December 1990, at 6.

82. *Id.* at 8.

83. *Prices for Wild Salmon Feel Pinch of Farmed Fish,* NATIONAL FISHERMAN WEST COAST FOCUS, October 1989, at 1.

84. Seattle Times, March 24, 1991, at A1.

85. *Outlook: Troll Salmon—Tighter Quotas Will Hurt Many,* NATIONAL FISHERMAN WEST COAST FOCUS, June 1989, at 1; Journal of Commerce, October 16, 1989, at 15; ALASKA BUSINESS MONTHLY, March 1990, at 44.

86. ALASKA BUSINESS MONTHLY, March 1990, at 64.

87. *Pacific Salmon on an Abundant Run; So are Worldwide Marketing Efforts,* QUICK FROZEN FOODS INTERNATIONAL, October 1990 at 100 [hereinafter cited as QUICK FROZEN FOODS INTERNATIONAL, October 1990]; Seattle Times, March 24, 1991, at A1; Anchorage Daily News, July 4, 1989 at D1.

88. *Don't Let Fish Farmers Fool You, Wild Pacific Salmon is Still King,* QUICK FROZEN FOODS INTERNATIONAL, April 1990, at 102.

89. Alaska Salmon Markets, *supra* note 26 at 3.

90. G. Knapp & T. Smith, *supra* note 1 at 38, 105, 109, and 111.

91. BILL ATKINSON'S NEWS REPORT, January 31, 1990; THE JAPANESE SEAFOOD MARKET: SALMON, *supra* note 56 at 21.

92. J.L. Anderson, J.T. Gledhill & Y. Kusakabe, The Japanese Seafood Market. Herring Roe 25–28 (February 1989) (prepared for the Canadian Department of Fisheries and Oceans by J.L. Anderson & Co.).

93. A. Alley, *Speculation, Risk and Consumer Demand in Japanese Markets for Herring Roe*, Proceedings of the International Seafood Trade Conference 123 (September 1982); *id.* at 29–30.

94. A. Alley, *id.* at 117.

95. THE JAPANESE SEAFOOD MARKET: SALMON, *supra* note 56 at 19–25 and at 29.

96. G. Knapp & T. Smith, *supra* note 1 at 110–112.

97. *Id.* at 113; J. Hastie *supra* note 46 at 1, 2, and 24.

98. J. Hastie, *supra* note 46 at 12.

99. Oral communication with Bill Gazey, fisheries biologist, W.J. Gazey Research (May 23, 1991).

100. CFEC MMT Reports indicate that fishermen using pot gear target spot shrimp.

101. J. Doll, *An Econometric Analysis of Shrimp Ex-Vessel Prices: 1950–1968,* 54 AMERI-

CAN JOURNAL OF AGRICULTURAL ECONOMICS No. 3 at 431–440 (1972).

102.   G. Knapp & T. Smith, *supra* note 1 at 107–108.

103.   CFEC Annual Report 1990, *supra* note 3 at 12.

104.   Boroughs were combined to correspond with fishing areas as follows: Cook Inlet includes plants in Kenai Peninsula; Southeast includes plants in Prince of Wales-Outer Ketchikan, Sitka and Wrangell-Petersburg; Kodiak Island includes plants in Kodiak Island; and Bristol Bay includes plants in Bristol Bay and Dillingham. Many of the unlisted boroughs contained no processing plants. BUREAU OF THE CENSUS, U.S. DEPARTMENT OF COMMERCE, 1988 COUNTY BUSINESS PATTERNS, ALASKA, (1991) [hereinafter cited as 1988 COUNTY BUSINESS PATTERNS]. *County Business Patterns* was not used to estimate employment because it counts employment only in mid-March, thus not accounting for the substantial seasonal variation. Knapp and Smith provide an annual average. G. Knapp & T. Smith, *supra* note 1 at 181.

105.   The McDowell Group, *supra* note 44 at 45–46.

106.   *Id.* at 42. The increase in year-round processing is due, in part, to growth in shore-based groundfish processing.

107.   Natural Resource Consultants, Investigation of Market Conditions and Events Related to the 1987 In-Season Decline in Sockeye Salmon Grounds Price in Upper Cook Inlet 34 (October 1990) (prepared for Faegre & Benson) [hereinafter cited as *Glacier Bay* NRC Study], at 46.

108.   W. Wahpepah, *supra* note 25 at C10.

109.   Natural Resource Consultants, Investigation of Effect of Ex-Vessel Sockeye Prices in Upper Cook Inlet Related to the *Exxon Valdez* Oil Spill, Appendix Table 1 (March 1991) (prepared for Faegre & Benson) [hereinafter cited as *Exxon Valdez* NRC Study]. It is not possible to determine from the table whether these sixteen parents may be parties related to one another.

110.   Puget Sound Business Journal, November 20, 1989, at 18. For firms that were ranked in the list, but did not provide a revenue figure, we assigned the average of the revenue of the next-larger and next-smaller firms.

111.   *See, Exxon Valdez* NRC Study, *supra* note 109 at 7, 24, for characterization of the salmon trade with Japan and distribution of salmon within Japan in language that is suggestive of non-competitive behavior. No supporting evidence or documentation is provided for this language.

112.   *Glacier Bay* NRC Study, *supra* note 107 at 35.

113.   *Id.* at 35.

114.   *Glacier Bay* NRC Study, *supra* note 107 at 35.

115.   *Id.* at Section III.

4

Qualitative Evidence Concerning Price Effects

This chapter describes qualitative evidence from news accounts and other sources on the effects of various factors including the oil spill on the price of Alaskan seafood. Subsequent chapters present quantitative analyses of the effects of the oil spill on seafood prices. Using electronic databases, we searched for articles in U.S. and Japanese publications concerning the effects of the spill on prices of salmon and other seafood. Articles searched included those with information on factors affecting prices of seafood, those that discussed contamination or safety of seafood, and those that mentioned the oil spill.[1]

The first part of this chapter examines evidence on demand for seafood that could be consistent with one or more of the theories of direct price effects postulated in chapter 2. These theories include the possibility that consumers' fears about the safety of seafood caused the demand for seafood to decline, thus reducing prices. We summarize a survey conducted soon after the oil spill and describe press reports related to the oil spill. In order to assess the plausibility of a price effect caused by consumers avoiding seafood from Alaska, we look at evidence concerning region-specific labeling.

The second part of the chapter discusses the effect of the oil spill on the supply of seafood. We consider evidence of increased prices caused by reduced quantities of seafood available due to closures. Finally, we discuss factors unrelated to the oil spill that could explain the observed decreases in prices of some of the species of Alaskan seafood in 1989.

EFFECT OF THE OIL SPILL ON THE DEMAND FOR SEAFOOD

One price effect theory is that consumers reduced their consumption of seafood because of fear of contamination. Dramatic reductions in consumer demand have occurred with other products following reports of actual product contamination in retail trade. In 1982, milk in Hawaii was contaminated by a pesticide. More recently, apples were contaminated with alar, and Perrier was contaminated by benzene. Reports of contamination of those products appeared in the press. Unlike these cases, however, there were no reports of contaminated Alaskan seafood reaching retail consumer markets.[2] Nevertheless, the Alaska Seafood Marketing Institute (ASMI), an arm of the state of Alaska, conducted surveys soon after the oil spill to find out whether worldwide consumers and traders were concerned about the safety of Alaskan seafood, and if so, what ASMI could do to reassure them. (We assume that ASMI sought accurate information to formulate its policies rather than used this report to influence public opinion.)

ASMI Surveys

ASMI commissioned Burson-Marsteller Research to conduct surveys in the United States, Japan, the United Kingdom, and France to determine the effect of the *Exxon Valdez* oil spill on consumers and "traders" (retailers and wholesalers) who purchase seafood likely to have come from Alaska.[3] At the time of the surveys in May and June of 1989, all seafood being sold internationally had been harvested prior to the March 24 spill or was caught from areas of Alaska known to be uncontaminated. All fisheries located in the contaminated areas of Prince William Sound were closed for the summer.[4] Consumers, however, might not have known when the seafood they purchased was harvested, and thus might have responded to news of the oil spill.

The surveys included questions to determine the following: (1) awareness of the oil spill, (2) the effect of the spill on purchase intent and behavior, (3) the effect of the spill on attitudes toward Alaskan seafood, and (4) steps that, if taken, would reassure the public about the safety of Alaskan seafood. All four surveys yielded similar results. In brief, the surveys found that (1) consumer behavior at the time of the interviews was unaffected by the spill, (2) nearly half of the "traders" said they *expected* consumers to purchase less Alaskan seafood because of the spill, and (3) whatever their expectations, traders as a whole reported no spill-related change in consumers' behavior. Of those traders who had recently reduced purchases (an equal number actually increased purchases), virtually none gave the *Exxon Valdez* oil spill as a reason. We report below the results of the surveys in Japan, where the bulk of Alaskan seafood is marketed, and in the United States.

Survey in Japan

The Japanese survey took place between June 3 and June 19, 1989. By this time, some seafood harvested from areas of Alaska unaffected by the spill had been shipped to Japan. The first air shipment of fresh chinook salmon from the Copper River had been placed on the Tokyo market by May 24, 1989, as had Bristol Bay roe-herring.[5] Bristol Bay sockeye harvests did not begin until after the survey. The May 10, 1989 issue of Bill Atkinson's News Report indicated that sablefish had been imported from Alaska prior to the survey and that prices were still being negotiated.[6] Reportedly, many of the vessels that normally harvest sablefish in Prince William Sound were involved in the oil cleanup effort, contributing to the lower-than-normal Central District harvest. However, very little of the Central District's sablefish harvest actually comes from Prince William Sound (1.2 percent of the total in 1988).[7]

The ASMI Japanese survey included telephone interviews with 306 consumers, 82 wholesalers, and 103 retailers. Seventy-five percent of the consumers thought the spill had affected seafood from Alaska. Fifty-eight percent of Japanese consumers interviewed said they would not eat Alaskan seafood. Despite these statements about intent, consumers' actual behavior up to the time of the study did not reflect these fears. Although most consumers (83 percent) reported that they were aware of the oil spill, virtually none listed the spill as a reason for decreasing seafood consumption.

Nearly all of the wholesalers (95 percent) and retailers (81 percent) were aware of the oil spill in Alaska. Among wholesalers, 46 percent believed the spill would affect consumer purchases; 41 percent of retailers believed it would affect purchases. More than one quarter of wholesalers and 8 percent of retailers noted that some customers had indicated a concern about the oil spill; 6 percent of wholesalers and 2 percent of retailers said that a "great many" customers had indicated concern. The traders had more confidence than did consumers in assurances from public officials that seafood from Alaska would be safe. "The trade's fear that the spill will reduce consumer demand because of health concerns can become a self-fulfilling prophecy," the survey cautioned. "If the trade becomes sufficiently worried this is or will happen, as a precaution they may reduce their purchases on economic grounds, e.g., overstocks, excessive returns, etc., or litigation fears."[8]

Like consumers, no traders reported decreasing their purchases of seafood because of the oil spill. Thus, in spite of the fears of "self-fulfilling prophesies" following the spill, there was no apparent change in purchasing behavior either among consumers or in the trade. Still, the report recommended that the trade be reassured through statements by the State of Alaska or the U.S. Government.

Survey in the United States

ASMI's telephone survey in the United States took place between May 18 and May 23, 1989. It questioned 501 consumers, 101 wholesalers, and 106 retailers. Nearly all consumers (95 percent) reported that they were aware of the spill. Forty-five percent said they would eat Alaskan seafood, while 37 percent said they would not, and 13 percent were not sure. Although 27 percent reported reduced consumption of fish, the reduction was not directly or indirectly related to the spill. Only one of the 190 salmon consumers, two of the 401 shrimp consumers, and no cod or halibut eaters mentioned the oil spill as a reason for their eating less seafood. Price was named as the primary reason for reduced consumption.[9]

Among the trade, at least nine out of ten wholesalers and retailers reported that they were aware of the oil spill. Only 1 percent did not currently purchase Alaskan seafood because of the spill. Half of the wholesalers and nearly half of the retailers stated they were very concerned (as opposed to somewhat concerned or not at all concerned) about the effect of the spill on price. About half of the retailers stated they were very concerned about the effect on safety (51 percent) and appearance (46 percent). Somewhat fewer wholesalers shared those concerns (36 percent and 29 percent, respectively). Slightly more than one-third of both wholesalers and retailers reported they were very concerned about the effect on availability.

About two-fifths of the trade felt the spill would affect consumers' purchases. Twenty-seven percent of wholesalers and retailers believed that people would reduce purchases because of health or safety issues, while 15 percent felt it would lead to higher prices or make the fish more scarce. Finally, 81 percent of wholesalers and 72 percent of retailers were either very confident or somewhat confident that only safe seafood would be sold in stores or restaurants.

Summary of Results

Table 4.1 summarizes the answers to some of the questions that relate specifically to purchases of seafood from Alaska and the safety of that seafood following the oil spill. Many consumers indicated they would not eat seafood from Alaska (for example, 58 percent of Japanese consumers and 37 percent of U.S. consumers). Very few of these consumers, however, reported that they had actually reduced consumption due to safety concerns. No wholesaler or retailer who reduced purchases of Alaskan seafood listed the oil spill as the cause.

It is difficult to reconcile the apparent inconsistency between what consumers said and what they did. One possible explanation is that some consumers misinterpreted the question to be whether they would eat *contaminated* Alaskan seafood. Another explanation could be that consumers were unable to distinguish Alaskan seafood from other seafood. Third, there were no press reports of contaminated seafood actually reaching the market, and consumers may have been confident that inspections and other precautions prevented that from happening. Finally, the surveys took place soon after the spill and thus might not have fully traced consumers' attitudes and actions.

The surveys do not indicate that there was a significant downward shift in consumer or distributor demand for Alaskan seafood in May and June 1989 because of fears of contamination from the oil spill. The surveys are consistent, however, with some expectation in May and June 1989 that there might be a future downward shift in demand for Alaskan seafood. ASMI concludes: "While there is widespread awareness of the oil spill and concern about the safety of eating Alaskan seafood by some, it has not yet translated into reduced purchases or usage."[10]

Table 4.1
ASMI Survey Results

Number of Surveyed Consumers Who Decreased Consumption of Seafood and Mentioned the Oil Spill as the Reason

	France	United Kingdom	United States	Japan
Salmon	1/185	—	1/190	1/272
Halibut	1/44	0/54	0/140	2/210
Shrimp	4/253	0/131	2/401	2/276

Wholesalers and Retailers

	France	United Kingdom	United States	Japan
"Very/Somewhat Concerned" about the safety of Alaskan seafood	47%	53%	43%	15%
Spill will impact consumers' purchase/consumption	47%	56%	43%	43%
Customers have indicated concern	7%	5%	not reported	16%

— = no more than 1 out of 227

Sources: Burston-Marsteller Research, "The Impact of the *Exxon Valdez* Oil Spill on Japanese Consumers and the Trade," August 1989. Burston-Marsteller Research, "The Impact of the *Exxon Valdez* Oil Spill on American Consumers and the Trade," June 1989. Burston-Marsteller Research, "The Impact of the *Exxon Valdez* Oil Spill on British Consumers and the Trade," July 1989. Burston-Marstellar Research, "The Impact of the *Exxon Valdez* Oil Spill on French Consumers and the Trade," July 1989. All prepared for Alaska Seafood Marketing Institute.

Reports in the Press

The ASMI reports cautioned that if there were significant negative press coverage concerning contaminated seafood, consumers might reduce their demand for seafood. "While consumer concern has not yet translated into behavior, a significant percentage of consumers are worried. Extensive reporting of tainted Alaskan seafood found in stores, or illness caused by them, will move these worriers and others like them to action."[11]

We examined the press reports in the United States and Japan following the oil spill to determine if there were indications that contaminated seafood was being harvested or sold or that consumer purchasing patterns were reflecting fears about contaminated seafood. We have found no reports in the press that seafood sales were actually affected, although the head of the Prince William Sound Seiners Association attributed the fall in ex-vessel price to the oil spill. "Because buyer confidence in salmon from spill-affected areas was so low, few buyers came back to the Sound this year. . . . The oil-price adjustment was three times the botulism price adjustment. The damage to the state and to some individuals was huge. It will take a while for prices to come back up."[12]

On April 7, 1989, two weeks after the oil spill, the Pacific Seafood Processors Association noted that no orders had been canceled.[13] By the end of June, the *Seattle Times* reported that Seattle consumers were not concerned about where their fish came from.[14] An early July memorandum by an official of the Alaska Department of Commerce and Economic Development commented that the ASMI study showed the market was not very concerned about contaminated fish. The memo stated that "it should be fairly easy to detect contaminated fish, and most people in the trade seem to be aware of this."[15]

The Japanese press reported Alaskan fishermen's concern that contaminated fish should not reach the market. Writing about the closure of the Kodiak area, one author notes that "the local fishermen are afraid to lose their market by shipping oil-contaminated fish and have accepted the postponement of the opening [of the fishing season] quietly."[16] Another article quotes: "In order to establish safety and protect our own future, we will not go out fishing unsafely. Even if the fishing areas are opened, if a single fish contaminated with oil is caught, the area will be closed immediately."[17]

Like the American print media, the Japanese print media did not mention reduced salmon purchases due to fear of contamination. However, one *Journal of Commerce* article published in the United States immediately after the spill stated that press reports from Tokyo indicated Japanese buyers would not buy seafood from the Prince William Sound area.[18] One Japanese article that mentioned the safety of seafood appeared immediately after the oil spill and reported that ASMI had announced that seafood was safe. Fish affected by the oil spill were not yet on the market, the article said, and no fishing would be allowed in affected areas. All fish would be tested and "no polluted seafood is allowed to be exported from Alaska." In addition, the article noted that it was too early to say if the oil spill would affect the price and quality of Alaskan seafood.[19]

Another Japanese article cited research showing that Alaskan salmon after the oil spill were holding fewer than the average number of eggs, and many baby herring were deformed. Exxon denied these assertions. No mention was made of reduced purchases due to fear of contamination.[20]

Some reports pointed to reduced demand by processors, but most cited causes unrelated to the oil spill. One document described some of the factors that could increase the cost of processing seafood. It noted the narrowed margins of processors due to increased inventories, the higher cost of money (presumably higher interest rates), and increased labor cost. Only one oil-related effect was mentioned in this document: as a result of the oil spill clean-up activities, fewer tenders were available, which increased processing costs.[21]

Press reports indicated that considerable caution was taken to ensure that no contaminated halibut were sold following the *Exxon Valdez* oil spill.[22] One press article reported oil-tainted halibut from Kodiak.[23] This story, however, was refuted two days later. The methods used to test the supposedly contaminated fish were called into question. The fisherman's boat also was found to be free of oil.[24]

Press reports on herring roe, sablefish, and shrimp did not indicate a concern about the safety of those species of seafood, or any actual contamination.

The *Glacier Bay* oil spill in Cook Inlet on July 2, 1987, provides a contrasting example of events and press coverage. Following that spill, contamination became a problem. The spill occurred during the fishing season, and its magnitude was underestimated. Fisheries in Cook Inlet were not immediately closed. The *Seattle Post-Intelligencer* reported that on July 10, eight days after the spill, all fishing was halted on most of the traditional red salmon fishing grounds in Cook Inlet and halted on all Cook Inlet grounds on July 14.[25] Another article explained, "Despite the recovery effort, oil contaminated about 20,000 pounds of the more than 500,000 pounds of salmon caught on one of the fishery openings, July 13."[26]

Tainted fish evidently did not reach consumers following the *Glacier Bay* spill, but a number of press reports indicated that contaminated fish had been found at processors. "Officials discovered Monday night that routine screening failed to detect oil on perhaps 30,000 pounds of salmon already at a processor for canning," one article stated. It noted that fishing was going to be stopped due to the "high risk of widespread oil-contaminated fish."[27] Another noted that 22,000 pounds of oil-tainted fish had been destroyed and that another 20,000 were segregated pending further inspection. It also stated that three weeks after the accident, a drift vessel had 3,000 pounds of contaminated salmon.[28]

Labeling

According to the ASMI survey, one of the reasons seafood purchases were not affected by the *Exxon Valdez* oil spill was that consumers did not know the region or country of origin of the seafood they purchased.

> [C]onsumers will continue to buy Alaskan seafood because, we suspect, most do not know if what they are buying comes from the State. An indication the problem is becoming more serious is when substantial numbers of consumers demand to know if the seafood they are buying comes from Alaska. Therefore, until ASMI feels obliged to do so it should not label its products.[29]

The extent of labeling of the source of seafood is an important issue in determining the effects of the oil spill on consumer demand and price. If seafood is labeled as to specific location of harvest, then consumers can avoid seafood from oil-touched locations.[30] As some consumers steer away from seafood from oil-touched regions, the price of seafood from those regions will tend to fall, while the price of seafood from other regions might increase due to the increased demand.

The more specific the labeling, the easier it would have been to avoid salmon potentially affected by the oil spill. For example, if salmon in Japanese retail markets were labeled "Alaskan salmon" rather than labeled by specific area within Alaska, then Japanese consumers would have had to avoid all Alaskan salmon in order to avoid salmon potentially tainted by the spill. Similarly, if salmon were simply labeled "U.S." or "Pacific," then consumers wishing to avoid salmon from oil-touched areas would have had to shift to non-U.S. salmon or Atlantic salmon. This absence of labeling of the specific location of harvest would tend to depress the price of all Alaskan (or U.S. or Pacific) salmon, and there would be no separate effect on specific regions within Alaska.[31] In the absence of labeling, there could be reduced consumer demand for a species of seafood worldwide, but not a relative reduction in demand from Alaska or oil-touched regions of Alaska.

Fresh and frozen salmon is generally packaged at Japanese supermarkets in foam containers with plastic wrap, and the only labeling relates to species, degree of saltiness, price, and whether it was caught on the high seas. Wessells, citing a personal communication with Yuko Kusakabe, states that packages that are sold at retail fish markets and supermarkets are not labeled according to country of origin. Salmon sold in department stores is labeled by species, country of origin, and sometimes method of catch.[32] For chinook salmon, Kusakabe and Anderson found cases where the specific river was noted on labels.[33] Official statistics on holdings of frozen salmon are not differentiated by country of origin, but only between pink salmon ("masu") and the other four species ("sake").[34] Fresh salmon is labeled as "new," to indicate that it is not thawed fish from the previous year's inventories.[35]

Although some Japanese consumers of fresh or frozen seafood know the country of origin of their seafood as a result of labeling, most probably do not. Clues to the origin of seafood come not only from labels but also from the species and the season of the year. Most Japanese consumers realize that chum generally comes from Japanese fisheries, while most sockeye comes from the United States. In addition, Wessels notes that Japanese shoppers are aware of the seasons of the various species. Sockeye is available from July through September. In September, the Japanese fall chum begin to reach the market, and most salmon sold is domestic.[36]

Seafood from other countries sold in the United States must have a label indicating country of origin at the initial level of trade. However, fresh and frozen seafood in retail markets is unlikely to indicate country of origin unless it is prepackaged. Canned salmon processed in the United States has "U.S.A." embossed on the lid of the can.[37] Canned salmon from other countries may indicate the country, such as "Salmon Canada," or may have a code for the country embossed on the can.[38] Table 4.2 presents the results of our labeling survey of companies that sell canned salmon. Fewer than half of the companies included the word "Alaska" or

"Alaskan" on the label. None of the companies changed its labeling policy after the *Exxon Valdez* oil spill. U.S. consumers of canned seafood may be able to determine the country—but not necessarily the exact location—of origin. U.S. consumers of fresh or frozen seafood are not very likely to know the country of origin.

There were mixed reports on the labeling of seafood from Alaska in the press. In Seattle, one article reported that Safeway Stores Inc. and restaurants were boasting the arrival of fresh Alaskan halibut. A later article noted that "fishmongers in Seattle's Pike Place Market have been advertising their fish as 'Not from Alaska'."[39]

While the initial reaction to the spill by ASMI was to recommend against Alaskan labels in marketing seafood, more recently Alaskan marketers are attempting to increase labeling in Japan. ASMI sent a salmon trade mission to Japan in September 1990 to promote Alaskan salmon as "wild and natural" as opposed to "fatty" farmed salmon. "The special characteristics of Alaskan salmon will be promoted, including: (1) its rich color, (2) the firm flesh, (3) a clean and rich flavor only found in wild salmon, and so forth. And with the high-protein and omega-3 fatty acid content, Alaskan salmon is ideal for the fitness minded."[40] In the past, Alaskan salmon had been repackaged, especially by smokers in Hokkaido, as a "domestic" product.[41]

The evidence on labeling, then, is not consistent with a theory that consumers were attempting to avoid seafood from contaminated areas of Alaska. There is almost no evidence of efforts by marketers outside of Alaska after the oil spill to force labels on Alaskan seafood, most of which carries no retail label as to origin.

EFFECT OF THE OIL SPILL ON THE SUPPLY OF SEAFOOD

In addition to affecting the demand for seafood, the *Exxon Valdez* oil spill could have affected the price of seafood by affecting the supply. Significant closures of fishing areas could have reduced supply, tending to increase price.

Some early reports noted that salmon prices might rise as a result of the oil spill if the closure of fisheries in affected areas substantially reduced the supply of salmon.[42] Atkinson noted in some articles shortly after the spill that fishermen were emphasizing the effect of the spill as they tried to negotiate higher prices.[43] Processors were also reportedly faced with difficulty securing enough manpower, since they had to compete against the high wages Exxon was offering for clean-up work.[44]

Despite the closure of some herring fisheries in Prince William Sound, early post-spill articles on herring roe indicated that the overall supply of herring roe was expected to be unchanged from the previous year. However, more of the catch would be from British Columbia, and less from Alaska.[45]

Table 4.2
U.S. Retail Labeling of Canned Alaskan Salmon

Companies	Source	Label/Brand
With location labeling		
Alaska Sausage and Seafoods Co.	P	company name
Bumble Bee Seafoods, Inc.	S,P	Alaska Salmon (pink, sockeye), "Made in Alaska"
Peter Pan Seafoods, Inc.	S	Alaskan Pink Salmon
Salmon River Smokehouse	P	Smoked Alaska
Silver Lining Seafoods	P	
Taku Smokeries	P	
Without location labeling		
Alaska Sausage and Seafoods Co.	P	
MW Polar Foods	S	Polar Pink Salmon
North Pacific Seafoods	P	
Ocean Beauty Seafoods, Inc.	P	
Safeway Stores, Inc.	S	Sea Trader Pink Salmon
Van Camp Seafood Co., Inc.	S	Chicken of the Sea Pink Salmon

Sources: P - phone survey, S - supermarket survey.

EFFECTS ON SEAFOOD DEMAND CAUSED BY FACTORS OTHER THAN THE OIL SPILL

While few references in the press noted reduced demand for seafood as a result of the *Exxon Valdez* oil spill, numerous articles described alternative explanations for the depressed prices in 1989.

Salmon

Articles in the trade press generally attributed the decline of salmon prices in 1989 to the large harvest, the large stock of inventories, the decline in the value of the Japanese yen, and the increased supply of farmed salmon from Norway and other countries.

An article in June 1989 expressed surprise that salmon from Bristol Bay was fetching low prices, given the spill-induced curtailment of salmon fisheries. It attributed the low prices to a large harvest, the strength of the dollar against the Japanese yen, and an overall weak salmon market.[46]

In July 1989, a fisheries trade specialist at the U.S. Embassy in Tokyo listed the tremendous quantity of pen-reared salmon and the exchange rate as the primary causes of the low prices in the Japanese salmon market. The specialist also noted that Japanese demand for all seafood was depressed due to the Emperor's death and the introduction of a 3 percent consumption tax in April that shifted purchases to March (and earlier).[47]

An article in September 1989 noted that the Japanese supply of salmon and trout (including domestic sources, foreign sources, and inventories) reached a record 460,000 tons. This large supply caused a drop in prices steep enough that the Norwegians withdrew their offer to sell salmon in Japan.[48] Other articles in late 1989 pointed to increased farmed salmon and high inventories in Japan.[49]

Written nearly a year after the oil spill, one article that forecast the 1990 fishing season made no mention of reduced demand for Alaskan seafood as a result of the oil spill. It, too, blamed the low 1989 prices on increased supplies of farmed salmon primarily from Norway and Chile, high inventories, the value of the dollar, and increased Japanese hatchery production of chum salmon.[50]

An article in *Asahi Science,* published in July 1990, noted that the amount of salmon caught in Alaska was normal and that other fishing was better than expected following the oil spill.[51] An article in the *Seafood Trading and Marketing News* stated that fishing in Kodiak had been postponed several times after contaminated fish were caught during test fishing. The effect of the oil spill was minimal, it said, due to the size of overall supply.[52]

Bill Atkinson's News Report described a situation of chronic oversupply in Japanese markets for seafood in 1989–1990. Along with the trend of increasing supply, it mentioned increasing competition from alternatives to seafood. Other articles noted that the increased supply of Norwegian salmon was putting pressure on the market in Japan as well as Europe and the United States. Reasons for the fall in salmon prices in 1989 in Japan were given as follows:

1. Sales of small sizes [of salmon] were very poor last year, indicating a trend towards larger salmon sizes.

2. The rapid increase in "red-fleshed salmon" from farm operations has weakened the sales base for chum salmon, and other light-fleshed species.

3. The consumer has little resistance to farmed salmon, and supermarkets find the product easy to fit into their purchase forecasts—the product is always available.

4. High prices for fresh salmon has [sic] traditionally meant improved wholesale prices for both frozen and salted salmon. Now that fresh salmon is

available throughout the year, however, the traditional pattern has disap-
peared; the general stability of fresh salmon prices and supply is having
an influence on the market for frozen and salted salmon.

5.   The Japanese consumer is shifting from heavily salted salmon, to "light
salt" fillets.[53]

Another article noted that ocean-farm trout had become a major competitor of
wild sockeye salmon.[54]

One article written more than two years after the oil spill focused on the steep
decline in salmon prices since 1988. It attributed the price drop to dramatic changes
in supply and exchange rates, and it did not mention the oil spill.

- Since 1988, Alaska salmon fishermen have watched the bottom drop out of
  harvest prices. For several years before that, prices had soared. What caused
  the boom and bust in salmon prices?
- Prices boomed between 1985 and 1988 because there was a temporary drop
  in world salmon supply at the same time the value of the Japanese yen was
  rising sharply.
- Prices crashed between 1988 and 1991 because rapidly growing supply of
  both wild and farmed salmon outstripped demand.[55]

A study completed in late 1991 examined the drop in the price for Bristol Bay
sockeye since 1988. It cited three factors: size of the Bristol Bay catch, salmon
inventories in Japan, and increased farmed salmon production.[56]

Herring Roe

Changed demand for herring roe, like salmon, can be attributed to many factors
other than the oil spill. According to one article, there has been a general decline in
the old Japanese tradition of celebrating the New Year by exchanging high-priced
"kazunoko" or herring roe in December.[57] Another article contended that "salted
herring roe remains a popular gift item, resulting in good sales of brand name gift
packs." It noted, however, that "the Japanese travel more during the New Year
season and are not always willing to spend all of the time preparing traditional New
Year's food. This has resulted in a reduced demand for salted herring roe [typically
small- and medium-sized] for consumption in one's own home."[58] Because British Columbia supplies more large roes to Japan than does Alaska, this change may
have led to depressed Alaskan prices of roe herring relative to British Columbian
prices.

One article attributed a decline in the quantity of roes of all kinds handled at the
Tsukiji Market from April 1988 to April 1989 to the new consumption tax and a big
holiday.[59] Nevertheless, the total tonnage of herring roe handled in that same market increased 45 percent in May 1989 compared with the previous year.[60] "The

relatively good performance during 1989 was largely the result of lower costs, increased consumer activity (no 'self-restraint' [i.e., no restrained behavior due to the Emperor's ill health as in 1988]), and utilization of non-popular sizes in flavored roe and non-bleached roe products."[61]

Despite apparently strong Japanese demand for herring roe in general, the demand for roe on kelp in Japan appears to have fallen in 1989. Japanese imports of herring roe on kelp harvested from Canada and the United States grew from 250 metric tons in 1985 to 605 metric tons in 1988 before falling to 502 metric tons in 1989. Finland's shipments rose from 5 metric tons in 1987 to 38 metric tons in 1988, but fell to 23 metric tons in 1989.[62]

On the supply side, one article reported that the size of herring roe was smaller in 1989 than in 1988, but the quality was better.[63] Several other articles discussed the availability of roe herring. Closure of the roe herring fishery in Prince William Sound on April 3, 1989 was expected to reduce the total amount of roe available. However, because this fishery has historically produced mostly small- to medium-sized roe, the loss of tonnage was not expected to affect Japanese demand for roe herring.[64] A later article noted "a major reduction in the volume of roe-herring shipped to Japan. A greater volume is either being processed locally, or in Korea. In addition, the size assortment for Bristol Bay roe was different last year [1989]. The supply of extra large roe (1,650 tons) dropped from 22 percent of the total in 1988, to an estimated 16 percent of the total last year."[65]

Reportedly, by April 26, 1989, about three-quarters of the average amount of roe herring caught each year in Cook Inlet had already been harvested. Kodiak, however, was undergoing a slow pace of harvesting, reportedly due to bad weather.[66] A 10 percent reduction in roe produced in the Togiak region was reported to be due to a higher male ratio and an earlier fishing season.[67]

The availability of roe-on-kelp in 1989 was heavily influenced by inventories. Inventories of high-priced Alaskan roe on kelp remained high in early 1989, although the low-priced product had sold well.[68] Even as late as mid-May 1989, inventories of high-priced Canadian product had been slow to sell. "The inventory is expected to off-set any decrease in this year's [1989] supply caused by the oil spill in Prince William Sound."[69]

Another *Bill Atkinson's News Report* article noted that alternative sources of herring roe for salted products exist and that a "sizable quantity" of herring roe was imported into Japan from the Shetland fishery in the Atlantic.[70]

Reportedly, the processing industries for kazunoko, which buy herring roe from traders, postponed their 1989 purchase of herring roe until October or November, the peak demand time.[71] According to Atkinson, "The delay was aimed at keeping raw roe prices at lower workable levels. And the strategy was successful."[72] In spite of the late purchases, processors were able to process 10,000 tons of finished product in a short time. Another Japanese article stated that salted herring roe, 55 percent of which comes from Canada, was considerably cheaper in 1989 than in the previous year, due to the "market environment."[73]

Prices for roe-on-kelp had been high throughout the late 1980s, generating increased production from North America. In 1988 contract prices were high because of low inventories of the top-grade product.[74] However, in 1989, prices fell substantially in response to high inventory levels. By the end of April 1989, Japanese buyers had purchased a small volume of Canadian top-grade herring roe-on-kelp at prices about 15 percent lower than in 1988. With high inventories and a slow-moving, high-priced product, Canadian prices continued to drop sharply in May.[75]

Halibut

Prior to the 1989 season, the International Pacific Halibut Commission (IPHC) recommended a 15 percent reduction in the harvest from the previous year's level.[76] During the season, fewer fishermen participated in the first opening, probably due to bad weather and involvement in clean-up work.[77] In addition, more inspections and precautions were taken.[78]

Fishermen and processors appear to have been worried that consumer demand for halibut would drop as a result of the oil spill. This prompted the IPHC to conduct a test fishery to check for contamination of the fish. One trade publication reported "no indication that oil will or has affected any halibut. Just fear and worry."[79] The impact of the oil spill on retailers seems to have been mixed. Some stores and restaurants advertised the sale of fresh Alaskan halibut, while other sellers sold fish labeled "not from Alaska."

The majority of Alaskan halibut is consumed in the United States. Exports to Japan increased significantly in 1989 followed by a near doubling in volume in 1990.[80] According to *Bill Atkinson's News Report*, the price of halibut in Japan rose strongly through the second half of 1989. Part of this increase is likely due to relatively low inventory levels—only half as high in mid-1989 as at the same point in the previous year.[81]

Sablefish

One article from Japan reported that many expected the supply of sablefish in 1989 to be "slightly lower than last year as a whole, even though the catch for the first half has been filling the quota more quickly than last year. . . . Actual imports through customs show a pace similar to last year with the contract price dropping in the later months because of weak buy demands, predictions of late shipment and uncompleted contracts."[82]

According to *Bill Atkinson's News Report*, low prices and slow sales of sablefish in the fall of 1989 "were largely due to abundant domestic [Japanese] landings of fresh fall chum salmon and saury, as well as competition from cheap import salmon."[83] Atkinson noted a change in the sablefish market during the two years preceding 1991: "Traditionally, sablefish competed with sockeye salmon—both as sliced fish—on the Japanese market. Over the past couple of years, however, the importers have worked hard to expand the market within Japan and have been able to develop an independent market for sablefish."[84]

CONCLUSION

Although immediately after the oil spill there was considerable concern about how consumers would react, the ASMI survey, the reports in the press, and the evidence on labeling of seafood provide little or no support for the hypothesis that consumers' demand for seafood from Alaska or parts of Alaska declined because they feared it was contaminated. There were no reports of actual contamination in the press (except the one erroneous report about halibut), and by 1990 Alaska was marketing and promoting its seafood with Alaska labels. Moreover, the results of our review of press reports do not support findings of reductions in consumer demand for a group of seafood species worldwide. Finally, none of the articles in the press discusses oil spill-related supply factors (such as changes in the quality of the catch) that could have affected the price of seafood. Rather, the articles attribute reduced prices to Japanese buying patterns, large stocks of inventories, the value of the yen, competition from farmed salmon or other species, and other supply factors.

NOTES

1. For a list of key words searched (with the assistance of SCAN C2C), and a description of the databases searched, see Economists Incorporated An Economic Analysis of the Effect of the *Exxon Valdez* Oil Spill on Alaskan Seafood Prices, submitted to the Trans-Alaska Pipeline Liability Fund, Appendix 2 (December 1991) [hereinafter cited as Economists Incorporated Report].

2. There was only one—erroneous—report of harvesting contaminated seafood. *Initial Tests Call Halibut Untainted, but Reports of Oily Water Still Surfacing in Kodiak*, Seattle Times, June 16, 1989, at B1 [hereinafter cited as *Initial Tests Call Halibut Untainted*].

3. Burson-Marsteller Research, The Impact of the Exxon Valdez Oil Spill on Japanese Consumers and the Trade (August 1989) (Prepared for the Alaska Seafood Marketing Institute) [hereinafter cited as ASMI Japanese Survey]; *id*. The Impact of the Exxon Valdez Oil Spill on American Consumers and the Trade (June 1989) [hereinafter cited as ASMI American Survey]; *id*. The Impact of the Exxon Valdez Oil Spill on British Consumers and the Trade (July 1989); *id*. The Impact of the Exxon Valdez Oil Spill on French Consumers and the Trade (July 1989).

4. ASMI American Survey, *supra* note 3 at i.

5. BILL ATKINSON'S NEWS REPORT No. 300 at 1 (May 24, 1989).

6. *Id.* No. 298 at 2 (May 10, 1989).

7. R. MORRISON & N. DUDIAK, CENTRAL REGION GROUNDFISH REPORT TO THE ALASKA BOARD OF FISHERIES 8, 13 (Division of Commercial Fisheries, Central Region, Alaska Department of Fish and Game, Regional Information Report No. 2H88-6, November 1988).

8. ASMI American Survey, *supra* note 3 at xiv. In its report on the *Exxon Valdez* oil spill, NRC interpreted this statement as meaning "they would reduce purchases or price but not necessarily attribute this to the spill." Natural Resource Consultants, Investigation of Effect of Ex-Vessel Sockeye Prices in Upper Cook Inlet Related to the *Exxon Valdez* Oil Spill 1 (March 1991) (prepared for Faegre and Benson) [hereinafter cited as *Exxon Valdez* NRC Study]. The survey does not report the reasons for reduced purchase of seafood. It merely states that "no one reducing their purchases cites the Exxon oil spill as a reason."

9. A survey conducted in the United States in January 1989, prior to the *Exxon Valdez* oil spill, found consumers to be relatively sensitive to changes in price. Price elasticity for seafood purchased by consumers in retail outlets was estimated to be -3.5, indicating that a 10 percent increase in price would result in a 35 percent decrease in seafood purchases. D. EGAN & G. GISLASON, U.S. SALMON CONSUMER SURVEY 3-7 (Market Analysis Group, Canadian Department of Fisheries and Oceans, Economic and Commercial Analysis Report No. 23).

10. ASMI American Survey, *supra* note 3 at xi; *id.* ASMI Japanese Survey at xi.

11. ASMI American Survey, *supra* note 3 at xii–xiii; *id.* ASMI Japanese Survey at xi–xiii.

12. *Concerns Loom Despite Strong Runs in Prince William Sound*, WEST COAST FOCUS, November 1990, at 1, 15.

13. C. Lee, *Alaskan Fish Industry Tries to Repair Image*, Journal of Commerce, April 7, 1989, at 1A.

14. T. Morrow, *Oil-fearful Fishermen with Consumers Jumpy*, Seattle Times, June 27, 1989, at A1.

15. Fax from Paul Peyton, Program Manager with the Alaska Department of Commerce and Economic Development, to Jim Wakefield, Special Assistant, Department of Labor 2 (July 3, 1989) [hereinafter cited as Peyton to Wakefield]. Reproduced in Economists Incorporated Report, *supra* note 1 at Appendix 2.

16. *The Kodiak Red Salmon Fishing Season Opening Is Postponed Again Because of the Oil Spill*, Nikkan Suisan Tsushin (Fisheries News), June 21, 1989.

17. *Changing North America (Report 21)*, Hokkai Keizai Shinbun, September 20, 1989.

18. Journal of Commerce, April 11, 1989, at 1A.

19. *'Seafood is Safe' Alaska Seafood Marketing Institute Announced After the Oil Spill Incident*, Nikkan Suisan Keizai Shinbun (Daily Fisheries Economics Newspaper), April 14, 1989.

20. *Harmed Earth (part 30): Post Alaska Oil Spill Incident*, 50 KAGAKU ASAHI (ASAHI SCIENCE) No. 7 (July 1, 1990) [hereinafter cited as *Harmed Earth*].

21. Peyton to Wakefield, *supra* note 15.

22. *Halibut Season Will Proceed, But with Precautions*, Anchorage Times, April 26, 1989.

23. *Oil Spoils Fourth of Halibut Catch, Alaska Crew Says*, Seattle Times, June 14, 1989, at A1.

24. *Initial Tests Call Halibut Untainted*, *supra* note 2, at B1.

25. *Fishermen Told to Avoid Waters Where Oil Spilled*, Seattle Post-Intelligencer, July 11, 1987, at D2; and *Oil Spill Taints Salmon and Closes Down Fishing*, Seattle Post-

Intelligencer, July 15, 1987, at D2 [hereinafter cited as *Oil Spill*].

26. *Cleanup Conflict—Coast Guard, Tanker's Owner Split on Approach*, Anchorage Daily News, July 28, 1987, at A1.

27. *Oil Spill, supra* note 25.

28. *State Keeps Close Watch on Inlet—Fish Inspectors Go Where Salmon Go*, Anchorage Daily News, July 25, 1987, at B1.

29. ASMI American Survey at, *supra* note 3 at xii; *id.* ASMI Japanese Survey at xii.

30. If seafood were not labeled prior to the spill and enough people were concerned about the safety of the products, producers from unaffected regions would likely ask for labeling so that sales of their own seafood would not be affected.

31. Not all customers would likely avoid Alaskan salmon, however, since some might think that the probability of obtaining tainted salmon in retail markets was very low.

32. C. Wessells, An Economic Analysis of the Japanese Salmon Market: Consumption Patterns, the Role of Inventories and Trade Implications 64 (1990) (unpublished Ph.D. Dissertation, Dept. of Agricultural Economics, University of California, Davis) at 64. Consumers wishing to avoid the current year's seafood could avoid "new" salmon regardless of country of origin.

33. J. L. ANDERSON & Y. KUSAKABE, THE JAPANESE SEAFOOD MARKET: SALMON 79-80 (Market Analysis Group, Canadian Department of Fisheries and Oceans, Economic and Commercial Analysis Report No. 21, April 1989) [hereinafter cited as THE JAPANESE SEAFOOD MARKET: SALMON].

34. *Exxon Valdez* NRC Study, *supra* note 8 at 16.

35. C. Wessells, *supra* note 32.

36. C. Wessells, *supra* note 32 at 64. Nearly three-fourths of the world catch of sockeye is from the United States. *See* Table 3.3 above.

37. Phone interview with Chuck Noviseau, National Marine Fisheries Service (Seattle, Washington) (October 28, 1991).

38. I. DORE, SALMON: THE ILLUSTRATED HANDBOOK FOR COMMERCIAL USERS at 202–03 (1990).

39. *Reduced Catch, Low Price a Double Blow to Halibut Fishermen*, ALASKA FISHERMAN'S JOURNAL, July 1989; and *Oil Shows up in Cook Inlet and Ruins Promising Sockeye Season*, NATIONAL FISHERMAN, August 1989.

40. BILL ATKINSON'S NEWS REPORT No. 340 at 2 (March 21, 1990).

41. 32 QUICK FROZEN FOODS INTERNATIONAL at 100 (October 1990).

42. Peyton to Wakefield, *supra* note 15 at 2; Nation's Restaurant News, April 10, 1989 at 1.

43. BILL ATKINSON'S NEWS REPORT No. 304 at 1 (June 21, 1989).

44. Sasaki, *Report No. 22*, Hokkei Keizai Shinbun, September 21, 1989.

45. *North American Egg-Carrying Herring Expected to be 90 Thousand Plus, Same as Last Year*, Nikkan Suisan Tsushin (Fisheries News), June 21, 1989.

46. G. Frost, *Low Prices Rile Salmon Fishermen*, Anchorage Daily News, June 29, 1989 at C1.

47. Peyton to Wakefield, *supra* note 15 at 2.

48. *Salmon and Trout Supply Sets a Record: 21,000 tons. Prices drop steeply. The main focus of sales is fresh fish which have steady popularity*, Nikkan Suisan Keizai Shinbun (Daily Fisheries Economics Newspaper), September 19, 1989.

49. *Salmon, Pike, Mackerel, Squid are Triggers: Fish Price Drops*, Minato Shinbun, September 11, 1989. The article notes that the fall in the price of salmon and other fish is due to excessive inventories and abundant supply. *Salmon and Trout Enter Mass-supply*

Age, Minato Shinbun, November 28, 1989. The article notes that imports of farmed salmon and trout are expected to be double those of 1988.

50. C. Kleeschulte, *Fates Upon the Waters*, 6 ALASKA BUSINESS MONTHLY 64 (March, 1990).

51. *Harmed Earth*, *supra* note 20.

52. *Kodiak Red Salmon Ban Lifted Again*, Seafood Trading and Marketing News, June 19, 1989.

53. BILL ATKINSON'S NEWS REPORT No. 305 at 1 (June 28, 1989).

54. BILL ATKINSON'S NEWS REPORT No. 311 at 1 (August 9, 1989).

55. G. Knapp, *Alaska Salmon Markets and Prices*, Salmon News, November 1991, at 1.

56. U.S. General Accounting Office, Factors Affecting the Price of Alaskan Bristol Bay Sockeye Salmon (September 1991).

57. Seattle Post-Intelligencer, December 29, 1990, at B3.

58. BILL ATKINSON'S NEWS REPORT No. 335 at 2 (February 14, 1990).

59. *Salted and Processed Fish Eggs. Trade Amount Handled at the Tsukiji Market in April*, Nikkan Suisan Keizai Shinbun (Daily Fisheries Economics Newspaper), June 6, 1989.

60. *Id. Salted and Processed Fish Eggs. Trade Amount Handled at the Tsukiji Market in May*, July 20, 1989. The Tsukiji Market is part of the Tokyo Central Wholesale Market where much of Japan's seafood is sold. Volumes represent wholesale sales of processed product.

61. BILL ATKINSON'S NEWS REPORT No. 333 at 3 (January 31, 1990).

62. *Id.* No. 288 at 1–2 (March 1, 1989) and No. 372 at 3 (November 7, 1990).

63. *Salted Herring Roe Tendered the First Time (this year) in Osaka*, Nikkan Suisan Keizai Shinbun (Daily Fisheries Economics Newspaper), November 27, 1989.

64. BILL ATKINSON'S NEWS REPORT No. 293 at 3 (April 5, 1989).

65. *Id.* No. 333 at 3 (January 31, 1990).

66. *Primary Fishing Harvest is Large in Cook Inlet*, Hokkai Keizai Shinbun, April 29, 1989.

67. *Fishing of Herring in Togiak District Ended with Total Volume of 12,000 Tons*, Hokkai Keizai Shinbun, May 18, 1989.

68. BILL ATKINSON'S NEWS REPORT No. 288 at 1–2 (March 1, 1989). Presumably, low-priced product refers to wild herring roe on kelp and high-priced product refers to herring roe on kelp in pounds.

69. *Id.* No. 301 at 3 (May 31, 1989).

70. *Id.* No. 299 at 4 (May 17, 1989).

71. *Kazunoko Processing Industries Seem to Postpone Their Purchase of Herring Roe*, Minato Shinbun, August 18, 1989.

72. BILL ATKINSON'S NEWS REPORT No. 334 at 2–3 (February 9, 1990).

73. Nishi-nibon (Western Japan) committee of salted and dried fish of Zenkoku Suisanbutsu Oroshikumiai Rengo (National Marine Products Wholesale Organization), *Salted Herring Roe to be Popular Merchandise*, Nikkan Suisan Keizai Shinbun (Daily Fisheries Economics Newspaper), October 17, 1989.

74. BILL ATKINSON'S NEWS REPORT No. 288 at 1–2 (March 1, 1989).

75. *Id.* No. 301 at 3 (May 31, 1989).

76. SEAFOOD BUSINESS, March 1989.

77. *Test fishery shows no polluted halibut*, Anchorage Daily News, May 9, 1989; *Halibut season proceeds*, Anchorage Times, May 9, 1989.

78. *Halibut Season Will Proceed, But with Precautions*, Anchorage Times, April 26, 1989.

79. SEAFOOD TREND, May 1, 1989, at 2.

80. G. Knapp & T. Smith, The Alaska Seafood Industry (1991) at 110–12 (report prepared at the Institute of Social and Economic Research, University of Alaska, Anchorage, for the Alaska Department of Commerce and Economic Development & the Alaska Industrial Development and Export Authority); and BILL ATKINSON'S NEWS REPORT No. 362 at 3 (August 29, 1990).

81. SEAFOOD TREND, September 18, 1989, at 1.

82. *Sablefish Import Trend*, Nikkan Suisan Tsushin (Fisheries News), July 26, 1989.

83. BILL ATKINSON'S NEWS REPORT No. 333 at 1 (January 10, 1990).

84. *Id.* No. 402 at 3 (June 12, 1991).

5

Japanese Consumer Demand

The Japanese market is central to sales of several species of seafood caught in Alaska, most notably sockeye salmon. Over the past decade, Japan has imported much of the sockeye caught in Alaska. Most of these imports arrive in Japan during and following the Alaskan harvest (i.e., July, August, and September) and are either immediately injected into the retail sector or put into cold storage to be released over the following months. This chapter examines whether household demand for salmon changed in Japan after the Exxon Valdez oil spill. A change in Japanese household demand for salmon relative to other forms of seafood would be consistent with a theory that worldwide demand for salmon changed after the oil spill.

The product form of salmon in the Japanese retail market varies.[1] Salmon is not a typical dinner dish or common food eaten out in restaurants. Most salmon sold in Japan is salted, with cures ranging from light salt to heavy. Salted salmon is consumed in small portions, generally as a breakfast or lunch food, combined with other products. It may be purchased in supermarkets, fish stores, or department stores and typically is packaged in fillet portions of about 100 grams. Usually grilled in the home, these fillets are popular because of ease of preparation. Unsalted salmon, also sold in small portions, is often marinated with soy, rice wine, wine lees, bean paste, or other complementary sauces. For the most part, these products are staples in the diet of the Japanese rather than luxuries.

Alaskan sockeye salmon has a number of substitutes in Japan that change throughout the season and in different regions of the country. Salmon consumption is highest in the northern part of Japan, traditionally the landing point of Japan's important salmon fleet. In its coastal fisheries, Japan lands chum salmon, most of which originates in a highly productive salmon ranching system in Japanese river systems. Chum salmon are landed in the fall, beginning in September and lasting through January. Seasonal consumption patterns show a peak in fresh salmon consumption in the fall coincident with chum runs.[2] Seasonal salted salmon consumption patterns show a corresponding drop in the fall, when fresh chum is available, and a large increase in December, during the gift-giving period.

In addition to Japanese domestic fall chum harvests, there is a domestic pink salmon run in the spring. This contributes to the increased consumption of fresh salmon that begins in May. Although these alternative salmon species are the strongest substitutes for imported Alaskan salmon, there are other non-salmon substitutes and complements as well. In northern Japan, complements for salted salmon are cuttlefish, horse mackerel, and flounder. In southern Japan, summer-available species such as yellowtail compete most strongly for consumer expenditures.[3]

EXPENDITURE DATA

A substantial data base is available on expenditures by Japanese households on food items as well as other household purchases.[4] The Family Income and Expenditure Survey (FIES) is conducted every year with a random sample of about 8,000 households. Daily diary accounts of all expenditures are kept by households of all types, except those in agriculture, forestry, or fisheries, or one-person households. A stratified sampling procedure is followed that ensures coverage over the range of city sizes and over the entire year.

The detailed food expenditure records in the FIES include average quantities purchased (across Japan and on a regional basis), total expenditures, and estimated prices of the following products: tuna, horse mackerel, sardines, bonito, flounder, salmon, mackerel, saury, sea bream, cod, flatfish, yellowtail, cuttlefish, octopus, shrimp and lobsters, crabs, sashimi, clams, corbicula, oysters, scallops, as well as "other" and unclassifiable categories. These species form the so-called "fresh fish and shellfish" group. In addition, there is a "salted and dried fish" group, comprising salted salmon, salted cod roe, dried young sardines, dried horse mackerel, dried sardines, dried small sardines, dried cuttlefish, and an "other" category of salted and dried fish.

Detailed data thus exist on many seafood products purchased in Japan, including two salmon categories. In both the salted and fresh category, all species and product forms are mixed together, consistent with the typical consumer being unaware of the source of the species being purchased. The fresh category mixes truly fresh seafood with seafood taken out of frozen inventory and thawed for retail sale.

As a first step in looking for effects of the oil spill on Japanese consumer demand, we examine whether there were any obvious reductions in the total quantity of salmon purchased in 1989 compared with, for example, 1988. In Table 5.1, total quantities purchased of salted salmon and fresh salmon are shown for both years on a monthly basis. There was no general reduction in salmon purchases in the year of the oil spill. Total purchases of both fresh and salted salmon are larger in 1989 overall than in 1988. Moreover, except for a slight drop in salted salmon purchases in December, quantities purchased of both types of salmon are larger in every month in 1989 following the oil spill in March. We also analyze the substi-

Table 5.1
Salmon Purchases by Japanese Households,
1988 and 1989
(hundreds of grams per household)

Month	Fresh Salmon		Salted Salmon	
	1988	1989	1988	1989
January	54	51	170	171
February	67	55	196	196
March	73	80	214	226
April	73	80	223	233
May	94	98	233	273
June	108	117	246	271
July	108	144	266	311
August	102	142	269	322
September	110	175	265	306
October	131	174	278	304
November	129	167	282	311
December	86	119	664	656
TOTAL	**1,134**	**1,402**	**3,307**	**3,581**

Sources: Japan Statistics Bureau, Management and Coordination
Agency, Annual Report on the Family Income and
Expenditure Survey, 1988 and 1989.

tution relationships between salmon and other seafood categories in order to get a
more complete picture of consumption patterns in Japan.

CONSUMER DEMAND MODEL

To further examine the hypothesis that Japanese salmon demand was affected
by the Alaskan oil spill, we have applied the model described in Appendix 2 to
Japanese data on household seafood expenditures from 1980 to 1989. The basic
issue is whether there is any evidence of an abnormal drop in the quantity of salmon
purchased following the oil spill, after removing the effects of changes in other
factors expected to affect demand, such as income levels and prices of substitute
and complementary goods. We compiled data on average monthly household purchases of the most important seafood species reported in the FIES: fresh salmon,

salted salmon, tuna, salted cod roe, horse mackerel, flounder, yellowtail, sea bream, shrimp and lobster, shellfish, and "other" category. The individual species represent approximately 45 percent of the typical Japanese household's expenditures on seafood. We assume that these purchase decisions arise out of rational economic behavior.

Statistical estimation involves setting up a system of budget shares representing the array of relevant choices and estimating the system jointly. We estimate the model with the appropriate econometric and statistical corrections and restrictions. We also include variables to account for seasonal patterns of purchases (see Appendix 2).

RESULTS

Fresh salmon shows two peaks of purchases: the first in July, when fresh sockeye is arriving from Alaska, and the second in September/October, when the first fall chum hits the markets. Salted salmon purchases tend to increase steadily from January until the fall chum arrive, when the quantity purchased of salted salmon drops. Purchases of salted salmon peak in December during the holiday gift season. Purchases of other seafood follows similar patterns dictated by seasonal availability.

Our comparison of average household purchases in 1988 and 1989 showed that the quantities of salted and fresh salmon purchased did not decline in 1989, either for the year as a whole or during the months following the spill. However, for several reasons, this finding is not hard evidence of lack of oil spill effect. First, changes in quantities purchased could mask a demand shift by also being a result of a price drop or income increase. Second, because fresh and salted salmon are aggregates across all species and product types, there could be a shift away from Alaska salmon compensated for by an increase in spending on quantities purchased of other salmon species and products.

Utilizing a demand system approach addresses the first problem by incorporating both prices and expenditures, thereby enabling the sorting out of other effects. The second problem cannot be addressed with data reported in the FIES surveys. The simplest way to use the demand system estimation results to analyze whether changes in the quantities of salmon purchased in 1989 might be due to oil spill effects is to examine predicted shares in 1989. If the household demand system is indeed an adequate representation of average household behavior, then predicted shares of salmon purchases can be derived from the model. Actual budget shares significantly different from those that the model predicts would be consistent with the hypothesis of a change in demand.

Actual budget shares in fact are close to those predicted by the model, using only relative prices and expenditures as explanatory variables. Japanese purchases of both fresh and salted salmon were above, but not significantly different from, that predicted by the model for most of the year 1989. These results do not support the hypothesis of a change in the demand for salmon, at least over this aggregate consumption data.

CONCLUSION

The consumer retail demand model is useful in examining whether Japanese demand for salmon changed in 1989. Subject to normal caveats regarding accuracy of the data, validity of the aggregation procedure, and variance of the estimates, the results do not support the hypothesis that Japanese consumers' demand for salmon changed following the Alaska oil spill. The quantities purchased of both salted and fresh salmon were as great or greater than in previous years and consistent with a model of purchasing behavior that depends only on relative prices of other fish and total fish expenditures.

NOTES

1. *Cf.* J. L. Anderson & Y. Kusakabe, The Japanese Seafood Market: Salmon (Market Analysis Group, Canadian Department of Fisheries and Oceans, Economic and Commercial Analysis Report No. 21, April 1989).

2. C. Wessells, An Economic Analysis of the Japanese Salmon Market; Consumption Patterns, the Role of Inventories and Trade Implications (1990) (unpublished Ph.D. Dissertation, Dept. of Agricultural Economics, University of California, Davis).

3. *Id.*, Ch. IV.

4. *See* Statistics Bureau, Management and Coordination Agency, Japan, Annual Report on the Family Income and Expenditure Survey (various years).

6

Salmon Benchmark Studies

World trade in a specific species of seafood means that price differences for identical quality seafood across geographic regions should be no greater than transportation costs and tariffs, if any. If seafood prices in one region of the world were substantially higher than the prices in other regions, buyers from that region would purchase seafood from those other regions and pay the transportation costs. Similarly, if seafood prices in one region of the world were substantially lower than the prices in other regions, sellers from that region would sell seafood to those other regions and pay the transportation costs.

While seafood prices in different geographic regions are governed by the forces of supply and demand in the world market for seafood, price relationships across regions may vary slightly from year to year to reflect short-term changes in local demand and supply conditions. These short-term changes in relative price differentials exist in any given year because processing, transport, and storage capacity is allocated based on pre-season forecasts, and there might not be sufficient flexibility or time to adjust to the actual run size and location. In addition, the price differentials may be too transitory or too small relative to transportation costs to equilibrate different regional markets fully and instantaneously.

Nevertheless, the regional price differences for fish of similar quality should be fairly stable over time and reflect differences in transportation costs of bringing the seafood to market. Supply conditions will be calibrated by the entry of out-of-region suppliers at high price levels and the exit of regional suppliers to other regions if prices are too low. Demand conditions will be calibrated by the entry of out-of-region purchasers at low price levels and the exit of regional purchasers to other regions if prices are too high. These forces tend to link prices in local regions to prices in the global market.

During periods of stable demand and supply conditions, one would expect the pattern of movement of Alaskan seafood prices to be similar to the movement of prices for similar seafood from other regions. This similarity of pricing patterns is the basis for the benchmark technique explained in this chapter.

BENCHMARK APPROACH

To measure whether there was any significant change, relative to historical patterns in 1989 ex-vessel prices of salmon in Alaska, we use the benchmark technique. In its simplest form, the benchmark technique is an unadjusted relationship between prices in Alaska and prices in other reference regions. The relationship can be adjusted to account for local differences that might affect the benchmark comparison, such as changes in harvests, factor prices, and exchange rates. The benchmark technique can be applied to a single set of prices in Alaska specific to a species, gear type, and area, or it can be applied to pooled information from different species, gear types, and areas. It also can be used to test for changes in price patterns between Alaska and other regions or among specific regions within Alaska. The benchmark approach is general enough to be applied to either ex-vessel or processor prices and to any species of seafood.

When determining the appropriate benchmark, we look for a reference price series against which to gauge the performance of Alaskan prices. The reference price series must satisfy several criteria. First, it must have a similar pattern of movement to the Alaskan prices. Second, there must be sound economic reasons for the similar movements in the price series. Some price series may move together, but absent a sound economic basis for the correlations, there is no assurance that the observed parallel movement is anything more than coincidental. Third, there must be a good, stable statistical relationship between the reference price series and the Alaskan prices. The price series need not be identical, but they must maintain a stable relationship to each other over time.

We select British Columbia as the benchmark location for Alaskan salmon prices because it satisfies the above criteria. British Columbia is the closest non-Alaskan area with the same salmon species sold generally to the same markets as Alaskan-caught salmon.[1] A variety of economic factors explains why prices in the two areas have such a stable relationship: the species of salmon caught in British Columbia are identical to those species caught in Alaska; the fish are caught using the same fishing methods; and the fish are sold to the same group of wholesalers for resale to the same group of end users for the same end uses. Both Alaska and British Columbia harvest their salmon at roughly the same time of year. Consequently, the same demand and supply factors, such as inventories and salmon supplies from other locations, influence the determination of their prices.[2] We are not aware of unusual circumstances in British Columbia in 1989 that would significantly change the historical relationship between salmon prices in Alaska and in British Columbia.[3]

In a separate application of the benchmark technique, we use Bristol Bay as a benchmark for the oil-touched regions. Bristol Bay is a major Alaskan salmon fishery, particularly for sockeye. Bristol Bay satisfies the criteria for a good benchmark for the oil-touched regions in much the same manner that British Columbia satisfies the criteria for a good benchmark for the state of Alaska.[4]

We perform statistical tests to determine if the relationship between the 1989

Alaskan price and the 1989 price in the benchmark area is significantly different from the relationship we estimate for years other than 1989. If the relationship of the ex-vessel price of salmon in Alaska relative to the benchmark price in 1989 were not significantly different from the relationship in other years, we would conclude that this evidence is consistent with the absence of a 1989 effect on ex-vessel salmon prices in Alaska. If, on the other hand, we were to find that the ex-vessel price of salmon in Alaska relative to the benchmark price in 1989 was significantly different than would have been predicted given the relationship in other years, we would conclude that this evidence is consistent with ex-vessel salmon prices in Alaska being affected in 1989 relative to ex-vessel prices in other regions. In isolation, each statistical result does not provide a sufficient basis to evaluate whether any 1989 price effect may have been caused by the oil spill. Patterns of these statistical results, however, may support various hypotheses about price effects from the oil spill.

HYPOTHESES TO BE EXAMINED

Chapter 2 outlines several scenarios in which the 1989 ex-vessel price of salmon in Alaska could have been affected by the *Exxon Valdez* oil spill. The benchmark approach provides a methodology to test for evidence that is consistent with 1989 price effects in Alaska relative to British Columbia under any of these scenarios. The price change must be specific to Alaska to be identifiable with the benchmark technique. Global shifts in prices cannot be identified by this technique, since the benchmark prices would be affected as well.

One of the hypotheses presented in chapter 2 is that the oil spill affected 1989 seafood prices only in regions touched by the oil spill. If this theory were true, 1989 seafood prices in the regions of Alaska touched by the oil spill would be different from 1989 seafood prices in other regions of Alaska. Our analysis of prices in the regions touched by the oil spill relative to a benchmark of prices in Bristol Bay provides a basis to test this hypothesis.

We test for a shift in the benchmark pricing relationship by estimating the benchmark relationship for a period including 1989 with specific variables included to capture any 1989 year-specific changes in the benchmark relationship.

DATA

Two types of data are required for the benchmark technique: (1) price data for Alaska or the oil-touched region to be tested for price changes and (2) comparable data for the benchmark region or regions. More complex specifications that account for region-specific factors affecting harvests or local ex-vessel prices require correspondingly more data. Our data set consists of annual ex-vessel salmon prices and harvests for 1978 to 1990 for Alaska and 1982 to 1990 for British Columbia.[5] In our benchmark analyses we are compelled to restrict our examination to the 1984–1989 period to keep our two data sources comparable.[6] The data include prices by species and gear type from various fisheries in Alaska and British Columbia.[7] To allow for the possibility of different relationships between the benchmark and a certain species, gear type, or region, the regression analyses include variables and interaction terms specific to each species, gear type, and area.

MODEL SPECIFICATION AND ESTIMATION

We estimate the benchmark relationship using standard regression techniques. We pool the data across all species, regions, and gear types when performing the regression.[8] Our benchmark specification regresses the real ex-vessel price for a particular species, gear type, and region in Alaska against the real benchmark price for that species and gear type.[9] Real prices are obtained by deflating nominal prices with the implicit GNP price deflator. Our benchmark specification also regresses dummy variables to capture specific region, gear type, and species effects; region-specific variables to capture local effects; and other variables to determine if there was a change in the relationship in 1989. The species-specific 1989 dummy variable is especially important, since it measures the effect of a change in the ex-vessel prices for a specific species relative to the benchmark location in 1989, the year of the *Exxon Valdez* oil spill.

Additional variables are included in the regression to account for local supply and demand conditions that may affect the adjustment of the regional prices to world supply and demand conditions in any year. One variable is the size of a given year's salmon harvest in a particular region relative to the average salmon harvest in that region. This variable attempts to capture any capacity-related factors that might affect ex-vessel price. Another local variable is the percentage of the total salmon harvest in a region accounted for by each species in a given year. There is also a variable to account for the *Glacier Bay* oil spill in 1987.[10] For comparisons to British Columbia, we estimate the benchmark relationship based on two samples: (1) all of the regions in Alaska and (2) only regions that were touched by the oil spill (Chignik, Cook Inlet, Kodiak, and Prince William Sound). For comparisons to Bristol Bay, we estimate a benchmark relationship based only on the oil-touched regions.

We estimate the benchmark equations using weighted least squares. We choose pounds to weight each observation, based on our assumption that the variance of the residual for each observation is inversely proportional to pounds caught in each fishery. Weighted least squares is used to correct for heteroscedasticity. The magnitude of the error terms across observations is inversely related to the size of the harvest. This result is consistent with the notion that prices in regions with few pounds for a particular species and gear type may not have time to adjust fully to world market conditions. Hence, there may be more uncertainty about what the fully adjusted ex-vessel price would be in those instances. The weights are nor-

Table 6.1
British Columbia Benchmark Model,
1989 Price Effects for Salmon

Species	1989 Dollars Per Pound	*t*-Statistic	*p*-Value
State of Alaska			
Chinook	0.21	1.63	0.10
Sockeye	0.02	0.84	0.40
Coho	0.07	0.97	0.33
Pink	0.00	0.17	0.86
Chum	0.03	0.58	0.56
Oil-Touched Regions of Alaska			
Chinook	0.32	1.50	0.13
Sockeye	0.07	1.70	0.09
Coho	-0.11	-1.11	0.27
Pink	-0.02	-0.51	0.61
Chum	0.02	0.22	0.82

Dependent variable: Real Alaskan ex-vessel price.
Explanatory variable: Real British Columbia price in U.S. dollars, poundage of catch for region relative to average poundage, species catch relative to total region catch. Dummy variables for species, gear type, region, 1989, and Cook Inlet in 1987 (for *Glacier Bay* oil spill).

Note: For the 10 percent two-tailed test used in this book, large values of the *t*-statistic (in absolute terms) indicate statistically significant results.   Statistical significance is also indicated by *p*-values less than 0.10.

malized so that each year received the same weight.

Ordinary least squares weights equally each combination of Alaskan fishery, species, and gear type. Thus, a small fishery (such as chinook gill net in Northern Alaska) with ordinary least squares would receive the same weight as a large fishery (such as the sockeye drift gill net in Bristol Bay). In contrast, the weighted-least-squares procedure we employ gives greater weight and influence on our estimates to larger fisheries than to smaller fisheries. Smaller fisheries are potentially associated with more statistical error and less useful information. (See Appendix 1 for a detailed discussion of statistical language.)

RESULTS

British Columbia Benchmark

We find no significant systematic price effects for any species of salmon in 1989, either for all of Alaska or for the regions touched by the oil spill. Table 6.1 summarizes our results for effects on the five species of Alaskan salmon in 1989.[11] A positive (negative) coefficient indicates that the observed 1989 price was higher (lower) than what would have been expected given the 1989 British Columbia benchmark price. Since it is unlikely that the actual price will ever exactly equal the expected price, we must consider whether the actual price is significantly different statistically from the expected price. The t-statistic enables us to evaluate the statistical significance of the estimated price effects. The p-value is essentially the significance level of the estimated price effect.

Actual 1989 ex-vessel prices in the oil-touched regions were significantly higher than predicted for sockeye and pink, relative to their historical relationship with Bristol Bay prices. Prices for other species were not significantly different in 1989. Ex-vessel prices in Prince William Sound were significantly higher in 1989 than their historical relationship with Bristol Bay price would have predicted.

In only two instances—chinook for all of Alaska and sockeye for the regions touched by the oil spill—is the 1989 ex-vessel benchmark price effect significantly different from zero. In both instances, actual prices were higher than predicted. Because these results are isolated and do not show a regular pattern, we conclude that prices for salmon for the regions touched by the oil spill and for all of Alaska were not systematically different in 1989, relative to the usual relationship of those prices to British Columbian prices.

The benchmark models based on British Columbian prices fit very well the Alaskan ex-vessel salmon prices. The benchmark models for all of Alaska and for the oil-touched areas both account for 98 percent of the underlying variation in ex-vessel prices. This supports our a priori conclusion that the benchmark analysis based on British Columbian prices is a good method to estimate Alaskan prices.

Bristol Bay Benchmark

Table 6.2 presents the actual 1989 ex-vessel prices of each salmon species in the oil-touched areas relative to the prices predicted using the 1989 Bristol Bay prices. The table also presents the actual 1989 ex-vessel salmon prices in each of the oil-touched regions relative to the prices that would have been predicted for those areas given the 1989 Bristol Bay prices.

Table 6.2
Bristol Bay Benchmark Model,
1989 Price Effects in Oil-Touched Regions

Species	1989 Dollars Per Pound	*t*-Statistic	*p*-Value
	Species Effects		
Chinook	0.41	1.51	0.13
Sockeye	0.13	2.94	0.00
Coho	-0.15	-1.24	0.22
Pink	0.14	3.21	0.00
Chum	0.05	0.48	0.63
	Region Effects		
Prince William Sound	0.16	4.18	0.00
Cook Inlet	0.07	1.34	0.18
Kodiak	0.17	1.57	0.12
Chignik	-0.06	-0.55	0.58

Dependent variable: Real Alaskan ex-vessel price.
Explanatory variable: Real Bristol Bay price in U.S. dollars, poundage of catch for region relative to average poundage, and species catch relative to total region catch. Dummy variables for species, gear type, region, 1989, Cook Inlet in 1987 (for *Glacier Bay* oil spill), and 1982 (for botulism scare).

Note: For the 10 percent two-tailed test used in this book, large values of the *t*-statistic (in absolute terms) indicate statistically significant results. Statistical significance is also indicated by *p*-values less than 0.10.

CONCLUSION

Ex-vessel prices for salmon in the oil-touched regions and in all of Alaska tended to be no different in 1989 than predicted prices, relative to British Columbia. In a few instances, ex-vessel prices were significantly higher, but never lower, than predicted. These results are consistent with either price elevation in 1989 or the absence of an effect on salmon ex-vessel prices in 1989 in Alaska or regions of Alaska. These results are not consistent with claims of price suppression, unless the claim is that the effect reduced British Columbia prices as well.

The benchmark analysis for the regions touched by the oil spill relative to Bristol Bay reveals that ex-vessel prices for sockeye and pink tended to be significantly different from predicted values in 1989. Again, in both cases, actual prices were higher than predicted values. Ex-vessel prices in Prince William Sound in 1989 were also significantly higher than predicted values. These results are consistent with either price elevation in 1989 or the absence of a 1989 ex-vessel price effect in the regions touched by the oil spill. These results are not consistent with claims of ex-vessel price suppression in 1989.

Our conclusions are based on multiple and reinforcing findings rather than on isolated results. Overall, the results in this section do not show a consistent pattern of price effects in 1989 relative to the benchmarks. Consequently, we conclude that these results are consistent with the absence of a price effect as a result of the *Exxon Valdez* oil spill.

NOTES

1. The comparison is weakest for canned pink. The United Kingdom is the largest export market for both Alaskan and British Columbian canned pink; however, most canned Alaskan pink is consumed in the United States.

2. Contracts between processors and the labor union representing fishermen and processor workers are common in British Columbia. The contracts set minimum ex-vessel prices by species for some net-caught salmon and herring. Between 1984 and 1989, the actual prices paid by British Columbian processors were above the minimums established by the contract.

3. A strike by the 7,000-member United Fishermen and Allied Workers Union against four major British Columbian processors lasted from July 21, 1989, through August 8, 1989. *See Mediator-Directed Talks Reopen in B.C. Fish Strike*, Montreal Gazette, August 7, 1989, at A5; *Tentative Deal Breaks B.C. Fishing Stalemate*, Montreal Gazette, August 8, 1989, at B1; B.C. Fish Strike Over But Future's Grim, Montreal Gazette, August 9, 1989, at B7. The effect of the strike on British Columbia fish prices, if any, was to increase those prices by reducing the supply of British Columbian salmon. Thus, if the strike had any effect on prices it would tend to result in the benchmark procedure finding price suppression in Alaska in 1989.

4. The use of Bristol Bay as a benchmark tests for intra-Alaskan price effects. It cannot be employed to test for a price effect if the oil spill also affected prices in Bristol Bay.

5. Alaska: STATE OF ALASKA, COMMERCIAL FISHERIES ENTRY COMMISSION MMT REPORTS BY FISHERY, YEAR & SPECIES, PROJECT 90173.01 (August 7, 1990), *id*. PROJECT 91166 (August 20, 1991), *id*. PROJECT 91180 (September 17, 1991) [hereinafter cited as CFEC MMT Reports]; British Columbia: Canada Department of Fisheries and Oceans, Pacific Region, Vancouver B.C.

6. The Alaskan prices for 1990 are preliminary and do not include information from all processors. The British Columbian data for 1990 do not include end-of-season price adjustments and are not consistent with earlier data. British Columbian data prior to 1984 are not reported on a consistent basis with data from later years.

7. The British Columbia drift gill net price was used to predict both the drift gill net prices and the set gill net prices in Alaska. The British Columbia purse seine price was used to predict both the purse seine prices and the beach seine prices in Alaska. The British Columbian power troll price was used to predict both the power troll prices and the hand troll prices in Alaska.

8. The regions used in the analysis are Southeast, Prince William Sound, Cook Inlet, Kodiak, Chignik, Peninsula and Aleutians, Bristol Bay, and Northwest, which is an aggregation of Upper Yukon, Lower Yukon, Kuskokwim, Kotzebue, and Norton Sound. We chose these regions of Alaska based on the breakdown of prices contained in CFEC's MMT Reports, *supra* note 5.

9. For British Columbia, the benchmark price is an index of prices from three fishery districts (Fraser River, Northern British Columbia, and Southern British Columbia). First, the British Columbian price was converted into real U.S. dollars. Next an index price was computed for each species and gear type as a weighted average of the prices in the three districts, where the weights are computed by averaging the share of landed value (in dollars) for each district over the eight years in the sample. For Bristol Bay, the drift gill net price is used as the benchmark.

10. Based on our statewide benchmark analysis of ex-vessel salmon prices, 1987 Cook Inlet ex-vessel prices were 12 cents per pound lower than predicted. Using data from only the oil-touched areas, 1987 Cook Inlet ex-vessel prices were 21 cents per pound lower than predicted. In both instances, these price differences were statistically significant.

11. As we noted earlier, the British Columbian ex-vessel data for 1982, 1983, and 1990 are not reported on the same basis as the data from 1984 to 1989. The results reported in the text are from the best and most consistent data available. For a more complete description of the variables and the results, see Economists Incorporated Report, *supra* Ch. 3 note 13, Appendix 4.

7

Salmon Reduced Form Study

To better examine the major economic factors involved in determining Alaskan salmon prices, we construct an econometric model of ex-vessel prices. This model allows us to assess quantitatively the importance of local and world harvests, exchange rates, salmon inventories, and other supply and demand factors in determining prices in Alaska. Because we estimate neither a demand nor a supply curve but rather an equation reflecting elements of both, we refer to this analysis as a "reduced form" study. The reduced form model can help explain whether ex-vessel salmon prices were significantly different from their expected values in 1989. We apply the reduced form model to data from the regions of Alaska touched by the oil spill as well as to data from a combination of that region and British Columbia in order to detect differences in 1989 price effects between Alaska and British Columbia.[1]

PRICE-DETERMINING FACTORS

The first step in constructing the reduced form model is specifying those measurable factors that may reasonably be expected to influence salmon prices at the ex-vessel level. We consider the following factors:

- *Salmon Inventories.* Though wild-caught salmon is usually harvested during a small part of the year, it can be stored if it is frozen, canned, or salted. In the worldwide markets where Alaskan salmon is sold, inventories could influence ex-vessel price. We expect that higher levels of salmon inventories would have a suppressing influence on ex-vessel salmon prices.

- *Salmon Harvest.* The size of wild harvests varies from year to year as a result of environmental conditions and fishery management policies. We expect that larger global or local harvests will lead to lower prices. Because Alaskan salmon is traded in world markets, it is reasonable to expect that the level of world harvests affects Alaskan prices. Aquacultured fish appear to be substitutable for wild-caught fish. Therefore, world harvests of acquacultured fish are expected to influence Alaskan prices.

Harvests within a small region may influence local prices. For example, a given region may have a relatively fixed level of processing capacity. If harvests were unusually large during some season, the processing facilities might be overburdened, resulting in less efficient processing of fish, hence a lower value per pound of raw fish.

- *Macroeconomic Factors.* The economic conditions in the major consuming countries—Japan and the United States—can influence salmon prices. For example, the level of real (i.e., inflation-adjusted) exchange rates may affect salmon prices. If the value of the yen increases, the fixed-dollar price of Alaskan salmon would go down in terms of yen. This apparent price reduction would then stimulate Japanese consumption, leading to an increased demand (and higher U.S. dollar price) for salmon.

  The amount of income devoted to purchasing food in the consuming nations should affect demand for salmon. We assume that as food expenditures increase, salmon prices will also increase.

- *Species.* Although all five major species of Pacific salmon—chinook, chum, coho, pink, and sockeye—share common attributes and are to some extent substitutable, there are differences in demand and supply characteristics among species. Therefore, each species commands its own price, reflecting the relative desirability of the various species' attributes and the relative availability of the species. Pink and chum tend to be less expensive than chinook, coho, and sockeye.

- *Gear Type.* The gear type used influences the quality of the harvested fish and hence its value. For example, troll-caught fish are less damaged than fish caught in nets. Consequently, they command a premium price in the marketplace.

- *Region of Catch.* The region where fish are caught can influence price. The location of the catch affects its price in a variety of ways.

- *1989 Effect.* We also include a 1989 dummy variable that captures the effect on price of all factors that are not directly observable and that are not explicitly featured in the model. These factors include, among others, any price effect from the *Exxon Valdez* oil spill.

MODEL SPECIFICATION AND ESTIMATION

Once we identify the price-determining factors, we specify the mathematical relationship between ex-vessel price and these factors and use real-world data to estimate the model. Price and the other variables are related to each other in logarithmic form. This yields results in percentage terms rather than in absolute terms. Our model estimates the percentage price effect of a particular factor on prices, not a dollar amount.

Given the importance of end-of-season bonuses and adjustments to the final compensation of fishermen, grounds prices during the fishing season would be incomplete. We compute ex-vessel prices including post-season bonuses and adjustments on the basis of earnings and poundage data collected by the Alaskan Commercial Fisheries Entry Commission (CFEC) for the regions of Alaska touched by the oil spill and data collected by LGL Environmental Research for British Columbia.

We construct annual ex-vessel price indexes for the four regions touched by the oil spill and for British Columbia. (See Appendix 3 for a detailed discussion.) These indexes take into account the price-influencing effects of species, region, gear type, size of regional harvest, and general inflation. The indexes are computed for each species separately as well as for an aggregation of Pacific salmon as a whole. In simple terms, the price indexes may be thought of as averages of real ex-vessel prices.

We obtain annual values for the proposed explanatory factors from a variety of sources. For all inventory variables, we use the stocks as of April of the given year. We choose April because it reflects the state of inventories just prior to the beginning of the wild harvest season. We convert all price and income numbers to real 1989 U.S. dollars using exchange rates and implicit price deflators.

DETECTION OF PRICE DEVIATION

One important purpose of the reduced form model is to help determine whether there was a shift in prices in 1989 for Alaskan salmon relative to historical patterns. Was the actual price in 1989 lower or higher than what would be expected given the levels of the various price-determining factors? The fall in salmon prices from 1988 to 1989 is well known. Without the reduced form model, we cannot know to what extent the price drop can be attributed to changes in factors such as inventories and harvests.

This methodology, however, has an important limitation. While the econometric reduced form model can help determine whether 1989 prices were abnormal, it cannot prove in any dispositive sense that the oil spill *caused* any part of a price change. By itself, the statistical model only demonstrates association. Thus, the statistical finding of a significant 1989 price deviation merely means that prices were outside of the range that can be explained by the quantifiable variables in the model. Ultimately, the determination of causality must be made on the basis of additional corroborating evidence.

A second important purpose of the reduced form model is to determine whether any 1989 price deviations in the regions touched by the oil spill were different from those in British Columbia. The absence of a significant difference between 1989 price deviations in Alaska and British Columbia would be consistent with hypotheses that any price effect of the oil spill was not specific to Alaska.

Once the model is estimated, there are two closely related ways of detecting a 1989 price effect. One is to examine the difference between the actual 1989 price and the price predicted by the model without a 1989 dummy variable. This value is referred to as the 1989 "residual." The other is to include a 1989 dummy variable in the model and observe the estimated coefficient of this variable. This coefficient also indicates the difference between the actual price level in 1989 and that predicted by the model. The difference between the residual method and the dummy variable method is that the latter does not use 1989 data when estimating this specific model.

RESULTS

Based on different levels of aggregation of the underlying data, we estimate three types of reduced form models: the aggregate salmon price model, the pooled species price model, and the individual species price model. The first is a single regression of an aggregate price index for salmon on the explanatory variables. The second is a single regression pooled across species with separate price index observations for each species and a separate dummy variable for each species. The third model consists of five separate regressions, one for each of the salmon species.

We apply these three types of models to two data sets, one consisting of just the oil-touched regions of Alaska and one including British Columbia as well. For a discussion of the statistical terminology we use in describing our results, see Appendix 1.

Aggregate Salmon Price Model

We estimate an aggregate average ex-vessel price for salmon in the regions touched by the oil spill as a function of the following explanatory variables: world salmon harvest (also separate harvests for Pacific and Atlantic salmon), cold storage inventories, canned inventories, real U.S.-Japanese exchange rate, and real food expenditures. We estimate the model with annual data from 1978 to 1990.[2] The 1989 residual has a value of -0.097, which implies that actual 1989 prices are about 9 percent lower than those predicted by the model.[3]

To test whether the 1989 price discrepancy is statistically significant, we use the "standardized residual." There are a number of ways of standardizing residuals. We report an "externally studentized" residual. The value of the standardized residual for 1989 is -1.49. We use a 10 percent two-tailed test or a 5 percent one-tailed test as a standard for statistical significance (see Appendix 1). By these conventional standards, this standardized residual is too small to be considered statistically significant.

In addition, we estimate a 1989 price deviation by the alternative method of including a 1989 dummy variable in the model. The coefficient of the 1989 dummy variable is -0.232, which corresponds to an actual price about 21 percent lower than the predicted price. We obtain a t-statistic of -1.49 and a corresponding p-value of 0.19, which indicate that this result is not statistically significant.

We also estimate the same aggregate salmon price model with data from the regions of Alaska touched by the oil spill and with data from British Columbia.[4] The estimated 1989 price deviation in the regions touched by the oil spill is minus 17 percent; this result, however, is not statistically significant. Ex-vessel salmon prices in British Columbia had an additional 10 percentage points negative deviation in 1989. This additional deviation also is not statistically significant. These results are similar to our results for the benchmark studies. We find that 1989 ex-vessel salmon prices in the oil-touched regions of Alaska were not significantly different from those in British Columbia.

Pooled Species Price Model

The pooled species price model involves estimating adjusted average annual prices for each of the five species, pooling the species' price data into a single data set, and estimating a model. We use the same regressors as the aggregate salmon price model plus a separate 1989 dummy variable for each species. Table 7.1 presents results for this model as the estimated percentage deviation of actual and predicted 1989 price.

Table 7.1 shows variation among 1989 price deviations. For three of the five species—sockeye, pink, and chinook—the deviation is not significant. The sockeye 1989 price effect is positive but not significant. The negative deviations for chum and coho are statistically significant.

A question that naturally arises is whether a spill-caused price shift would have a differential effect on the five species. If this price shift should have affected all species, then a differential effect may be attributed to factors other than the oil spill or simply to perturbations in the data. Unless the oil spill had a substantially different effect on ex-vessel prices of different species, the absence of a similar price effect across all species of salmon would not be consistent with a theory of a spill-

Table 7.1
Pooled Species Model,
1989 Price Effects (1978–1990 Data)

Species	1989 Deviation	*t*-Statistic	*p*-Value
Chinook	-10%	-0.56	0.58
Chum	-33%	-2.15	0.04
Coho	-42%	-2.89	0.01
Pink	-10%	-0.57	0.57
Sockeye	3%	0.17	0.87

Dependent Variable: Log of the adjusted average price for individual species.
Explanatory Variables: Log of: world salmon harvest, including aquacultured Atlantic salmon; U.S. and Japanese cold storage salmon inventories; U.S. canned salmon inventories; real yen/dollar exchange rate; real U.S. and Japanese expenditures on food. Dummy variables for each species in 1989.

Note: For the 10 percent two-tailed tests used in this report, large values of the *t*-statistic (in absolute terms) indicate statistically significant results. Statistical significance is also indicated by *p*-values less than 0.10.

related price effect.

We also estimate the pooled species price model with data from the oil-touched regions of Alaska as well as British Columbia.[5] As with the results shown in Table 7.1 for the oil-touched regions alone, the only significant 1989 price effects are negative deviations for chum and coho. With the exception of chinook, the 1989 ex-vessel price deviations for salmon in British Columbia are not significantly different from those in the regions of Alaska touched by the oil spill. Chinook has a significantly negative price deviation in British Columbia relative to the oil-touched regions of Alaska. These results are consistent with those from the benchmark studies. There is little difference in the 1989 price effects in British Columbia and the regions touched by the oil spill.

Individual Species Price Model

Because of possible differences in the markets for the individual salmon species, we estimate a separate model for each species. To do this, we include a 1989 dummy variable in the five species models. Table 7.2 shows the 1989 price deviations derived from these models. All of the price deviations are negative, but none is statistically significant. We place slightly less emphasis on the results from the individual species models than from the aggregate salmon price model or the pooled

**Table 7.2
Individual Species Model,
1989 Price Effects (1978–1990 Data)**

Species	1989 Deviation	*t*-Statistic	*p*-Value
Chinook	-1%	-0.08	0.94
Chum	-36%	-1.44	0.20
Coho	-29%	-1.38	0.22
Pink	-22%	-1.06	0.33
Sockeye	-9%	-0.42	0.69

Dependent Variable: Log of the adjusted average price for individual species.

Explanatory Variables: Log of: world salmon harvest, including aquacultured Atlantic salmon; U.S. and Japanese cold storage salmon inventories; U.S. canned salmon inventories; real yen/dollar exchange rate; real U.S. and Japanese expenditures on food. Dummy variable for 1989.

Note: For the 10 percent two-tailed tests used in this report, large values of the *t*-statistic (in absolute terms) indicate statistically significant results. Statistical significance is also indicated by *p*-values less than 0.10.

species price model because with fewer observations the statistical tests are less powerful, and because the estimated values for some regressors are implausible.

In this model we again include data from the regions of Alaska touched by the oil spill and from British Columbia.[6] The results are like those shown in Table 7.2 for the oil-touched regions, and they are consistent with the findings of the benchmark studies. We find no significant 1989 price effects.

Moreover, the 1989 deviations for each species in British Columbia are not significantly different from the 1989 deviation in the regions touched by the oil spill.

EFFECTS OF FORGONE HARVEST

An independent team of biologists has produced estimates of what salmon harvests would have been in the oil-touched regions had the oil spill not occurred. Because some fisheries were closed due to the spill, the biologists estimate that harvests would have been greater than actually occurred. (See chapter 10 on supply effects.) Consideration of the 1989 forgone harvest (predicted harvest less than actual harvest) could change the price deviations presented above. The expected 1989 price would be lower when calculated using higher harvest levels. Therefore, a negative price deviation would be reduced, and a positive deviation increased, by taking into account the forgone harvest.

We examine two ways in which harvests influence ex-vessel prices: by means of a global effect and by means of a local effect. However, none of the results presented in this chapter is substantially altered by accounting for forgone harvests. The price deviations and the *t*-statistics are slightly smaller in magnitude, and the *p*-values are slightly higher, but not enough to change any conclusions that might be drawn from the results we present.

CONCLUSION

The econometric reduced form models of ex-vessel salmon prices are useful for assessing the level of 1989 prices because they take directly into account several important price-determining factors. The results can be summarized as follows. The aggregate salmon price in 1989 is not significantly different from the price our model predicts. For the pooled species price model, the 1989 price deviation varies substantially by species. Price deviations for chinook, pink, and sockeye are not significantly different from zero. The chum and coho price deviations—minus 34 and 42 percent, respectively—are statistically significant. The 1989 price deviations for chum, coho, pink, and sockeye in British Columbia were not significantly different from those in the oil-touched regions of Alaska. Price deviations for chinook were significantly lower in British Columbia.

Estimated 1989 price deviations from individual species models again show some variation by species, ranging from a minus 2 percent deviation for chinook to a minus 36 percent deviation for chum. None of the price deviations estimated from the individual species models is statistically significant, nor are there any significant differences between price deviations in British Columbia and the oil-touched regions of Alaska. The results of the salmon reduced form models are largely consistent with the results of the salmon benchmark models in that they rarely find any significant difference between 1989 price deviations in British Columbia and the oil-touched regions of Alaska.

The statistically significant negative coefficients for chum and coho in the oil-touched regions of Alaska in 1989 should not be construed as evidence consistent with a price-depressing effect from the *Exxon Valdez* oil spill for three reasons. First, only one of the eight regression models considered in this chapter produced significant negative price effects. Second, that model estimated significant effects for only two species. Most theories of oil spill effects would predict a consistent pattern across species. Third, prices in British Columbia also were lower in 1989 than can be explained by the factors in these models.

NOTES

1. For complete details on our econometric model (description of the data and their sources and the estimated coefficients of the regressions), see Economists Incorporated Report, *supra* Ch. 3 note 13, Appendix 5.

2. The data that were available for 1990 are not as reliable as data for earlier years. We also estimated this model with data from 1978 to 1989 and obtained practically the same results.

3. The percentage change estimated by the model is technically the "logarithmic percentage change," which is similar to, but not exactly the same as, the normal measure of percentage change. Percentage change = exp(log percentage change) - 1, where exp() is the exponential function.

4. We add to the model a dummy variable for British Columbia observations because we observe British Columbian data only for the years 1984 to 1989. In addition, we include a separate dummy variable for the 1989 British Columbia observation.

5. We add to the model a dummy variable for British Columbia observations and a separate British Columbia 1989 dummy variable for each species.

6. We add to the model a dummy variable for British Columbia observations and a separate British Columbia 1989 dummy variable.

8

Salmon Processor Prices

This chapter reviews Alaskan salmon processor prices and processor margins. The processor margin is defined as the difference between processor prices and ex-vessel prices, adjusted for the poundage of fish lost in processing. Salmon processor margins have not been constant in recent years. Our method uses annual data for 1984 through 1989 to predict processor prices for frozen and canned salmon based on ex-vessel prices.[1] Some processors were closed after the *Exxon Valdez* oil spill in 1989, and some processors allege that prices paid by wholesalers were suppressed because of the spill. Our results can be used to estimate what processor prices would have been had the oil spill not occurred. They also can be used to compare actual processor prices in 1989 with those that would have been expected if the oil spill had not occurred.

To analyze 1989 salmon processor prices, we also apply the benchmark approach. We estimate a relationship between the processor price for each salmon species in Alaska (fresh and frozen as well as canned salmon) and the contemporaneous processor price for that species in British Columbia.[2] We also estimate a benchmark model for salmon roe processor prices.

PROCESSOR MARGINS

Remarkably little has been published on the economics of the seafood processing industry in Alaska. A recent report, *The Alaska Seafood Industry*, claims to present the first measures of production margins in the industry. The authors define production margins as the difference in revenues or prices between the processing and harvesting industries. The report finds:

> With the exception of chinook salmon for the period 1987–1988, the [nominal] production margin per pound for all species of salmon has remained relatively constant over the 9-year period [1980–1988]. This means that processors are, in

general, selling at a constant markup [in nominal terms], with fluctuations in production or harvest prices passed through to the fisherman or buyer of the processed product, respectively.[3]

This conclusion appears to be based more on a simple interpretation of graphical data than on statistical tests of competing hypotheses. Several issues are not addressed by the report. Are there regional differences in margins? Are there differences in margins between fresh and frozen processing and canning? These issues are important in considering whether the oil spill had any effect on processor prices in 1989.

Nominal Margins

The Alaska Seafood Industry claims that margins are fixed values per pound, constant in nominal terms. Table 8.1 presents the margin per pound of harvest as calculated by this report for the five salmon species for the period 1984 to 1988. Nominal margins clearly are not constant, and the 1984–1988 average nominal margin is not a reliable predictor of the nominal margin each year. Chinook margins displayed the most variation, ranging from 51 cents per pound in 1985 to $2.24 per pound in 1988. The period average of 95 cents per pound is less than half the margin in 1988 and nearly twice the margin of 1985. The reported margin for chinook in 1988 is unusually large, primarily because processors sold more processed chinook in that year than they purchased harvested chinook. Based on the formula for margins from *The Alaska Seafood Industry,* changes in the quantity of

Table 8.1
Alaska Statewide Nominal Margin:
Data from *The Alaska Seafood Industry*
(dollars per pound of harvested fish)

Year	Chinook	Sockeye	Coho	Pink	Chum
1984	0.57	0.67	0.47	0.48	0.36
1985	0.51	0.61	0.51	0.37	0.44
1986	0.66	0.49	0.72	0.42	0.32
1987	0.95	0.53	1.01	0.61	0.61
1988	2.24	0.68	0.69	0.65	0.46
Average	0.95	0.60	0.65	0.48	0.43

Source: G. Knapp and T. Smith, *The Alaska Seafood Industry,* Tables III-4 through III-8, based on Commercial Fisheries Entry Commission Production Report.
Note: These data cover all processors in Alaska.

Table 8.2
Alaska Statewide Nominal Margin: CFEC Data
(dollars per pound of harvested fish)

Year	Chinook	Sockeye	Coho	Pink	Chum
1984	0.70	0.75	0.60	0.50	0.42
1985	0.59	0.64	0.66	0.41	0.47
1986	0.75	0.58	0.83	0.47	0.37
1987	1.00	0.60	1.07	0.67	0.65
1988	2.39	0.81	0.82	0.66	0.56
1989	2.67	0.93	1.54	0.75	0.65
Average	1.35	0.72	0.92	0.58	0.52

Source: Commercial Fisheries Entry Commission, Ex-Vessel Price Estimates, Report III (1984–89).
Note: The data cover all processors in Alaska.

fish sold relative to fish purchased—such as through changes in inventories—can result in large changes in margins.[4]

Margins for other salmon species vary less than those for chinook, but the variation is still substantial. Margins for coho range from 51 cents to $1.01 per pound, for pink from 37 cents to 65 cents per pound, for chum from 32 cents to 61 cents per pound, and for sockeye, which had the most constant margins, from 49 to 68 cents per pound. Moreover, the highest and the lowest margins were not consistent in the same years across species. The margins for each species in Table 8.1 have a slight upward movement over time but not a constant upward trend. Nominal margins in 1988 are uniformly higher than in 1984 but not uniformly higher than in 1987. Consequently, part but not all of the increase seems attributable to general inflation.

The average margins for the 1984–1988 period indicate that margins per pound of harvested chinook tended to be the highest followed by coho, sockeye, pink, and chum. However, this order held in only one of the five years, 1988, when the reported margin for chinook showed a very large increase. Three different species—chinook, sockeye, and coho—had the highest margin in at least one of the five years. Three different species—chum, pink, and sockeye—had the lowest margin in at least one of the five years. Not only did nominal margins for the same species vary substantially from year to year, but the margins did not vary in the same manner across species.

The pattern of processor margins presented in *The Alaska Seafood Industry* is consistent with the pattern of processor margins based on data that we have obtained independently from the State of Alaska's Commercial Fisheries Entry Com-

Table 8.3
Alaska Statewide Real Margin: CFEC Data
(1989 dollars per pound of harvested fish)

Year	Chinook	Sockeye	Coho	Pink	Chum
1984	0.82	0.88	0.70	0.59	0.49
1985	0.67	0.73	0.76	0.46	0.54
1986	0.84	0.64	0.92	0.53	0.41
1987	1.08	0.65	1.15	0.72	0.70
1988	2.49	0.85	0.85	0.69	0.58
1989	2.67	0.93	1.54	0.75	0.65
Average	1.43	0.78	0.99	0.62	0.56

Source: Commercial Fisheries Entry Commission, Ex-Vessel Price Estimates, Report III (1984–89).
Note: The data cover all processors in Alaska. The margins are adjusted using the GNP implicit price deflator.

mission (CFEC). Table 8.2 presents statewide margins calculated from CFEC data for the period 1984 to 1989. The calculated margins are slightly higher than in Table 8.1, but the pattern is similar.

The 1989 processor margins displayed in Table 8.2 were higher than the sample average for each species. Use of a constant nominal margin to predict the 1989 processor prices based on prior information, however, might lead to substantial errors. As noted above, margins for the same species varied substantially from year to year. Moreover, the relative ranking of margins across species varied substantially from year to year.

Real Margins

Table 8.3 presents the CFEC margins of Table 8.2 in 1989 dollars, adjusted for the effects of inflation by deflating using the GNP implicit price deflator. This adjustment removes some of the upward movement in margins. For example, 1988 margins are not uniformly higher than 1984 margins. But the 1989 margins are still higher than the sample averages for all species. Margins for each species still show substantial variation over time, and the period average is a poor predictor of margins in individual years.

ESTIMATION OF PROCESSOR PRICES BASED ON EX-VESSEL PRICES

Another way to evaluate the potential impact of the oil spill on processors is to examine processor prices. We approach this using two models. One estimates processor prices based on ex-vessel prices. The other compares Alaskan processor prices with benchmarks from British Columbia.

We examine several model specifications to estimate real processor prices for frozen salmon as a function of ex-vessel prices, quantities of processed fish, regions within Alaska, and species.[5] The regions are Southeast, Prince William Sound, Cook Inlet, Kodiak, Chignik, Peninsula-Aleutians, and Bristol Bay. Processor prices were examined for chinook, sockeye, coho, chum, and pink salmon.

We also examine the specific effect of the year 1989 on processor prices by species and by region. Our data set is drawn from annual CFEC data on processor prices, ex-vessel prices, and quantities of processed fish for 1984 through 1989. Each combination of region, species, and year is represented by a single observation in our data set. Because the regions of Alaska by which the CFEC data are organized are not of equal size, we employ weighted least squares in our regression analyses using the quantity of processed fish as weights.

Analysis by Species

Our preferred specification uses species and regional dummy variables in all years prior to 1989. In 1989 we use either species dummy variables or regional dummy variables.

As Table 8.4 indicates, real prices in 1989 for fresh and frozen processed salmon of all species were slightly lower than predicted but not significantly different.[6] Results for canned salmon were substantially different from those for fresh and frozen salmon. Processor prices rose for all canned species, except chinook, in 1989. The increase was significantly different from zero for sockeye, pink, and chum. That is, accounting for the variables in our model, processor margins for canned sockeye, pink, and chum increased in 1989.

Analysis by Region

We also estimate the effect of the year 1989 on processor prices by region (Table 8.5).[7] The results are similar to those discussed above. None of the real prices of fresh and frozen processed salmon was significantly affected in 1989 for any region except Cook Inlet, where processor prices for fresh and frozen processed salmon were 22 cents lower per pound than can be explained by the other factors that we take into account in the regression. This result is statistically significant.

Results for canned salmon in 1989 reveal regional price effects in Southeast Alaska, Prince William Sound, and Bristol Bay. Cannery prices in 1989 in these

Table 8.4
1989 Processor Price Effects by Species

Species	1989 Effect Based on Ex-Vessel Prices (dollars per pound of processed fish)	*t*-Statistic	*p*-Value
	Fresh and Frozen Salmon		
Chinook	-0.20	-0.62	0.53
Sockeye	-0.09	-0.89	0.37
Pink	-0.21	-1.50	0.13
Coho	-0.08	-0.42	0.67
Chum	-0.09	-0.53	0.60
	Canned Salmon		
Chinook	-0.83	-0.56	0.57
Sockeye	0.58	5.06	0.00
Pink	0.29	4.62	0.00
Coho	1.11	1.61	0.11
Chum	0.65	2.73	0.01

Dependent variable: Real processor price.
Explanatory variables: Species dummies (sockeye, coho, pink, and chum); region dummies (Prince William Sound, Cook Inlet, Kodiak, Peninsula/Aleutian Islands, and Bristol Bay); real ex-vessel price; processor output in quantity (fresh and frozen or canned); and constant.

Note: For the 10 percent two-tailed test used in this book, large values of the *t*-statistic (in absolute terms) indicate statistically significant results. Statistical significance is also indicated by a *p*-value less than 0.10.

regions are higher (and significantly higher for all regions except Cook Inlet) than can be explained by the variables in the model.

BENCHMARK ANALYSIS

The benchmark analysis for processor prices closely follows the benchmark analysis for ex-vessel salmon prices described in chapter 6. For fresh and frozen salmon as well as canned salmon, we estimate a relationship between the processor price for each salmon species in Alaska and the contemporaneous processor price for that species in the benchmark area, British Columbia.

Table 8.5
1989 Processor Price Effects by Region

Species	1989 Effect Based on Ex-Vessel Prices (dollars per pound of processed fish)	*t*-Statistic	*p*-Value
Fresh and Frozen Salmon			
Southeast	-0.07	-0.69	0.49
Prince William Sound	-0.19	-0.88	0.38
Cook Inlet	-0.22	-1.74	0.08
Kodiak	0.03	0.13	0.90
Peninsula/Aleutian Islands	0.04	0.20	0.84
Bristol Bay	-0.37	-1.15	0.25
Canned Salmon			
Southeast	0.34	4.63	0.00
Prince William Sound	0.22	2.40	0.02
Cook Inlet	0.08	0.17	0.86
Bristol Bay	0.68	6.15	0.00

Dependent variable: Real processor price.
Explanatory variables: Species dummies (sockeye, coho, pink, and chum); region dummies (Prince William Sound, Cook Inlet, Kodiak, Peninsula/Aleutian Islands, and Bristol Bay); real ex-vessel price; processor output in quantity (fresh and frozen or canned); and constant.

Note: For the 10 percent two-tailed test used in this book, large values of the *t*-statistic (in absolute terms) indicate statistically significant results. Statistical significance is also indicated by a *p*-value less than 0.10.

Methodology

Our data set consists of annual processor prices and quantities for 1984 to 1989. The data are organized by species and type of processing from various fisheries in Alaska and British Columbia. The Alaskan data are divided between canned salmon and fresh and frozen salmon. The British Columbia data are divided three ways: canned, fresh, and frozen. We weighted the fresh and frozen prices by pounds and averaged them to obtain a fresh-frozen benchmark price. The data are pooled across all species and regions to perform the regression.

Table 8.6
1989 Processor Price Effects for Fresh and Frozen Salmon:
British Columbia Benchmark Model

Species	1989 Effect Based on Ex-Vessel Prices (dollars per pound of processed fish)	*t*-Statistic	*p*-Value
	State of Alaska		
Chinook	0.05	0.19	0.85
Sockeye	0.06	0.82	0.41
Coho	0.36	2.29	0.02
Pink	0.02	0.24	0.81
Chum	0.07	0.54	0.59
	Regions of Alaska Touched by Oil Spill		
Chinook	0.44	1.23	0.22
Sockeye	0.01	0.17	0.86
Coho	0.24	1.14	0.26
Pink	0.08	0.48	0.63
Chum	0.12	0.77	0.44

Dependent variable: Real processor price for fresh and frozen salmon.
Explanatory variables: Dummy variables for species, region, and Cook Inlet in 1987.

Note: For the 10 percent two-tailed test used in this book, large values of the t-statistic (in absolute terms) indicate statistically significant results. Statistical significance is also indicated by a p-value less than 0.10.

Our benchmark specification estimates the real processor price for a particular species and region in Alaska based on the real British Columbia benchmark price for that species. Real prices were obtained by deflating nominal prices by the implicit GNP price deflator. To allow for the possibility of different relationships between the benchmark and a certain species or region, the regression analysis includes variables and interaction terms specific to each species and region. It also includes a variable to account for the *Glacier Bay* oil spill in 1987. We estimate the benchmark relationship separately for canned salmon and for fresh and frozen salmon.

The benchmark relationship is based on two samples: (1) all of the regions in Alaska and (2) those regions that were touched by the oil spill (Chignik, Cook

Table 8.7
1989 Processor Price Effects for Canned Salmon:
British Columbia Benchmark Model

Species	1989 Effect Based on Ex-Vessel Prices (dollars per pound of processed fish)	*t*-Statistic	*p*-Value
State of Alaska			
Chinook	-1.61	-0.08	0.94
Sockeye	-0.20	-1.06	0.29
Coho	-1.65	-1.14	0.26
Pink	-0.23	-2.50	0.02
Chum	-0.15	-0.37	0.71
Regions of Alaska Touched by Oil Spill			
Chinook	0.66	0.08	0.94
Sockeye	0.09	0.19	0.85
Coho	-1.20	-0.98	0.34
Pink	-0.29	-2.92	0.01
Chum	-0.52	-1.26	0.22

Dependent variable: Real processor price, canned salmon.
Explanatory variables: Dummy variables for species, region, and Cook Inlet in 1987.

Note: For the 10 percent two-tailed test used in this book, large values of the t-statistic (in absolute terms) indicate statistically significant results. Statistical significance is also indicated by a p-value less than 0.10.

Inlet, Kodiak, and Prince William Sound). Pounds of processed salmon are used as weights for weighted least squares. The effect of change in the processor prices for a specific species in Alaska relative to British Columbia in 1989 is measured by the coefficient on the species-specific 1989 dummy variable.

Fresh and Frozen Salmon

With the possible exception of coho, the results from the benchmark analysis of processor prices for five species of Alaskan fresh and frozen salmon are consistent with theories that these prices were unaffected in 1989. Coho processor prices in

1989 were higher and significantly different from predicted values based on a benchmark analysis for the entire state of Alaska, but they were not significantly different from predicted values based on an analysis of just those regions touched by the oil spill (Table 8.6).

We also tested with the benchmark model whether fresh and frozen processor prices were different from their expected value in Cook Inlet in 1987, the year of the *Glacier Bay* oil spill. Based on the statewide sample, Cook Inlet prices were not significantly different in 1987; however, based on the sample of just the oil-touched regions, fresh and frozen processor prices were 16 cents per pound lower in Cook Inlet in 1987 than can be explained by the benchmark model. This price difference is statistically significant.

Canned Salmon

Table 8.7 summarizes our benchmark results for the effects on processor prices for canned salmon for the five species of Alaskan salmon in 1989. While all of the estimated coefficients are negative in the all-Alaska sample, the *t*-statistics indicate that none of the observed prices, except for pink, is below the normal range of price fluctuation. The 1989 processor prices for canned pink salmon in Alaska were about $0.23 per pound below their expected value given what processors were paid for canned pink salmon in British Columbia, and this difference is statistically significant. As noted earlier, however, 1989 canned pink salmon processor prices in Alaska were significantly higher than expected based on ex-vessel prices. One possible explanation for the difference between Alaskan and British Columbian canned pink salmon price movements in 1989 is the difference in the markets to which canned pink salmon is sold. Relatively more Alaskan pink salmon is sold to domestic markets.

As with the all-Alaska sample, the coefficient for pink canned salmon in the oil-touched sample is negative and statistically significant. The 1989 processor price for canned pink salmon in the affected areas was about $0.29 per pound below its expected value. None of the other coefficients is statistically significantly different from zero.

Our benchmark analysis of processor prices for canned salmon is consistent with theories that suggest that 1989 canned processor prices for pink salmon were suppressed in Alaska, or in the regions of Alaska touched by the oil spill.

Our benchmark analysis also is consistent with theories that suggest canned processor prices for the other species of salmon were unaffected, either in Alaska as a whole or in the regions of Alaska touched by the oil spill.

The benchmark results, in combination with the regression results based on ex-vessel prices, do not support a finding of processor price suppression even for pink salmon because processor prices are not lower relative to both ex-vessel prices and British Columbian processor prices for any species.

Salmon Roe

We estimate a benchmark model of Alaskan processor prices for salmon roe for the period from 1984 through 1989. CFEC data do not distinguish salmon roe by species, and consequently the prices in our model reflect an aggregation of processor prices that include all salmon species.[8] The results of the benchmark model indicate that salmon roe processor prices in the oil-touched areas were significantly higher statistically in 1989, relative to prices in British Columbia, the benchmark area. Salmon roe processor prices in the oil-free areas were relatively low in 1989, but the price decrease is not statistically significant.[9]

CONCLUSION

As shown in Table 8.3, real salmon processor margins per pound of harvest in Alaska were not constant during the 1984–1989 period, and they were higher in 1989 than the average for the period. The pattern of processor margins in 1989 is not substantially different, however, from the 1984–1988 period. The pattern does not support a theory that processor margins in 1989 were uniformly affected.

Our regression analysis of salmon processor prices based on ex-vessel prices indicates that prices for fresh and frozen salmon were not unusually high or low for any species in 1989. This result is consistent with a theory that processor prices for fresh and frozen salmon of all species in Alaska were unaffected in 1989. Prices of fresh and frozen salmon were lower, however, in Cook Inlet in 1989 than can be explained by the factors in our model. Because it is difficult to explain why processor prices in the other regions touched by the oil spill were not also affected in 1989, we do not consider the isolated Cook Inlet price effect to be consistent with claims that the oil spill suppressed processor prices in all of the regions of Alaska touched by the oil spill. Nevertheless, it is possible, in principle, that some local supply-side effect of the oil spill specific to Cook Inlet might account for this result.

For several regions of Alaska (Southeast, Prince William Sound, and Bristol Bay) and for certain species (sockeye, pink, and chum), processor prices of canned salmon (based on ex-vessel prices) were often significantly higher than predicted values in 1989. Some of these results are consistent with a finding that canned salmon processor prices were elevated in 1989. However, as we discuss in the introduction, isolated results do not form the basis of our conclusions; rather, we rely on reinforcing patterns of evidence.

Processor prices in 1989 for fresh and frozen salmon in Alaska, with the exception of coho, were not affected relative to what would have been predicted given British Columbian prices. Coho prices were significantly higher than predicted. Processor prices in 1989 for canned pink salmon were significantly below what would have been expected given the canned pink price in British Columbia. However, canned pink processor prices in Alaska in 1989 were significantly higher than can be explained by ex-vessel prices. The canned prices for other species in 1989 were not significantly different statistically from their predicted values based on British Columbian prices. In other words, 1989 canned pink prices in Alaska reflected unusually high mark-ups that were nonetheless lower than those observed in British Columbia. Salmon roe processor prices were not significantly different in 1989 based on a benchmark analysis. In general, the results of our analyses do not display the consistent pattern of price effects in 1989 on which we base our conclusions and consequently do not support claims that processor prices were affected by the *Exxon Valdez* oil spill in 1989.

NOTES

1. State of Alaska, Commercial Fisheries Entry Commission, Ex-Vessel Price Estimates, Report III (1A &1B, 2A & 2B, 3A & 3B) (1984–89).

2. Alaska and British Columbia export a large quantity of canned pink salmon to the United Kingdom, but most canned Alaskan pink is consumed domestically.

3. G. Knapp & T. Smith, The Alaska Seafood Industry (1991) at 61 (report prepared at the Institute of Social and Economic Research, U. of Alaska, Anchorage for the Alaska Department of Commerce and Economic Development and the Alaska Industrial Development and Export Authority). Footnotes omitted.

4. Processor margin = (Processor revenue - cost of harvested fish) / pounds of harvested fish.

5. The estimation based on real prices performed slightly better than the estimation based on nominal prices. Real prices were obtained by deflating nominal prices by the GNP implicit price deflator. The implicit price deflator was from the Economic Report of the President 290 (February 1991).

6. The equation using species for 1989 dummy variables is as follows:

real processor price = $a + b_1$ real ex-vessel price + b_2 total processed weight

$$+ g_1 \, D_{pink} + g_2 \, D_{sockeye} + g_3 \, D_{chum} + g_4 \, D_{coho}$$
$$+ d_1 \, D_{Prince \, William \, Sound} + d_2 \, D_{Cook \, Inlet} + d_3 \, D_{Kodiak}$$
$$+ d_4 \, D_{Chignik} + d_5 \, D_{Peninsula/Aleutian \, Islands} + d_6 \, D_{Bristol \, Bay}$$
$$+ z_1 \, D_{chinook1989} + z_2 \, D_{sockeye1989} + z_3 \, D_{chum1989} + z_4 \, D_{coho1989}$$
$$+ z_5 \, D_{pink1989}$$

where $D_{species}$ represents a dummy variable for species throughout the sample period; D_{region} represents a dummy variable for regions throughout the sample period; and $D_{species1989}$ represents a dummy variable for each species in 1989.

7. The equation using region for 1989 dummy variables is as follows:

real processor price = $a + b_1$ real ex-vessel price + b_2 total processed weight

$$+ g_1 \, D_{pink} + g_2 \, D_{sockeye} + g_3 \, D_{chum} + g_4 \, D_{coho}$$
$$+ d_1 \, D_{Prince \, William \, Sound} + d_2 \, D_{Cook \, Inlet} + d_3 \, D_{Kodiak}$$
$$+ d_4 \, D_{Chignik} + d_5 \, D_{Peninsula/Aleutian \, Islands} + d_6 \, D_{Bristol \, Bay}$$
$$+ z_1 \, D_{Prince \, William \, Sound1989} + z_2 \, D_{Cook \, Inlet1989}$$
$$+ z_3 \, D_{Kodiak1989} + z_4 \, D_{Chignik1989}$$
$$+ z_5 \, D_{Peninsula/Aleutian \, Islands1989} + z_6 \, D_{Bristol \, Bay1989}$$
$$+ z_7 \, D_{Southeast1989}$$

where $D_{species}$ represents a dummy variable for species throughout the sample period;

D_{region} represents a dummy variable for regions throughout the sample period; and $D_{region}1989$ represents a dummy variable for each region in 1989.

8. Because CFEC salmon roe price data are aggregated across all species, we cannot compare processor prices directly with ex-vessel prices, which are disaggregated by species.

9. See Economists Incorporated Report, *supra* Ch. 3 note 12, Appendix 7 for details.

Non-Salmon Species Studies

This chapter analyzes ex-vessel prices for herring, halibut, sablefish, shrimp, and crab, and processor prices for herring. As with salmon, we use two types of models to examine the relationship between various economic factors and ex-vessel prices: a benchmark price model (which relates Alaskan ex-vessel prices to ex-vessel prices in a benchmark area using historical prices) and a reduced form model (which relates Alaskan ex-vessel prices to demand and supply conditions using historical data). Using these two models, we can predict what ex-vessel prices in various Alaskan fisheries would have been in 1989 based on the historical relationships. We can also predict what ex-vessel prices would have been in the four herring roe fisheries in Prince William Sound that were closed in 1989 and had no harvests. For processor prices, we use a model that relates processor prices to ex-vessel prices.

Although these models do not provide tests of a direct causal linkage between measures of price effects in 1989 and the *Exxon Valdez* oil spill, they provide information that may be consistent or inconsistent with theories of price effects associated with the spill. We can use the benchmark models to evaluate whether ex-vessel prices in Alaska were affected in 1989 relative to those in the benchmark location. The results of these models can also be used to test the plausibility of whether price effects from the oil spill, if any, were limited to Alaska or regions of Alaska. The models based on demand and supply factors enable us to evaluate whether ex-vessel prices in Alaska changed in 1989 relative to historical patterns. Similarly, the processor price model allows us to evaluate whether 1989 processor prices differ significantly from what the historical pattern of ex-vessel prices predicts.

Information and literature on these non-salmon species are much scarcer than those on the salmon species. Our data set for each species includes fewer observations than the salmon data set, thereby limiting the number of factors that we can take into account. Except for most of the herring roe fisheries, we lack 1990 Alaskan price data.

Following a description of the price models, this section presents and discusses the results from the models for each non-salmon species. We end with our conclusions about 1989 Alaskan ex-vessel and processor prices for these species.[1]

DESCRIPTION OF THE PRICE MODELS

Benchmark Price Model

Our benchmark analysis estimates a relationship between the price of a species in Alaska and the contemporaneous price of the same species in a comparable location. Using statistical tests, we evaluate whether the relationship of prices in the two locations in 1989 differs significantly from the relationship in other years.

We use British Columbia as the benchmark location for most non-salmon species because the species caught there are the same as in Alaska, the harvests occur at roughly the same time, the same harvesting methods are used, and the seafood is sold through the same channels of wholesalers to the same types of consumers. Our benchmark models use annual Alaskan ex-vessel prices and annual 1982–1990 British Columbian ex-vessel prices (see Economists Incorporated Report, *supra* Ch. 3 note 12, Appendix 8). The pricing methodology for these species does not change over this time period in contrast to salmon species.

For roe herring in gill nets, we use annual 1986–1990 ex-vessel prices from Tomales, California, as a benchmark. British Columbian roe herring caught in gill nets have larger roes than the Alaskan herring caught in gill nets. The Tomales, California roe herring, however, are a similar size. For wild roe-on-kelp in Prince William Sound, we use annual price data broken out by kelp species from the Alaska Department of Fish and Game in Cordova. Roe size is computed by multiplying average herring weight (in grams) by roe content. We cannot use British Columbia as a benchmark for wild roe-on-kelp because that method of harvesting is unlawful in British Columbia; instead we choose Bristol Bay. (Wild roe-on-kelp fisheries are uncommon, giving us few benchmarking alternatives.) For crab we also use ex-vessel prices from Alaskan locations. British Columbia combines information on several crab species rather than reporting each species separately, thus preventing us from using British Columbia as a benchmark.

For each species, we estimate prices by gear type in the areas affected by the oil spill (Prince William Sound, Cook Inlet, Kodiak, and Chignik).[2] Each year economic conditions simultaneously influence prices in Alaska and prices in the benchmark area, making them move together. Both location dummy variables and interaction terms take into account price differences among Alaskan locations.[3] The 1989 dummy variable allows us to measure the difference between actual Alaskan prices in 1989 and the prices predicted by the historical relationship with the benchmark's prices. In some cases, we use additional factors to account for species-specific conditions that influence price.

Reduced Form Price Model for Halibut

We relate annual ex-vessel prices of halibut to demand and supply factors in a reduced form model. As explained above, we estimate a relationship between the price of a species in Alaska and contemporaneous economic conditions for years other than 1989. In this model, like the benchmark models, we evaluate whether the relationship of prices to economic conditions in 1989 differs significantly from the relationship in other years.

Prices in a market are determined by demand and supply. In order to estimate the relationship of price to economic factors, supply must shift in response to different factors than those that shift demand. For fisheries where the amount harvested depends on biological and environmental conditions as well as harvest regulations, that condition appears to hold, enabling us to estimate the price relationship.[4]

Most of the economic factors in these price models—harvest, inventories, food expenditures, and 1989 price effect—were discussed in chapter 7 on the salmon reduced form model. One other economic factor that we include in the halibut model is price of a substitute.[5]

A close substitute for halibut offers an alternative to consumers of halibut. Consequently, when consumers establish their demand for halibut, they take into account the price of the substitute. If the price of the substitute were to decline relative to halibut prices, consumers would purchase a larger volume of the substitute and, at each possible halibut price, purchase less halibut. As a result, the quantity of halibut demanded would decline and so would its price. Thus, the prices of a product and its substitutes tend to decline and to rise together. In the price models, the effect of the price of a substitute should be positive.

Processor Price Model

Our roe herring processor price analysis estimates a relationship between processor prices and ex-vessel prices in Alaska. Processors try to sell frozen roe herring at prices that cover their costs, including a return on capital, and the herring price that processors pay fishermen is one important cost. Although ex-vessel prices fluctuate considerably from year to year, other costs such as labor and capital are probably more stable over a limited time period, after adjusting for inflation. Consequently, we can derive a useful relationship between processor prices and ex-vessel prices with adjustment factors for regional differences. Regional differences may reflect not only transportation costs but also differences in processing quality. We include a 1989 dummy variable in the model to measure the difference between actual price for Alaskan frozen herring in 1989 and the prices predicted from the historical relationships with ex-vessel prices.

Table 9.1
1989 Ex-Vessel Prices for Non-Salmon Species
in Fisheries Open for at Least Part of the 1989 Season
(in 1989 dollars per pound)

Non-Salmon Species, Gear	1989 Ex-Vessel Prices
Sac Roe Herring, Seine	
Cook Inlet	$0.33*
Kodiak	$0.46*
Sac Roe Herring, Gill Net	
Cook Inlet	$0.29*
Kodiak	$0.38*
Halibut, Long Line	
Prince William Sound	$1.47
Cook Inlet	$1.48
Kodiak	$1.51
Chignik	$1.46
Sablefish, Long Line	
Prince William Sound	$1.48
Cook Inlet	$1.40
Dungeness Crab, Pot Gear	
Prince William Sound	$1.00

* The price at 10 percent roe content. See discussion at footnote 10.

EX-VESSEL PRICES: NON-SALMON SPECIES

We find no pattern of significant 1989 ex-vessel price effects for non-salmon species. This conclusion is based on the detailed evidence presented in this section. We estimate that the 1989 ex-vessel prices in fisheries that were open are the same prices that would have prevailed without the oil spill. Table 9.1 presents these prices for fisheries that were open for at least part of the 1989 season. Estimates of ex-vessel prices for non-salmon fisheries that were closed for the entire 1989 season are presented in chapter 10.

Sac Roe Herring

"Roe herring" refers to fish containing roe, while "herring roe" refers to the roe itself. Inside the fish, roe is encased in a membrane or sac. In the sac roe herring fishery, fishermen catch herring before the fish spawn and sell the entire fish.

Due to oil-spill closures, Prince William Sound's sac roe herring fisheries had no harvests in 1989. Two districts in Cook Inlet, a small fishery along the Kenai Peninsula, and 35 of 56 management districts at Kodiak Island also were closed.

Differences in roe content contribute to variations in the prices of sac roe herring from different areas. Roe content is the weight of mature roe divided by total fish weight. Herring buyers reportedly establish a base price at 10 percent roe content and then revise the price by a fixed amount for each percentage-point increase or decrease in roe content.[6] The price structure creates an economic incentive for fishermen to increase roe recovery.[7]

Price also differs by gear type. Roe herring caught in gill nets tend to have higher roe content than those caught in purse seines, thus leading to a higher gill net price. The higher roe content of gill net-caught fish stems from several factors. Gill netting occurs close to shore where the fish spawn. The fish tend to have more mature eggs, and consequently higher roe content, as they move inshore. Gill net fishermen also can adjust the size of the mesh of their nets, giving them greater control than seiners over the size of the fish harvested. On the other hand, purse seine-caught roe herring tend to have lower roe content because the harvesting occurs farther offshore. In addition, purse seines harvest larger catches, which are transferred to tender boats for shipment to processors. The time needed to pump the large quantity of fish into the tender reduces freshness, and the weight of all the fish in the seine increases the likelihood of damaging and breaking the egg sacs.

Even after taking into account roe content and gear type, roe herring prices from different areas do not follow each other closely. Differences in roe characteristics across areas and over time help explain ex-vessel price variation. Aside from price, important roe characteristics for Japanese buyers include roe size and shape, percentage of whole skeins, roe texture, region of origin, lack of blood, and color.[8] Changes in roe characteristics in one area could cause prices to diverge from prices in other areas. For example, prior to 1987, the price of Sitka herring exceeded the price of Prince William Sound herring. In recent years Sitka has harvested very small fish, causing Sitka's price to drop below Prince William Sound's. Even when roe characteristics in an area do not change, the relative supply of roe sizes can vary and alter the price differential between roe sizes and consequently between areas.

To account for these differences to the greatest extent possible, we select as a benchmark an area in British Columbia or California with the same gear type and with roe sizes (in grams) closest to those in each Alaskan area.[9] In addition, we adjust prices for roe content.[10]

The results using 1982–1990 Alaskan seine prices from the oil-touched areas indicate that actual prices in Cook Inlet, Kodiak, and Chignik were lower in 1989, relative to the benchmark prices from regions in British Columbia, than predicted by the model. As Table 9.2 shows, adjusted seine prices of roe herring with 10 percent roe content were 10 cents per pound lower than predicted, but the price

Table 9.2
1989 Price Effects for Sac Roe Herring in
Oil-Touched Areas: Benchmark Model

Gear	1989 Dollars Per Pound	*t*-Statistic	*p*-Value
Seine	-0.10	-1.18	0.27
Gill Net	-0.20	-5.28	0.00

Dependent Variable: adjusted Alaska price at 10 percent roe content in 1989 dollars.
Explanatory Variables: adjusted benchmark price at 10 percent roe content in 1989 dollars, dummy and interaction variables for oil-touched areas.

Note: Seine data are from 1982 to 1990. Prince Rupert and West Coast Vancouver Island are the benchmark areas. Gill net data are from 1986 to 1990. Tomales, California, is the benchmark area. For the 10 percent two-tailed tests used in this report, large values of the *t*-statistic (in absolute terms) indicate statistically significant results. Statistical significance is also indicated by a *p*-value of less than 0.10.

difference is not statistically significant.[11] The same model predicts, for Prince William Sound in 1989, seine prices at 10 percent roe content of 18 cents per pound.[12] The model accounts for 58 percent of the variation in the seine prices in the oil-touched areas.

Table 9.2 also presents the results for 1986–1990 Alaskan gill net prices from the oil-touched areas. Prices in Cook Inlet, Kodiak, and Chignik were lower in 1989—relative to Tomales, California, prices—than predicted by the model. Adjusted gill net prices of roe herring with 10 percent roe content were 20 cents per pound lower than predicted, and the price difference is statistically significant.[13] The same model predicts, for Prince William Sound in 1989, gill net prices at 10 percent roe content of 31 cents per pound.[14] The model accounts for 83 percent of the variation in the gill net prices in the oil-touched areas.

These mixed results do not support a hypothesis of price effects in the oil-touched areas because only one gear, gill net, has a statistically significant price difference in 1989. If prices were affected for demand-side reasons, we would expect both gears to have statistically significant 1989 effects. Some supply-side factors could account for these results, but we have no information to support that hypothesis.

The price of herring caught in Kodiak is higher than the price of herring caught in Prince William Sound. Using our prices adjusted for roe content, we find that seine prices in Kodiak usually exceed seine prices in Prince William Sound, but the ratio varies from year to year and is not usually as high as double (see Figure

9.1 and Table 9.3). In 1988, the ratio was 1.78, but in many other years the ratio was lower. (The ratio for herring gill net prices is even lower.)

Herring Roe-on-Kelp

Fishermen harvest herring roe-on-kelp in two ways. In the roe-on-kelp in pounds fishery, fishermen fill floating net cages (or pounds) with *Macrocystis* kelp harvested in Southeastern Alaska, seine pre-spawning herring, transport the fish to the pounds, and release them to spawn on the kelp. In the wild roe-on-kelp fishery, divers gather kelp after the herring have laid their eggs on kelp growing wild. In the wild fisheries, the harvest consists of ribbon, sieve, hair, or rockweed kelp, which fetch lower prices than *Macrocystis*. The prices in the pound fishery substantially exceed the prices in the wild fishery in part because the pound fishermen do their own marketing. Due to oil-spill closures, Prince William Sound's pound and wild fisheries had no harvests in 1989.

We have no model for herring roe-on-kelp relating ex-vessel prices to demand and supply factors because we have been unable to locate any data on inventories in Japan other than general indications in the trade press (e.g., "high," "low"). In addition, to the extent that the harvest depends on demand conditions (see below),

Figure 9.1
Roe Herring Prices at 10 Percent Roe Content:
Ratio of Kodiak to Prince William Sound

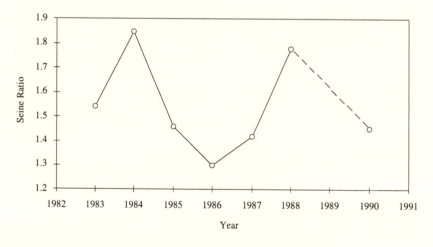

Source: Table 9.3.

Table 9.3
Roe Herring Prices at 10 Percent Roe Content:
Ratio of Kodiak to Prince William Sound

Year	Seine	Gill Net
1983	1.54	1.00
1984	1.85	1.83
1985	1.46	1.41
1986	1.30	1.14
1987	1.42	1.17
1988	1.78	1.00
1989	*	*
1990	1.45	1.32

Note: See Economists Incorporated Report, *supra* Chapter 3 note 12, Appendix 8 for explanation of prices.
* Prince William Sound roe herring fishery was closed in 1989.

rather than on biological conditions or regulations, we cannot estimate a stable price relationship. Consequently, this section presents herring roe-on-kelp results from benchmark models only.

Benchmark Analysis of Herring Roe-on-Kelp in Pounds Prices

We estimate a relationship between prices in Prince William Sound's roe-on-kelp in pounds fishery and prices in British Columbia's roe-on-kelp in pounds fishery during the 1980–1988 period. All prices are in 1989 dollars. At the time we wrote this book, Alaska's Commercial Fisheries Entry Commission (CFEC) did not yet have a preliminary 1990 price for roe-on-kelp in pounds in Prince William Sound. We use unweighted least squares to give each year an equal weight in the regression.

We omit location factors (and their interactions) from the model because there are no other Alaskan roe-on-kelp in pounds fisheries.[15] We omit a 1989 dummy variable from the model because there is no 1989 price for Prince William Sound. The model predicts that Prince William Sound's 1989 price would have been $9.75 per pound. The model fits the historical data relatively well, accounting for 83 percent of the variation in Prince William Sound's prices.

Benchmark Analysis of Wild Herring Roe-on-Kelp Prices

The benchmark model takes into account an additional feature of the wild herring roe-on-kelp fishery: kelp species. In the wild roe-on-kelp fishery in Prince

William Sound, the harvest has involved three types of kelp: ribbon, sieve, and hair. Roe on ribbon kelp earns a premium price over roe on the other types of kelp. By contrast, the harvest in Bristol Bay (Togiak) has been almost entirely rockweed kelp. Despite differences in prices of kelp species, the prices of these products have moved together over time.[16] The model includes factors indicating kelp species and interactions between the kelp species factors and the Bristol Bay price.

We estimate a relationship between prices in Prince William Sound's wild roe-on-kelp fishery and prices in Bristol Bay's wild roe-on-kelp fishery during 1980, 1983, 1986–1988, and 1990.[17] We omit location factors (and their interactions) from the model because there are no other wild roe-on-kelp fisheries. We omit a 1989 dummy variable from the model because there is no 1989 price for Prince William Sound.

This model predicts the 1989 price per pound of wild roe-on-kelp in Prince William Sound as $2.00 for ribbon, $1.35 for sieve, and $0.89 for hair. The model accounts for only 42 percent of the variation in Prince William Sound's prices. However, excluding 1990 prices from the model improves the fit to 70 percent and results in higher predicted prices for each kelp species in 1989: $2.15 for ribbon, $1.40 for sieve, and $1.10 for hair.

The relatively poor fit when the model includes 1990 prices could be due to changing demand structure. The share of ribbon kelp harvested has steadily declined along with its price since 1986. In addition, ribbon's price premium has declined as the prices of other species have risen. This may indicate a decline in relative demand. If relative demand has declined in recent years, the model (which relies on historical data) will tend to inflate the 1989 price of ribbon kelp and deflate the 1989 price of other species.

Halibut

Most halibut is harvested in deep water away from the oil-touched areas. No halibut fisheries were closed in 1989. Halibut prices rose from 1988 to 1989.

Benchmark Analysis of Halibut Prices

The benchmark model enables us to take into account two additional features of this fishery: size categories and the location of the first opening. Fish tickets for halibut have several size categories: chicken (under 10 lbs), medium (10–59 lbs), large (60 lbs and over), No. 2 (bruised), and mixed (no size limit). CFEC began in 1985 to compute one price for all halibut sizes in Alaska, but prices in Canada continue to differ by size. We exclude the data for chicken, No. 2, and mixed halibut because these categories comprised only about 2 percent of the halibut catch in the oil-touched areas from 1980 to 1984.

The model includes a factor indicating size and an interaction between the size factor and the British Columbian price.[18] The model also includes a dummy vari-

Table 9.4
1989 Price Effects for Halibut:
Benchmark Model

Area	1989 Dollars Per Pound	t-Statistic	p-Value
Oil-Touched Areas Only (Excluding Chignik)	0.23	6.61	0.00
All Alaska			
Oil-Free Areas	0.25	6.28	0.00
Oil-Touched Areas	0.18	2.97	0.00

Dependent Variable: Alaskan ex-vessel price in 1989 dollars.
Explanatory Variables: British Columbian ex-vessel price in 1989 U.S. dollars, dummy and interaction variables for each area, dummy and interaction variables for halibut size, dummy variable for first opening in Canada, and dummy variable for 1989.

Note: For the 10 percent two-tailed tests used in this book, large values of the t-statistic (in absolute terms) indicate statistically significant results. Statistical significance is also indicated by a p-value of less than 0.10.

able indicating whether the United States or Canada had the first opening of the season.[19] Fishermen receive a price premium for fish sold to the fresh market, rather than to processors, and the country with the earlier opening sells a larger share of the harvest to the fresh market. In addition, when Canada has the first opening, it temporarily enjoys the relative scarcity of halibut. (The U.S. catch is substantially larger over a shorter period of time.) This situation boosts the price for the first opening, generating a price differential between U.S.-caught halibut (primarily frozen market-bound) and Canadian-caught halibut (primarily fresh market-bound). By contrast, when the United States has the first opening, Canadian prices are closer to, and sometimes below, U.S. prices.

As Table 9.4 shows, actual prices were 23 cents higher in 1989 than predicted by the benchmark model, and the price difference is statistically significant.[20] The model accounts for 94 percent of the variation in the Alaskan prices.

We also have price effects with the model accounting for other Alaskan locations (Ketchikan, Petersburg/Wrangell, Sitka, Juneau, Yakutat, Alaskan Peninsula, Dutch Harbor, Bering Sea, Adak, and Kuskokwim) and an additional 1989 factor to indicate the oil-free areas. We use unweighted least squares because we lack data on pounds harvested outside the oil-touched areas.

Prices in the oil-free areas were 25 cents per pound higher in 1989 than predicted by the model, and the price difference is statistically significant. Prices in the oil-touched areas were 18 cents per pound higher in 1989, and the price difference is statistically significant. However, prices in oil-touched and oil-free areas did not differ significantly from each other in 1989. After adding the oil-free locations, the model accounts for 71 percent of the variation in the Alaskan prices. This evidence is consistent with the proposition that halibut prices were elevated in 1989.

Reduced Form Analysis of Halibut Prices

Our reduced form halibut model is based on the work of Lin *et al.*[21] They estimated the demand for halibut using annual data from 1955 to 1984. We have extended their data to cover the 1955–1990 period. Our model (hereafter referred to as the Extended Lin Model) estimates U.S. ex-vessel halibut price from harvests in Canada and the United States, U.S. inventories of halibut prior to the opening of the fishing season, the price of a substitute (proxied by wholesale price of finfish), U.S. expenditures on food, and the length of the halibut season.

With extremely short seasons in recent years, only a small share of the catch could be consumed fresh. Because fish shipped to the fresh market enjoy a price premium over fish destined for processing, the decline in the share of catch consumed fresh reduces the average price of halibut. The Extended Lin Model aggregates the halibut catch in the United States, rather than distinguishing locations.

There are two other reasons, not discussed by Lin *et al.*, that shorter seasons are associated with lower prices. First, during the shortest seasons, fishermen and processors have difficulty handling a large harvest. Consequently, the quality of the harvest declines.[22] For example, during a 24-hour opening, fishermen may neglect to clean some fish, and ice-packed halibut may pile up on a dock for several days before processing. Compressed seasons, in addition to reducing the share of the harvest consumed fresh, depress the quality of halibut and hence its price.

Second, during the long time period covered by the model, technological changes in fishing have enabled fishermen to catch fish more quickly. For example, circle hooks have greatly increased harvesting efficiency.[23] The season length has been shortened, in part, to offset the improvements in technology. For this reason, season length also accounts for technological improvements that lower the cost of fishing and ultimately ex-vessel prices in all types of markets (competitive, monopolistic, or monopsonistic). Thus, the positive relationship between ex-vessel price and season length may also reflect a higher cost structure during longer seasons that raised price in earlier years.

Our replication of the Lin model for 1955 to 1984 produced results close to those of Lin, *et al.* In that model, all the factors except food expenditures affect halibut prices as expected. The Extended Lin Model also yields the result that the actual 1989 price is higher than predicted, but the price difference is not statistically significant (Table 9.5).

We also estimate the model with three revisions: a different version of inventories, the price of swordfish as a substitute, and, instead of length of season, factors

Table 9.5
Regression Analysis Results from Halibut Demand Model

1989 Dummy Variable	Percentage Effect	*t*-Statistic	*p*-Value
Extended Lin Model	44	1.36	0.19
Revised Model	22	0.72	0.48

Dependent Variable: Ex-vessel halibut prices
Explanatory Variables for Extended Lin Model: harvest in Canada and the United States, season length, inventories, wholesale price index of unprocessed finfish, and U.S. food expenditures.
Explanatory Variables for Revised Model: harvest in Canada and the United States, Canadian first opening dummy variable, U.S. first opening dummy variable, revised inventories, swordfish price, and U.S. food expenditures.
Note: We compute the percentage effect from exp(coefficient)-1.

indicating whether Canada or the United States had the first opening. We use the price of swordfish instead of the wholesale price index of unprocessed finfish, which is based on salmon, halibut, and haddock prices. It is inappropriate to use that index to estimate halibut price because halibut price is included in the index. We use swordfish as a substitute for halibut because both are steakfish.

The practice of giving one country the first opening began in 1980 when the season length had been shortened to 20 days. During the 1980s, prices declined 50 percent compared with earlier years, and U.S. prices declined an additional 6 percent when Canada had the first opening.[24]

The results of the Revised Model indicate that actual prices were higher in 1989 than predicted, but the price difference is not statistically significant. All the other factors affect halibut prices as expected and, except for the swordfish price, are statistically significant. The Revised Model accounts for 71 percent of the variation in halibut prices (less than the other models primarily because the Revised Model does not include the wholesale price index for unprocessed finfish). The evidence supports a finding that halibut prices were unaffected in 1989.

Sablefish

Although some sablefish fishing occurs in a few pockets of deep water in the oil-touched areas, most is done in oil-free areas. Fisheries were closed in Prince William Sound (for two months) and in Cook Inlet.

Alaskan sablefish prices in the oil-touched areas were 35 cents per pound higher in 1989 than predicted by the benchmark model, and the difference is statistically significant (Table 9.6).[25] The model fits the historical data well, accounting for 97 percent of the variation in the Alaskan prices.

Table 9.6
1989 Price Effects for Sablefish:
Benchmark Model
(in 1989 dollars per pound)

Area	1989 Dollars Per Pound	*t*-Statistic	*p*-Value
Oil-Touched Areas Only	0.35	8.16	0.00
All Alaska			
Oil-Touched Areas	0.34	6.38	0.00
Oil-Free Areas	0.29	7.26	0.00

Dependent Variable: Alaskan ex-vessel price in 1989 dollars.
Explanatory Variables: British Columbian ex-vessel price in 1989 U.S. dollars, dummy and interaction variables for each area, and dummy variable for 1989.

Note: For the 10 percent two-tailed tests used in this report, large values of the *t*-statistic (in absolute terms) indicate statistically significant results. Statistical significance is also indicated by a *p*-value of less than 0.10.

When we include other Alaskan locations (Ketchikan, Sitka, Juneau, Petersburg/Wrangell, Yakutat, and Bering Sea) and an additional 1989 factor to indicate the oil-free areas, the model accounts for 95 percent of the variation in the Alaskan prices.[26] The actual price was 29 cents per pound higher in oil-free areas and 34 cents per pound higher in oil-touched areas in 1989 than predicted by the model. These price differences are statistically significant, but prices in oil-touched and oil-free areas did not differ significantly from each other in 1989. This evidence is consistent with price elevation for sablefish in 1989.

Shrimp in Pot Gear

Fishermen catch several different species of shrimp in the shrimp fisheries using different gear types, but this study focuses on spot and pink shrimp caught in pot gear. Pot gear shrimp fisheries were closed in Prince William Sound and part of Cook Inlet in 1989. The prices of shrimp in pot gear rose in 1989 relative to 1988. In recent years Alaska's harvest of pink shrimp caught in pot gear has been small: 416 pounds in 1987, 127 pounds in 1988, and 7 pounds in 1989.[27] For reasons explained below, we were unable to evaluate whether shrimp prices were affected in 1989.

Benchmark Analysis of Shrimp Prices

In our benchmark model, we estimate the prices of spot and pink shrimp caught in pot gear from prices in another location. However, the model does not account for much of the variation in Alaskan prices. The erratic behavior of shrimp prices over time contributes to problems in estimating prices. We found little relationship between prices in one Alaskan location and prices in another Alaskan location, prices in British Columbia (for spot shrimp), or prices in the State of Washington.[28] Although prices outside of Alaska may impose a ceiling on Alaskan prices (after taking into account transportation costs), the price movements of locally marketed shrimp in pot gear may not follow price movements outside of Alaska.

Estimating Shrimp Prices from Demand and Supply Factors

Spot shrimp are primarily sold locally in Anchorage and Seward to the fresh market, such as restaurants. Although shrimpers using pot gear focus on large shrimp, they sometimes harvest smaller pink shrimp in the process.[29] For pot gear, the pink shrimp harvest is minor, and pink shrimp prices have occasionally been as high as or higher than spot shrimp prices, although the relationship is erratic.

Because of the local marketing, we estimate a price for spot shrimp in pot gear from local economic conditions: Alaskan catch, Alaskan income, and the price of substitutes, such as spot shrimp that could be transported from other locations. The model accounted for 94 percent of the variation in Alaskan prices. Although the historical relationship between price and local economic conditions provides a useful benchmark for many purposes, it is unlikely to provide a good comparison for a year when local conditions change dramatically. In 1989, the Alaskan harvest of spot shrimp in pot gear dropped to about half of the harvest in each of the previous two years. With such a large decline in the harvest, restaurants would, in all likelihood, purchase shrimp from other locations and thereby mitigate Alaskan price increases.

Crab in Pot Gear

The crab fisheries have several species and gear types, but this study focuses on brown king crab and Dungeness crab caught in pot gear. In our benchmark model, we estimate crab prices in Prince William Sound from prices in other Alaskan locations.[30] We use the location that, in addition to having a 1989 price, accounts for the largest amount of variation in Prince William Sound's prices: Juneau for brown king crab and Kodiak for Dungeness crab. Based on Juneau's prices from 1982 to 1988, the price of brown king crab in Prince William Sound would have been $3.81 in 1989. The model accounts for 75 percent of the variation in prices in Prince William Sound. Based on Kodiak's prices from 1969 to 1989 and a 1989 factor, the actual price of $1.00 per pound for Dungeness crab in Prince William

Table 9.7
1989 Processor Price Effects for Frozen Roe Herring

Variable	1989 Dollars Per Pound	*t*-Statistic	*p*-Value
All Alaska	-0.16	-4.66	0.00
Region			
Southeast	-0.11	-1.63	0.12
Prince William Sound/			
Cook Inlet	-0.15	-1.60	0.13
Western (incl. Kodiak)	-0.36	-4.14	0.00
Bristol Bay	-0.12	-2.55	0.02
Arctic/Yukon/			
Kuskokwim	-0.16	-2.24	0.04

Dependent Variable: frozen roe herring processor price in 1989 dollars.
Explanatory Variables: ex-vessel price in 1989 dollars, dummy variables for regions, and constant.

Note: For the 10 percent two-tailed tests used in this report, large values of the *t*-statistic (in absolute terms) indicate statistically significant results. Statistical significance is also indicated by a *p*-value of less than 0.10.

Sound in 1989 did not differ significantly from the price predicted by the model. The model accounts for 93 percent of the variation in Prince William Sound's prices.

PROCESSOR PRICES: NON-SALMON SPECIES

We examine processor prices and margins for only one non-salmon species: roe herring. The vast majority of Alaskan sac roe herring are frozen whole. By contrast, processors outside of Alaska generally remove the roe from the herring. Because of these differing processing methods, we do not attempt to compare herring processor prices in Alaska with prices in areas outside of Alaska. Instead, using annual data by area from 1984 to 1990, we predict processor prices for frozen roe herring based on ex-vessel prices.

Processor margins and ex-vessel prices for frozen roe herring both fluctuate over time, but processor margins generally exhibit less variation.[31] Our model estimates frozen roe herring prices based on ex-vessel prices in 1989 dollars and based on regions within Alaska.[32] We also examine the effect of the year 1989 on processor prices.

As Table 9.7 indicates, processor prices for frozen roe herring were lower in 1989 than predicted by ex-vessel price and region alone, and the price decline is statistically significant.[33] A model that separates 1989 price effects for each region confirms that all regions exhibited a price decline in 1989. Frozen roe herring processor prices declined in 1989 by 11 cents per pound in the Southeast, 15 cents per pound in Prince William Sound/Cook Inlet, 36 cents per pound in Western (including Kodiak and Chignik), 12 cents per pound in Bristol Bay, and 16 cents per pound in Arctic/Yukon/Kuskokwim, relative to prices that would have been expected to prevail.[34] The 1989 price declines by region do not differ significantly from the Alaska-wide price decline of 16 cents per pound in 1989, which is consistent with theories of Alaska-wide processor price suppression in 1989.

CONCLUSION

Roe herring ex-vessel prices in the oil-touched areas (adjusted for roe content) were lower in 1989, relative to benchmark prices, than predicted by the model. However, only the price difference for gill nets was statistically significant. The lack of a statistically significant price difference for seines makes it difficult to attribute price differences to demand-side effects of the oil spill. We do not expect—and are unaware of any claim or basis for believing—that the oil spill had gear-specific, supply-side effects. The interpretation of these results should be qualified because our ability to perform benchmark analysis of roe herring prices is weaker than for other species due to greater price variation induced by quality differences. As discussed above, we base our conclusions on consistent patterns of findings. Because the roe herring results present no such pattern, we conclude that they do not support hypotheses of price effects in 1989.

Halibut prices in 1989 were significantly higher statistically than predicted by the benchmark model using British Columbian prices. Our model based on demand and supply conditions shows that actual halibut prices were higher in 1989 than predicted, but the difference is not statistically significant.

Actual prices for sablefish were higher in 1989, relative to British Columbian prices, than predicted by the model, and the price difference is statistically significant. Our results for Dungeness crab show that prices in Prince William Sound were not significantly different in 1989, relative to prices in Kodiak (which were not affected by the spill), than predicted by the model.

Our quantitative analyses of ex-vessel prices for non-salmon species of seafood in Alaska provide no support for theories that find price effects in 1989 from the *Exxon Valdez* oil spill. Alaskan ex-vessel prices in 1989, with the exception of some roe herring prices, were not affected relative to economic factors that influence prices. Moreover, factors unrelated to the oil spill, particularly factors affecting demand in Japan as reported in the trade press, may account in part for price changes for roe herring.

Herring roe processor prices showed Alaska-wide price suppression in 1989. We have not undertaken further analysis or investigation to see if the price effect is spill-caused, a hypothesis that would be difficult to understand in light of the preponderance of qualitative evidence.

NOTES

1. For a detailed description of our data souces, see Economists Incorporated Report, *supra* Ch. 3 note 13, Appendix 8.

2. We use weighted least squares for wild herring roe-on-kelp, sac roe herring, halibut, and sablefish in the oil-touched areas. Each year is weighted equally. The weight for an area is the percentage of pounds harvested that year from the areas included in the regression that year. For herring roe-on-kelp in pounds and crab, we use unweighted least squares to give each year an equal weight. In the Alaska-wide models for halibut and sablefish, we use unweighted least squares because we lack data on pounds harvested for those fisheries.

3. A location dummy for Cook Inlet equals 1 when the price is from Cook Inlet, and it equals 0 otherwise. In this case, an interaction is a location factor multiplied by a benchmark price. The price difference from a location dummy variable is a fixed dollar value (in 1989 dollars), while the price difference from an interaction term is in percentage terms.

4. Different agencies regulate the harvesting of different species, as described in chapter 3. In addition, other regulations, such as Japanese import restrictions on roe herring, could potentially affect the harvest.

5. We converted all prices and food expenditures to 1989 dollars using the GNP Deflator reported in ECONOMIC REPORT OF THE PRESIDENT 290 (February 1991).

6. Phone interview with Kristi Nelson, herring buyer, Juneau, Alaska (September 1991); Phone interview with Paul Reilly, Biologist, California Department of Fish and Game (August 29, 1991).

7. *See* L. Brannian & K. Rowell, Biological and Sampling Considerations when Maximizing Roe Recovery for Alaska's Herring Fisheries, Proceedings of the International Herring Symposium, Anchorage, Alaska (October 21–23, 1990) (Alaska Sea Grants College Program, University of Alaska, Fairbanks).

8. J. L. Anderson, J. T. Gledhill & Y. Kusakabe, The Japanese Seafood Market: Herring Roe 104 (February, 1989) (prepared for the Canadian Department of Fisheries and Oceans by J.L. Anderson & Co.) [hereinafter cited as The Japanese Seafood Market: Herring Roe].

9. For seine, roes from Prince William Sound (13 to 16 g.), Kodiak (14 to 18 g.), and Chignik (16 to 19 g.) are closest in size to those from Prince Rupert (14 to 19 g.). Roes from Lower Cook Inlet (19 to 22 g.) are closest in size to those from West Coast Vancouver Island (17 to 22 g.). For gill nets, roes from Prince William Sound (15 to 18 g.) and Upper Cook Inlet (12 to 20 g.) are closest in size to those from Tomales (16 to 18 g.). We lack data for Kodiak roes in gill nets, but we use Tomales as the benchmark.

10. We assume that the price for each percentage-point change in roe content is one-tenth of the base price at 10 percent roe content. Using this relationship, we compute the base price at 10 percent roe content from the average price and the average roe content in each location in each year.

Base Price = Average Price/(1 + .1 (Roe Content -10))

11. The model uses weighted least squares with the weight for a region equal to the percentage of pounds of roe herring caught in seines in the oil-touched areas that year.

12. This seine price includes the 10 cent decline in 1989.

13. The model uses weighted least squares with the weight for a region equal to the percentage of pounds of roe herring caught in gill nets in the oil-touched areas that year.

14. This gill net price includes the 20 cent decline in 1989.

15. A pound fishery opened in Sitka, but not until 1990.

16. Because CFEC averages the roe-on-kelp price for all kelp species in Prince William Sound, we have used prices from the Alaska Department of Fish and Game. As a check on the comparability of CFEC and ADF&G prices, we averaged the ADF&G prices for each year (weighted by the percentage harvest of each type of kelp) and subtracted that average from the CFEC price. The difference varies by year: -6, 3, -1, -2, 8, 20, and 2 cents per pound. For two years, ADF&G had a price range, and we used the top end of the range to bring the average closest to CFEC's price. The differences between the two price series are relatively small except in one year.

17. Prices are not available from both locations every year. All prices are in 1989 dollars, and Bristol Bay's prices come from STATE OF ALASKA, COMMERCIAL FISHERIES ENTRY COMMISSION, EX-VESSEL PRICE ESTIMATES, REPORT 1A (undated report received May 30, 1991). We use weighted least squares with the weight for a kelp species equal to the percentage of tons of wild roe-on-kelp harvested in Prince William Sound that year.

18. The size factor equals 1 for large halibut and 0 for medium halibut.

19. The Canadian opening factor equals 0 in 1982 and 1986 when the United States had the earliest opening and equals 1 in 1983–1985 and 1987–1989 when Canada had the earliest opening.

20. We use weighted least squares with the weight for each observation equal to the percentage of the annual harvest (in pounds) of medium or large halibut in Prince William Sound, Cook Inlet, or Kodiak. Chignik is excluded because we have no information on pounds harvested there.

21. Biing-Hwan Lin, H. Richards, & J. Terry. *An Analysis of the Ex-vessel Demand for Pacific Halibut*, 4 MARINE RESOURCE ECONOMICS 305–314 (1988).

22. H. Bernton, *Halibut Fleet Caught Up in Short Fishing Frenzy*, Washington Post, May 18, 1991; The McDowell Group, Alaska Seafood Industry Study: An Economic Profile of the Seafood Industry in Alaska (May, 1989) (prepared for the Alaska Seafood Industry Study Commission).

23. INTERNATIONAL PACIFIC HALIBUT COMMISSION, SCIENTIFIC REPORT NO. 72. METHODS OF POPULATION ASSESSMENT OF PACIFIC HALIBUT.

24. The Canadian opening factor equals 0 when either the openings occurred on the same dates or the United States had the earliest opening, and it equals 1 when Canada had the earliest opening. The U.S. opening factor equals 0 when the openings occurred on the same dates or Canada had the earliest opening, and it equals 1 when the United States had the earliest opening.

25. Note that sablefish fishery regulations for the Gulf of Alaska require long line gear. Chignik generally has no sablefish fishery, so the model has no data from Chignik. We use weighted least squares with the weight for a region equal to the percentage of pounds of sablefish harvested in the oil-touched areas that year.

26. We use unweighted least squares because we lack data on pounds harvested outside the oil-touched areas.

27. Fax from Elaine Dinneford, CFEC, Sept. 13, 1991.

28. British Columbia does not report pink shrimp (*Pandalus borealis*) separately; it groups together five species of shrimp. The State of Washington has data on another pink shrimp (*Pandalus jordani*).

29. CFEC MMT Reports indicate that fishermen using pot gear harvest only a small volume of pink shrimp, as compared with spot shrimp.

30. We use unweighted least squares to give each year an equal weight in the regression.

31. Margin is defined as the difference between processor price and ex-vessel price, adjusted for fish weight lost in processing. Because most roe herring is frozen whole, we assume no weight loss from processing.

32. The five regions include Prince William Sound/Cook Inlet, Western (Kodiak, Chignik, and Alaska Peninsula), Southeast, Bristol Bay, and Arctic-Yukon-Kuskokwim (Kuskokwim, Kotzebue, Yukon, and Norton Sound). For processor prices, region refers to the processing area; for ex-vessel prices, region refers to the harvesting area. To maintain the comparability of the processor and ex-vessel prices, we have used broad regions. Because of their fragility, we do not expect roe herring to be shipped long distances from the harvesting area, but, for example, processors in Prince William Sound might buy roe herring harvested in Cook Inlet and vice versa.

33. The model uses weighted least squares with the weight for a region equal to the percentage of pounds of roe herring frozen that year in Alaska.

34. The Western harvest is dominated by Kodiak, and the Prince William Sound/Cook Inlet harvest came entirely from Cook Inlet in 1989.

10

Supply Effects

The *Exxon Valdez* oil spill may have affected differently the supply conditions for fisheries in each of the regions it touched—Prince William Sound, Cook Inlet, Kodiak, and Chignik—as well as subregions within them. Seafood prices may have been affected by the following: seafood quality differences, closure of local fisheries, reduced harvests, and the oil spill clean-up operation.

QUALITY DIFFERENCES

The oil spill may have affected 1989 ex-vessel prices by changing fish quality (size, appearance, freshness, etc.) in regions where some local districts may have been closed for part or all of the season. For example, the Prince William Sound Area Management Report for 1989 asserts that as a result of certain closures for periods of up to 10 days in Prince William Sound, there were perceived spill-related declines in the quality of the harvest.[1] Spill-related closures of some local districts in some regions may have led to an increased prevalence of fishing near river mouths or hatcheries where salmon tend to be lower in quality. It is also possible in principle that fish quality increased because local fisheries associated with small fish or fish with low oil content were closed.

We have no data with which to measure changes in seafood quality in 1989 or any other year, nor do we have information with which to distinguish any quality changes caused by the oil spill from those resulting from other factors. Any price effect in 1989 as the result of changed seafood quality, whatever the cause, should be reflected in our quantitative analyses of ex-vessel prices, particularly our bench-mark studies. Because these quantitative analyses provide little if any support for the existence of a significant price effect in 1989, they do not support claims of substantial local price effects as the result of changes in seafood quality caused by the oil spill.

Table 10.1
Regional Salmon Fisheries for which 1989 Price Data
Are Missing from Official State of Alaska Publications

Region	Species	Gear	Missing from Source
Cook Inlet	Chinook	Drift gill net	MMT Report
	Pink	Drift gill net	MMT Report
	Sockeye	Drift gill net	MMT Report
Kodiak	Chinook	Beach seine	MMT Report and CFEC Report 1A
	Chinook	Purse seine	MMT Report and CFEC Report 1A
	Chum	Beach seine	MMT Report and CFEC Report 1A
	Chum	Purse seine	MMT Report
	Coho	Beach seine	MMT Report
	Coho	Purse seine	MMT Report
	Pink	Beach seine	MMT Report and CFEC Report 1A
	Pink	Purse seine	MMT Report
	Sockeye	Purse seine	MMT Report
	Sockeye	Beach seine	MMT Report
Prince	Chinook	Set gill net	MMT Report and CFEC Report 1A
William	Chum	Set gill net	MMT Report and CFEC Report 1A
Sound	Coho	Set gill net	MMT Report and CFEC Report 1A
	Pink	Set gill net	MMT Report and CFEC Report 1A
	Sockeye	Set gill net	MMT Report and CFEC Report 1A

CLOSURE OF FISHERIES

Several local fisheries were closed for part or all of the 1989 season as a result of the oil spill. Many local districts of salmon fisheries were closed for part of the season, but relatively few fisheries appear to have been closed throughout an entire region for the entire season. Similarly, for non-salmon species, some fisheries were closed in local districts or for part of the season, but the only fisheries that appear to have been closed throughout a region for the entire season were in Prince William Sound. These were fisheries for roe herring and wild herring roe on kelp, spot shrimp and pink shrimp in pot gear, and king crab.

Salmon

Table 10.1 lists the Alaskan salmon regional fisheries for which ex-vessel prices in 1989 are missing from official publications of the State of Alaska: Report 1A of the Commercial Fisheries Entry Commission and MMT Reports.[2] Other fishery

Table 10.2
Estimated 1989 Ex-Vessel Prices for Salmon Fisheries for which Data Are Missing from Official State of Alaska Publications

Region	Species	Gear	Basis for Estimate	Price Estimate (1989 dollars per pound)
Kodiak				
	Chinook	Purse seine	Kodiak set net	$1.17
	Chinook	Beach seine	Kodiak set net	$1.17
	Chum	Beach seine	Kodiak purse seine	$0.37
	Pink	Beach seine	Kodiak purse seine	$0.55
Prince William Sound				
	Chinook	Set gill net	Prince William Sound drift gill net	$2.28*
	Chum	Set gill net	Prince William Sound drift gill net	$0.44*
	Coho	Set gill net	Prince William Sound drift gill net	$0.66
	Pink	Set gill net	Prince William Sound drift gill net	$0.39*
	Sockeye	Set gill net	Prince William Sound drift gill net	$2.30*

* In 1988, the ex-vessel prices for this fishery and the basis fishery were the same.

closures affected only some districts within a region or did not last for the entire season. The two data sets provided by the state are not completely consistent as to which 1989 ex-vessel prices are missing for salmon species in the regions touched by the oil spill. The absence of official data would be consistent with the notion— but would not prove—that the fishery was closed in 1989.

Closures may have affected prices in at least three different ways.

- First, some regional fisheries may have been closed for the entire season. Table 10.2 presents the 1989 price estimate and the basis for the estimate for regional fisheries for which we have no 1989 price information.

  To obtain estimates of missing salmon prices, we employ a simple procedure that substitutes the actual 1989 prices from regional salmon fisheries that were open at least part of the season. For these substitute prices, we use salmon fisheries that are as similar as possible to the closed fishery. In all cases, the substitute prices were available from the same region and for the same species as the missing price. Only the gear type is different. Among gear types, we use the most similar gear type to provide the substitute price. For example, if a drift gill net price is missing, we used a set gill net price when available.

We have assessed the validity of this approach by comparing prices from the missing and substitute regional salmon fisheries for those years when both are available. We find that in most cases, prices are identical, particularly in the latter half of the 1980s. In those cases where prices are not identical, we find that the average differences are small, and there is no consistent pattern in the differences between prices.

- Second, some fisheries were closed within districts and large areas of the broader CFEC regions. For example, drift net fisheries were closed for most of the season in much of the Upper Cook Inlet, yet the State of Alaska reports ex-vessel prices for some drift net fishing in Cook Inlet during the 1989 season.[3] The oil spill may have affected average 1989 regional ex-vessel prices in regions where some fisheries were closed for part or all of the season. The effect of closing fisheries could be either to increase or suppress season average ex-vessel prices. Any price effects in 1989 caused by fishery closures should be reflected in our quantitative analyses of ex-vessel prices (see chapters 5, 6, 7, and 9). These quantitative analyses provide little if any support for the existence of a significant price effect in 1989. Consequently, they do not support claims of local price effects related to fishery closures from the oil spill.

- Third, reductions in fish harvest as the result of fisheries being closed for part or all of the season may have reduced local fish supply, thereby raising prices. We examine the effect of changed abundance on price below.

Non-Salmon Species

Several non-salmon fisheries in Prince William Sound were closed for the entire 1989 season. We estimate the 1989 ex-vessel prices for these closed fisheries based on benchmark price models presented in chapter 9.

Table 10.3 presents our estimates of 1989 ex-vessel prices for the closed non-salmon fisheries in Prince William Sound. The model of roe-on-kelp in pounds using British Columbia as the benchmark accounts for a large percentage of the

Table 10.3
Estimated 1989 Ex-Vessel Prices for
Non-Salmon Fisheries Closed for the 1989 Season

Region	Species	Gear	Basis for Estimate	Price Estimate (1989 dollars per pound)
Prince William Sound				
	Sac Roe Herring	Seine	British Columbia	$0.18*
	Sac Roe Herring	Gill net	Tomales, Calif.	$0.31*
	Wild Roe on Kelp			
	Ribbon Kelp		Bristol Bay	$2.00
	Sieve Kelp		Bristol Bay	$1.35
	Hair Kelp		Bristol Bay	$0.89
	Roe on Kelp in Pounds		British Columbia	$9.75
	Brown King Crab	Pot gear	Juneau	$3.81

* Adjusted for roe content and represents the price at 10 percent roe content.

variation in Alaskan ex-vessel prices and predicts a 1989 price per pound of $9.75, which is much lower than the 1988 price of $17.10. The model of wild roe-on-kelp using Bristol Bay as the benchmark does not fit the historical prices well, accounting for less than half of the variation in Alaskan ex-vessel prices.[4] However, the model's 1989 price predictions of $2.00 per pound for ribbon kelp, $1.35 for sieve kelp, and $0.89 for hair kelp are higher than prices in 1988, when ribbon kelp sold for $1.50 per pound and sieve and hair sold for $0.75 to $1.00. Changing demand structure for wild roe-on-kelp may account for the poor fit and may inflate the 1989 price estimates for ribbon kelp. The roe herring model using British Columbian prices indicates that in Prince William Sound 1989 roe herring prices at 10 percent roe content would have been 18 cents per pound for seines. The roe herring model using Tomales, California, prices indicates that, in Prince William Sound, 1989 roe herring prices at 10 percent roe content would have been 31 cents per pound for gill nets. This model accounts for a large percentage of the variation in Prince William Sound's gill net prices. The model for brown king crab using Juneau's prices predicts Prince William Sound's price as $3.81 per pound in 1989.

REDUCED HARVESTS

For the quantitative studies in this report, measures of a 1989 effect are usually based on the assumption that 1989 harvests are held constant, at their actual levels.

Table 10.4
Price Effects from Forgone
Salmon Harvests in Regions Touched by the Oil Spill

Oil-touched Region	Percentage Reduction in Harvest	Percentage Increase in Price
Chignik	37%	2.3%
Cook Inlet	25%	1.4%
Kodiak	70%	5.8%
Prince William Sound	1%	*

* Less than 0.1 percent.

These measures do not reflect the price effect of reduced harvest from the oil spill.

Common sense and the laws of supply and demand compel the conclusion that an increase in the harvest of any seafood species would, if anything, lower both the ex-vessel and processor price of that species. Thus if forgone harvests were substantial, our predicted 1989 price would be at least somewhat lower. This implies that the magnitude of any estimated 1989 price suppression will be reduced. On the other hand, if the actual price in 1989 is *higher* than the predicted price (a positive price effect), then accounting for the forgone harvest will likely increase the spread between actual and predicted prices.

For salmon ex-vessel prices, we have estimated both local and global harvest effects. The local harvest effect is assumed to be related to the capacity utilization of fish processors. We construct a simple capacity utilization variable as the ratio of the total salmon poundage in a given area to the 1978–1990 average salmon poundage for the same area. As capacity utilization increases, ex-vessel price will tend to fall.

The possible price effects of changes in local harvest are likely to be constrained by transportation costs and a market force known as price arbitrage. Prices for comparable quality seafood in two regions cannot persistently differ by more than transportation costs because buyers and sellers in each region will engage in the markets of the other region until prices are equal, net of transportation costs. Consequently, local price effects will not be very large unless peak harvest years in one region are highly correlated with peaks in nearby regions.

We estimate the local harvest effect using data from CFEC. The model includes dummy variables representing year, species, region, and gear type, as well as the log of the ratio described above as explanatory variables.[5] If the capacity utilization variable increases by 10 percent, the price will fall by 0.5 percent. This estimate is highly significant statistically.

Our estimates of the global harvest effect are very sensitive to changes in the model specification. However, the effect is small in magnitude and is never statistically significant.

An independent team of biologists has estimated the size of the 1989 Alaskan seafood harvest in each fishery had the oil spill not occurred. Their estimates of the 1989 seafood harvest provide the basis for our estimates of the 1989 forgone harvest—estimated 1989 harvest minus the actual 1989 harvest (see Appendix 4).

Table 10.4 presents the percentage reduction in the actual 1989 salmon harvest relative of the estimated 1989 salmon harvest in each of the four regions touched by the oil spill. It also presents the percentage increase in ex-vessel prices as a result of the reduced local harvests. These estimates do not account for any price effect from the reduction in global harvest. The largest harvest reduction was in Kodiak, where we estimate that 1989 ex-vessel salmon prices would have been 5.8 percent lower had harvests not been curtailed. The price effects of the forgone harvest are smaller in Chignik and Cook Inlet and are likely to have been inconsequential in Prince William Sound.

OIL SPILL CLEAN-UP OPERATIONS

The clean-up operation for the *Exxon Valdez* oil spill may have elevated the prices of Alaskan seafood. First, Exxon offered substantial payments to vessels and crews for clean-up work related to the oil spill. Processors may have had to offer fishermen higher ex-vessel prices than usual to induce them to fish. Second, to the extent that some boat owners and crew participated in the clean-up operation rather than the seafood harvest, the 1989 Alaskan seafood harvest may have been reduced. As discussed above, reductions in the harvest in 1989 increased seafood prices.

The oil spill clean-up operations also may have exerted some downward pressure on ex-vessel prices. The demand for workers on the clean-up operation may have bid up wages for workers at seafood processors. Selling seafood in a global market, seafood processors could not easily, if at all, translate increased wages into higher processor prices. To accommodate the higher wage payments, processors may have reduced ex-vessel prices for seafood.

We do not have sufficient information to isolate the effect of the clean-up operation on 1989 Alaskan seafood prices or to determine whether the effect was to raise or to lower those prices. Whatever the effect may have been in 1989, it would be included in any 1989 price effect as measured in our quantitative studies.

CONCLUSION

The *Exxon Valdez* oil spill may have affected the global supply of seafood or of certain seafood species. In addition, the spill may have affected local supply conditions in several regions—and subregions within them. We have developed techniques to estimate ex-vessel prices for fisheries that were closed by the oil spill and to estimate changes in ex-vessel prices attributable to changes in fish abundance as a result of the oil spill. Price effects from changes in quality and many local conditions would be reflected in our quantitative analyses of ex-vessel prices in 1989. Reductions in harvest in 1989 attributable to the oil spill *increased* ex-vessel prices. The magnitude of this price increase is likely to be small but difficult to measure exactly. The price increase from a local harvest effect is bounded by price arbitrage from other regions of Alaska. The price increase from a global harvest effect in our present models is small and not significantly different from zero.

NOTES

1. Prince William Sound Area Management Report, 1989, at 2.

2. STATE OF ALASKA, COMMERCIAL FISHERIES ENTRY COMMISSION, EX-VESSEL PRICE ESTIMATES, REPORT 1A (undated). CFEC data do not distinguish between Upper and Lower Cook Inlet. The second data set is state of Alaska, 1980–1990 MMT REPORTS BY FISHERY, YEAR & SPECIES, PROJECT 90173.01 (August 7, 1990), *id.* PROJECT 91166 (August 20, 1991), *id.* PROJECT 91180 (September 17, 1991).

3. CFEC Report 1A data.

4. A model excluding 1990 accounts for a large percentage of the variation in wild roe-on-kelp prices.

5. This model is identical to the one used to obtain the annual average adjusted prices used in chapter 7.

11

Fishing Permit Values

The relationship between future earnings associated with an asset and the current price of the asset is a standard principle of financial economics.[1] Fishing permit prices provide a convenient measure of the expected future benefits of Alaskan commercial fishing. Permit prices not only incorporate all currently available information about the expected future profitability of fishing, but they also provide a monetary measure of other benefits, such as the aesthetic pleasures of fishing on a commercial boat.

To the extent that the *Exxon Valdez* oil spill inflicted long-term damages on commercial fishermen, changes in permit prices should reflect all available information regarding the monetary value of the loss.[2] This chapter examines permit price data to determine what changes, if any, occurred subsequent to the oil spill. A significant reduction after the oil spill in the prices at which permits were traded would be consistent with claims of future losses. A change in prices for permits in areas touched by the oil spill—Prince William Sound, Cook Inlet, Kodiak, and Chignik—relative to other areas of Alaska would be consistent with the theory that commercial fishing was particularly affected in these regions.

Most commercial fishing in Alaska is subject to state government regulation that limits entry.[3] Fishermen must obtain special permits that are specific to a geographic region and gear type in order to fish. These permits are valuable assets for several reasons: the total number of these permits is limited; more fishermen want to fish than there are permits; and the permits are tradable.

Economists have examined how the price of Alaskan fishing permits is determined.[4] The price of a permit primarily reflects the expected future profitability of fishing under the permit. As expected profitability increases, fishermen will be willing to pay more to acquire a permit, and the price of the permit increases. As expected profitability decreases, fishermen will be willing to pay less to acquire a permit, and the price of the permit decreases. Expected non-monetary benefits may also be a consideration. The revenue earned by some fishermen is sufficiently low that earnings alone do not explain the fishermen's willingness to incur the cost of owning a permit (i.e., either to purchase one or to forgo selling one). Overall, fishermen will be willing to pay as much for a permit as the expected total benefit, both monetary and non-monetary, that the permit provides them.

ANALYSIS OF PROFITABILITY OF FISHING

Expected profitability depends on many factors. Expectations are substantially influenced by current and recent profitability.[5] Two important influences on current and expected future profitability are recent fish price movements and changes in fish harvests. Higher (lower) fish prices, holding all else constant, should increase (decrease) permit prices. Similarly, higher (lower) fish harvests, holding all else constant, should increase (decrease) permit prices. In both cases the effect is on expectations of future prices. If the spill increased uncertainty about future harvests, this would be reflected in lower prices for permits in the affected areas than would have occurred otherwise. The reverse would be true if, for some reason, the spill decreased uncertainty about future harvests. Other factors, such as a loan subsidy program for purchasing permits, also affect current profitability and may thus affect the price of fishing permits.[6]

Expected profitability depends not only on past profitability but also on expectations about future changes. Some fishermen in the *Exxon Valdez* case claim expected future losses as a result of the oil spill. These future losses, if realized, might result from lower prices or lower harvests than would have occurred absent the oil spill—or both. (They also could stem from lower prices due to *higher* harvests, tied for example to higher predator mortality.) To the extent fishermen expected future losses, such expectations would seem more likely in the fisheries physically affected by the oil spill—Prince William Sound, Cook Inlet, Kodiak, and Chignik—than in other Alaskan fisheries. Expected future losses may also stem from an increase in uncertainty about future harvests. If fishermen are risk averse, they would be better off avoiding an uncertain future and would be willing to pay to do so.[7]

A related approach to assess fishermen's expected future profitability is to consider the aggregate value of the stock of fishing permits over time. An increase in the expected profitability of owning a permit will increase the market price of permits, which will increase the wealth of all permit holders, holding all else constant. If the oil spill reduced the expected future profits of the fishermen, the total permit value should fall, reflecting the lost asset value for all fishermen, not just those who transfer their permits.

These phenomena should be observable in the data in a number of different ways. An observed change in the price of permits in 1989 relative to 1988 or in the oil-touched areas of Alaska relative to the oil-free areas would be consistent with the hypothesis that the expected profitability of fishing changed or that uncertainty changed as a result of the oil spill. In order to conclude that changes in expected profitability cause differences in permit price movements between oil-touched and oil-free areas, we must assume that there are no significant non-monetary effects to fishermen in the oil-touched areas. Such an assumption is generally consistent with the work referenced above that expected profitability is the primary determinant of permit prices.

Most of the comparisons of permit prices are on an annual basis. For several reasons, including the limited number of permit sales, we do not regard monthly data as reliable enough to measure short-run effects of the oil spill. Movement in the profitability of fishing over a relatively short time may not be reflected in the annual pricing data. Even if monthly permit prices were available, they might not respond to temporary changes in ex-vessel prices or to changes that were expected to be temporary.

RESULTS

The State of Alaska's Commercial Fisheries Entry Commission (CFEC) publishes data on fishing permit prices. The data are classified by species, gear type, and fishery. This analysis focuses on salmon, herring, and herring roe. Entry to the crab fisheries has been limited only since 1989. So few crab permits have been transferred that CFEC is unable to disclose transfer price information. The analysis focuses on eight gear types (purse seine, beach seine, drift gill net, fishwheel, set net, power troll, hand troll, and pound) and on 13 fisheries (Southeast, Yakutat, Prince William Sound, Cook Inlet, Kodiak, Chignik, Alaska Peninsula, Bristol Bay, Kuskokwim, Upper Yukon, Lower Yukon, Norton Sound, and Kotzebue). Herring fishing permit prices for Nelson Island and Nunivak Island fisheries are reported only in 1990 and thus are not included. The three seafood categories, combined in different ways, yield 34 species-gear-fishery combinations (e.g., fishing salmon by purse seine in Southeast).

The permits data are published on both a monthly and an annual basis. The estimated permit values reported on a monthly basis could potentially allow for a comparison of permit values immediately preceding and immediately following the spill. However, the averaging method used by CFEC makes it impossible to separate pre-spill and post-spill observations within 1989.[8] We restrict our comparisons to 1988 average annual prices that are clearly pre-spill and 1990 average annual prices or 1991 monthly estimated permit values that are entirely post-spill. Permit prices do not include the transfer of physical assets such as boats and gear. CFEC reports that most financed permit transfers were made without a transfer of physical assets. CFEC surveys request permit transfer prices separately from asset transfer prices.[9]

The permits data reveal the following:

- *Most fishing permit prices increased from 1988 to 1990* (Table 11.1). Average real permit prices for permits in 31 of 34 species-gear-fishery combinations were greater in 1990 than in 1988.[10]

Table 11.1
Average Prices for Fishing Permits: Salmon, Herring, and Herring Roe, 1988–1991

Gear and Region	1988 Number of Monetary Transfers	1988 Average Permit Price	1989 Number of Monetary Transfers	1989 Average Permit Price	1990 Number of Monetary Transfers	1990 Average Permit Price	June 1991 Estimated Permit Value (e)	Percentage Change 1988-89	Percentage Change 1988-90	Percentage Change 1988-91
SALMON										
Purse Seine										
Southeast	18	$71,369	29	$81,678	18	$104,667	$90,528	14.4%	46.7%	26.8%
Prince William Sound	19	$146,523	6	$246,063	5	$228,000	$208,956	67.9%	55.6%	42.6%
Cook Inlet	9	$71,646	3	$93,705 (b)	4	$177,500	$159,010	30.8%	147.7%	121.9%
Kodiak	34	$72,082	22	$138,262	17	$146,588	$119,989	91.8%	103.4%	66.5%
Chignik	1	$390,272 (a)	2	$386,969 (b)	2	$416,667 (c)	$399,378	-0.8%	6.8%	2.3%
Alaska Peninsula	4	$162,207	2	$223,331 (b)	2	$226,667 (c)	$226,808	37.7%	39.7%	39.8%
Beach Seine										
Kodiak	5	$30,788	6	$36,267	3	$46,000 (c)	$39,996	17.8%	49.4%	29.9%
Drift Gillnet										
Southeast	30	$82,345	16	$130,797	28	$106,500	$83,504	58.8%	29.3%	1.4%
Prince William Sound	50	$82,176	15	$143,508	27	$160,523	$130,037	74.6%	95.3%	58.2%
Cook Inlet	28	$136,745	35	$175,333	24	$203,063	$172,277	28.2%	48.5%	26.0%
Alaska Peninsula	2	$254,761 (a)	5	$358,163	11	$356,136	$344,749	40.6%	39.8%	35.3%
Bristol Bay	77	$181,543	53	$243,010	60	$212,855	$210,615	33.9%	17.2%	16.0%
Fishwheel										
Upper Yukon	5	$9,432	3	$13,189 (b)	6	$11,667	$10,633	39.8%	23.7%	12.7%
Set Net										
Yakutat	17	$30,657	5	$34,567	12	$36,458	$42,923	12.8%	18.9%	40.0%
Prince William Sound	2	$54,023 (a)	1	$66,809 (b)	1	$86,667 (c)	$87,797 (d)	23.7%	60.4%	62.5%
Cook Inlet	46	$44,611	49	$60,069	42	$91,171	$72,676	34.7%	104.4%	62.9%
Kodiak	3	$85,580 (a)	6	$72,405	6	$85,000	$97,552	-15.4%	-0.7%	14.0%
Alaska Peninsula	3	$92,735 (a)	1	$82,415 (b)	3	$121,667 (c)	$126,818	-11.1%	31.2%	36.8%
Bristol Bay	47	$50,419	39	$66,355	33	$60,545	$58,726	31.6%	20.1%	16.5%
Power Troll										
Southeast	68	$32,286	56	$33,782	51	$33,142	$37,167	4.6%	2.7%	15.1%
Hand Troll										
Southeast	97	$6,988	66	$7,625	98	$8,322	$8,292	9.1%	19.1%	18.7%

Table 11.1 (cont.)
Average Prices for Fishing Permits: Salmon, Herring, and Herring Roe, 1988–1991

Gear and Region	1988		1989		1990		June 1991 Estimated Permit Value (e)	Percentage Change		
	Number of Monetary Transfers	Average Permit Price	Number of Monetary Transfers	Average Permit Price	Number of Monetary Transfers	Average Permit Price		1988-89	1988-90	1988-91
Gillnet (AYK)										
Upper Yukon	3	$9,467 (a)	4	$10,282	4	$11,250	$11,023	8.6%	18.8%	16.4%
Kuskokwim	18	$10,482	20	$12,546	18	$12,056	$13,462	19.7%	15.0%	28.4%
Kotzebue	11	$8,136	3	$7,983 (b)	8	$8,250	$7,999	-1.9%	1.4%	-1.7%
Lower Yukon	13	$22,407	11	$26,578	9	$24,778	$22,339	18.6%	10.6%	-0.3%
Norton Sound	3	$11,022 (a)	7	$9,593	2	$11,000 (c)	$8,097	-13.0%	-0.2%	-26.5%
HERRING										
Gillnet										
Southeast	11	$52,933	4	$57,004	2	$54,333 (c)	$25,754	7.7%	2.6%	-51.3%
Prince William Sound	2	$61,432 (a)	3	$96,482 (b)	0	$92,667 (c)	$84,773	57.1%	50.8%	38.0%
Kodiak	18	$17,899	12	$23,752	8	$29,000	$30,729	32.7%	62.0%	71.7%
Purse Seine										
Southeast	3	$458,931 (a)	0	$440,762 (b)	2	$330,000 (c)	$239,002	-4.0%	-28.1%	-47.9%
Prince William Sound	10	$173,996	1	$255,087 (b)	3	$216,667 (c)	$233,149	46.6%	24.5%	34.0%
Cook Inlet	4	$178,875	4	$219,948	1	$228,333 (e)	$165,838	23.0%	27.6%	-7.3%
Kodiak	2	$25,837 (a)	3	$56,223 (b)	5	$70,500	$76,188	117.6%	172.9%	194.9%
HERRING ROE										
Pound										
Prince William Sound	32	$26,581	13	$49,855	2	$51,833 (c)	$61,458	87.6%	95.0%	131.2%

Note: Transfers with a sale price higher than $500 are counted as a monetary transfer. Average permit prices are based on the average permit sale prices during each year. When there are fewer than four transfers in a given year, no average value is reported in the annual report. Estimated permit values are calculated by averaging the price of permit transfers that occurred from January through December. Estimated permit values for 1991 are found by averaging the price of permit transfers for the current month as well as those for the preceding two months. Where insufficient data exists, additional data from earlier months are included until a sufficient number of observations are obtained. Bold print indicates highest real permit value between 1975 and June 1991. Adjustments made with implicit price deflators for gross national product, Department of Commerce, Bureau of Economic Analysis. Prices based on 1990 dollars. June 1991 value adjusted with February 1991 deflator.

Source: Unless otherwise noted, "1990 Annual Report, Commercial Fisheries Entry Commission, State of Alaska."
a) From CFEC "1988 Estimated Monthly Permit Value Report, Year End, 1988."
b) From CFEC "1989 Estimated Monthly Permit Value Report, Year End, 1989."
c) From CFEC "1990 Estimated Monthly Permit Value Report, Year End, 1990."
d) Estimated value includes transfers before April 1989.
e) From CFEC "June 1991 Estimated Monthly Permit Value Report, June 1991."

Table 11.2
Total Values for Fishing Permits: Salmon, Herring, and Herring Roe, 1988–1990

Gear and Region	1988		1989		1990		Change in Permit Value	
	Average Permit Price (d)	Value of Permits	Average Permit Price (e)	Value of Permits	Average Permit Price (f)	Value of Permits	1988–1989	1988–1990
SALMON								
Purse Seine								
Southeast	$71,369	$29,689,504	$81,678	$33,978,048	$104,667	$43,646,139	$4,288,544	$13,956,635
Prince William Sound	$146,523	$38,535,549	$246,063	$64,714,569	$228,000	$60,192,000	$26,179,020	$21,656,451
Cook Inlet	$71,646	$5,874,972	$93,705 (b)	$7,683,810	$177,500	$14,555,000	$1,808,838	$8,680,028
Kodiak	$72,082	$27,535,324	$138,262	$52,816,084	$146,588	$55,996,616	$25,280,760	$28,461,292
Chignik	$390,272 (a)	$35,124,480	$386,969 (b)	$34,827,210	$416,667 (c)	$37,500,030	($297,270)	$2,375,550
Alaska Peninsula	$162,207	$19,302,633	$223,331 (b)	$26,576,389	$226,667 (c)	$26,973,373	$7,273,756	$7,670,740
Beach Seine								
Kodiak	$30,788	$1,016,004	$36,267	$1,196,811	$46,000 (c)	$1,518,000	$180,807	$501,996
Drift Gillnet								
Southeast	$82,345	$38,537,460	$130,797	$61,212,996	$106,500	$49,842,000	$22,675,536	$11,304,540
Prince William Sound	$82,176	$44,046,336	$143,508	$77,063,796	$160,523	$86,200,851	$33,017,460	$42,154,515
Cook Inlet	$136,745	$76,713,945	$175,333	$98,361,813	$203,063	$113,918,343	$21,647,868	$37,204,398
Alaska Peninsula	$254,761 (a)	$40,252,238	$358,163	$56,589,754	$356,136	$56,269,488	$16,337,516	$16,017,250
Bristol Bay	$181,543	$317,518,707	$243,010	$431,585,760	$212,855	$379,946,175	$114,067,053	$62,427,468
Fishwheel								
Upper Yukon	$9,432	$1,254,456	$13,189 (b)	$1,754,137	$11,667	$1,551,711	$499,681	$297,255
Set Net								
Yakutat	$30,657	$5,027,748	$34,567	$5,703,555	$36,458	$6,015,570	$675,807	$987,822
Prince William Sound	$54,023 (a)	$1,620,690	$66,809 (b)	$2,004,270	$36,667 (c)	$2,600,010	$383,580	$979,320
Cook Inlet	$44,611	$33,145,973	$60,069	$44,631,267	$91,171	$67,740,053	$11,485,294	$34,594,080
Kodiak	$85,580 (a)	$16,003,460	$72,405	$13,612,140	$85,000	$15,980,000	($2,391,320)	($23,460)
Alaska Peninsula	$92,735 (a)	$10,479,055	$82,415 (b)	$9,312,895	$121,667 (c)	$13,748,371	($1,166,160)	$3,269,316
Bristol Bay	$50,419	$47,444,279	$66,355	$66,819,485	$60,545	$61,271,540	$19,375,206	$13,827,261
Power Troll								
Southeast	$32,286	$30,413,412	$33,782	$31,822,644	$33,142	$31,219,764	$1,409,232	$806,352
Hand Troll								
Southeast	$6,988	$12,990,692	$7,625	$13,786,000	$8,322	$14,746,584	$795,308	$1,755,892

Table 11.2 (cont.)
Total Values for Fishing Permits: Salmon, Herring, and Herring Roe, 1988–1990

Gear and Region	1988		1989		1990		Change in Permit Value	
	Average Permit Price (d)	Value of Permits	Average Permit Price (e)	Value of Permits	Average Permit Price (f)	Value of Permits	1988–1989	1988–1990
Gillnet (AYK)								
Upper Yukon	$9,467 (a)	$662,690	$10,282	$709,458	$11,250	$787,500	$46,768	$124,810
Kuskokwim	$10,482	$8,679,096	$12,546	$10,388,088	$12,056	$9,994,424	$1,708,992	$1,315,328
Kotzebue	$8,136	$1,781,784	$7,983 (b)	$1,748,277	$8,250	$1,798,500	($33,507)	$16,716
Lower Yukon	$22,407	$15,774,528	$26,578	$18,710,912	$24,778	$17,443,712	$2,936,384	$1,669,184
Norton Sound	11,022 (a)	$2,215,422	$9,593	$1,928,193	$11,000 (c)	$2,200,000	($287,229)	($15,422)
HERRING								
Gillnet								
Southeast	$52,933	$4,816,903	$57,004	$5,244,368	$54,333 (c)	$5,324,634	$427,465	$507,731
Prince William Sound	$61,432 (a)	$1,474,368	$96,482 (b)	$2,315,568	$92,667 (c)	$2,224,008	$841,200	$749,640
Kodiak	$17,899	$1,145,536	$23,752	$1,615,136	$29,000	$2,088,000	$469,600	$942,464
Purse Seine								
Southeast	$458,931 (a)	$20,192,964	$440,762 (b)	$19,393,528	$330,000 (c)	$14,520,000	($799,436)	($5,672,964)
Prince William Sound	$173,996	$17,921,588	$255,087 (b)	$26,273,961	$216,667 (c)	$22,316,701	$8,352,373	$4,395,113
Cook Inlet	$178,875	$13,057,875	$219,948	$16,056,204	$228,333 (c)	$16,668,309	$2,998,329	$3,610,434
Kodiak	$25,837 (a)	$1,162,665	$56,223 (b)	$2,586,258	$70,500	$3,243,000	$1,423,593	$2,080,335
HERRING ROE								
Pound								
Prince William Sound	$26,581	$3,402,368	$49,855	$6,381,440	$51,833 (c)	$6,634,624	$2,979,072	$3,232,256
Oil-touched Areas	$95,030	$317,781,133	$134,927	$452,140,337	$151,781	$509,375,545	$134,359,204	$191,594,412
Oil-free Areas	$65,846	$607,033,571	$86,079	$797,264,487	$79,734	$737,299,485	$190,230,916	$130,265,914
TOTAL	$73,614	$924,814,704	$99,057	$1,249,404,824	$98,919	$1,246,675,030	$324,590,120	$321,860,326

Note: Average permit prices are based on the average permit sale prices during each year. When there are fewer than four transfers in a given year, no average value is reported in the annual report. Estimated permit values are calculated by averaging the price of permit transfers that occurred from January through December. Where insufficient data exists, additional data from earlier months are included until a sufficient number of observations are obtained. Adjustments made with implicit price deflators for gross national product, Department of Commerce, Bureau of Economic Analysis. Prices are based on 1990 dollars.

Source: Unless otherwise noted, "1990 Annual Report, Commercial Fisheries Entry Commission, State of Alaska."

a) From CFEC "1988 Estimated Monthly Permit Value Report."
b) From "1989 Estimated Monthly Permit Value Report."
c) From CFEC "1990 Estimated Monthly Permit Value Report, Year End, 1990."
d) From CFEC "1988 Annual Report."
e) From CFEC "1989 Annual Report."
f) From CFEC "1990 Annual Report."

More than two-thirds of the combinations in which permit prices rose showed increases in excess of 20 percent. In 6 combinations, the increase was at least 95 percent. Average real permit prices in 15 out of 34 combinations reached record high levels in either 1990 or 1991.[11]

- *The increase in permit prices was strongest in the oil-touched areas* (Table 11.1). Average real permit prices in 15 of 16 combinations in the oil-touched areas increased between 1988 and 1990. The 12 largest percentage increases in permit prices occurred in the oil-touched areas. The average permit price in the areas touched by the spill rose 59.7 percent from 1988 to 1990, compared with a 21.1 percent increase in the oil-free areas.

- *Total permit value rose substantially from 1988 to 1990* (Table 11.2). The total value of permits (average permit price multiplied by total number of permits) rose by $322 million from $925 million in 1988 to $1.247 billion in 1990. Nearly $192 million of the increase is accounted for by the oil-touched areas; the remaining $130 million is from the oil-free areas. Very little of the increase is attributable to an increase in the number of permits; practically all of it is due to an increase in permit prices.

- *Many fishing permit prices continued to rise in early 1991.* In 27 of the combinations, the June 1991 estimated permit value was greater than the 1988 average annual price, according to Table 11.1.[12] Although there are some signs that prices began to soften in early 1991, approximately one-third of combinations saw an increase in real fishing permit prices from 1990 to June 1991.

The claims of some fishermen involve reduced profitability of fishing and reduced value of fishing permits. The price of a permit is normally determined by the profitability of fishing. However, the profitability of holding a permit may also be affected by compensatory payments that have been made, or possibly will be made, by Exxon, the Trans-Alaska Pipeline Liability Fund, and others.

Payments by Exxon have been to individuals who held a permit at the time of the oil spill, and the payments were only for losses incurred during 1989. Some adjustments were allowed for permit transfers if transfers affected more than one-third of the season. Payments like this for one-period losses in 1989 would not likely have an effect on permit prices in 1990 and thus would not affect our analysis.

CONCLUSION

Fishing permit prices reflect all available information regarding the expected future benefits (both monetary and non-monetary) of owning a permit to fish commercially in Alaska. This chapter has examined the pattern of Alaskan fishing permit prices before and after the *Exxon Valdez* oil spill. Fishing permit prices did not fall after the *Exxon Valdez* oil spill, a finding that is not consistent with fishermen's claims of expected long-term losses. Indeed, fishing permit prices rose to record levels after the oil spill for many combinations of species, gear, and fishery. This increase in permit prices was stronger in areas touched by the oil spill than in other areas of Alaska. This finding does not support the theory that fishermen in these areas suffered long-term losses.

NOTES

1. *See, e.g.,* the valuation of common stock in, R.A. BREALY AND S.C. MEYERS, PRINCIPLES OF CORPORATE FINANCE 49–52 (3rd ed. 1988).

2. Current short-term losses of perhaps just a few months might not be reflected in the prices of permits in a market with infrequent transactions, such as the Alaskan fishing permit market. Long-term reductions in the future profitability should reduce current prices under a wide range of market conditions. For the absence of a need for perfectly efficient markets in order to conduct an analysis of the effect of an event on market prices, see J. Macey, G. Miller, M. Mitchell & J. Netter, *Lessons from Financial Economics: Materiality, Reliance, and Extending the Reach of Basic v. Levison*, 77 VIRGINIA LAW REVIEW No. 5 1017-49 (1991).

3. Two exceptions are the halibut and shrimp fisheries. Entry to the halibut fisheries is open, but the season is limited to a few one-day derbies. Entry into the shrimp fisheries requires a permit, but the number of permits is unlimited.

4. *See, e.g.,* B. MUSE, PERMIT VALUES AND FISH STOCKS (STATE OF ALASKA, COMMERCIAL FISHERIES ENTRY COMMISSION, Report No. 90-9, 1990); J.M. KARPOFF, LIMITED ENTRY PERMIT PRICES (State of Alaska, Commercial Fisheries Entry Commission Report No. 83-6, 1983) [hereinafter cited as PERMIT PRICES]; *id. Non-Pecuniary Benefits in Commercial Fishing: Empirical Findings from the Alaska Salmon Fisheries*, ECONOMIC INQUIRY, January 1985, at 159–73 [hereinafter cited as *Non-Pecuniary Benefits*].

5. *Non-Pecuniary Benefits, supra* note 4 at 159–73.

6. PERMIT PRICES, *supra* note 4 ; B. MUSE, *supra* note 4; Telephone interview with Ben Muse (July 17, 1991). The loan subsidy program began in 1979. We are unaware of any significant changes in the program that would have caused the permit price increase in the late 1980s.

7. B. MUSE, *supra* note 4.

8. Estimated permit values from the monthly reports are calculated as the average of the transactions that occurred in the current month plus the previous two months. If there is an insufficient number of transactions in that time period to prevent disclosure of confidential information, additional transactions from previous months are added until a sufficient number is reached. The average annual price includes just those transactions that occur in the

calendar year, and it is not reported if there were an insufficient number of transactions to prevent disclosure. We use monthly data only in 1991 (since annual data are not available) and omit the 1991 monthly average for salmon set net in Prince William Sound because it includes a pre-spill observation.

9. Phone interview with Al Tingley, Commercial Fisheries Entry Commission (July 24, 1991).

10. Inflation-adjusted or real values are more appropriate for comparisons of prices in two time periods.

11. Table 11.1 shows 16 record high average permit prices, but the record high price for salmon set net in Prince William Sound is excluded because the average contains at least one pre-spill observation.

12. This does not include the June 1991 estimated permit value for salmon set net in Prince William Sound because the average contains at least one pre-spill observation.

12

Summary of Results

This chapter presents our conclusions about the possible price effects of the *Exxon Valdez* oil spill. We summarize the statistical and economic evidence that is consistent with each of three conclusions: (1) price suppression in 1989, (2) price elevation in 1989, and (3) the absence of a 1989 price effect. Based on our review of the evidence, we conclude that Alaskan seafood prices were unaffected by the oil spill. This conclusion ignores possible supply-side effects of harvests that were reduced by the oil spill. If 1989 Alaskan harvests had been larger, seafood prices would have been lower.

SUMMARY OF EVIDENCE

In preparing this book, we have reviewed a formidable array of evidence bearing on the possible economic effects of the *Exxon Valdez* oil spill. Our conclusions are based on evidence from both quantitative and qualitative analyses. Although the economic evidence is not perfectly consistent, our findings are based on multiple and complementary pieces of evidence. No single piece of evidence in isolation leads us to our central conclusion; instead, we rely on the overall pattern of evidence, giving due weight according to the credibility of each piece.

To determine whether Alaskan seafood prices were unusually low or high in 1989, we have applied statistical tests to economic models based on market data. A statistically significant 1989 price deviation in a single economic model does not, by itself, provide a causal linkage to the oil spill, but the presence of a 1989 price effect would be consistent with hypotheses that associate the oil spill with a significant change in price. Conversely, the absence of a statistically significant 1989 price effect in an economic model would be consistent with hypotheses of the absence of price effects resulting from the oil spill.

Many of the theories of demand-side effects of the oil spill on Alaskan seafood prices imply a regular pattern of 1989 price effects across different fisheries and species. A regular pattern of statistically significant 1989 price effects across different economic models and across different species of seafood would be consistent with a demand-related price effect from the oil spill. The absence of a regular pattern of 1989 price effects would not support demand-related theories of price effects.

Evidence Consistent with Price Suppression from the Oil Spill

Table 12.1 summarizes statistical evidence of significantly lower Alaskan seafood prices in 1989 regardless of the cause. Each individual result in isolation is consistent with suppressed 1989 Alaskan seafood prices. However, with one possible exception, the statistical evidence in Table 12.1 consistent with a negative 1989 price effect is isolated and does not present a clear and persistent pattern across species, regions, or models. Much of the evidence is for individual species of salmon, but no model finds evidence consistent with price suppression for all species of salmon. Evidence of 1989 price suppression for one species with one analysis is not corroborated with evidence from a different analysis. For example, statistical evidence for some reduced-form ex-vessel price regressions in which species are pooled is consistent with suppression of 1989 Alaskan chum and coho ex-vessel prices. Similar evidence from regressions for individual species is consistent with the absence of a 1989 price effect. Similarly, consistent with the absence of a 1989 price effect for chum and coho are the results of the benchmark analysis and the preponderance of the qualitative evidence.

The one exception to this conclusion is processor prices for frozen roe herring. We find that prices were significantly lower in 1989 than predicted by our model, and we have no evidence to offset that finding. Because we understand that there are no claims by processors of price suppression in connection with roe herring processing, we have not undertaken further analysis or investigation to see if the price effect is spill-caused, a hypothesis that would be difficult to understand in light of the preponderance of qualitative evidence.

Economic evidence consistent with 1989 Alaskan seafood price suppression as a result of the oil spill tends to be isolated and anomalous (Table 12.2). The survey by the Alaska Seafood Marketing Institute does not provide strong or unambiguous support for a 1989 price suppression hypothesis. The same evidence may be interpreted to support a finding of no 1989 price effect. Price suppression stemming from reduced demand for Alaskan seafood as a result of the oil spill would be likely to result in a regular pattern of price suppression across species, regions, and gear types. We do not observe a pattern of statistical evidence consistent with price suppression in 1989 for any species or region. The specific effect of 1989 processor prices for fresh and frozen salmon in Cook Inlet, however, might be consistent with local supply-side effects related to the oil spill.

Table 12.1
Statistical Evidence Consistent with Significantly Lower 1989 Alaskan Seafood Prices

Species	Price	Model	Region	Benchmark Area	Reference
Chum	Ex-Vessel	Salmon Reduced Form Price Model, Pooled	Regions touched by the oil spill	—	Table 7.1
Coho	Ex-Vessel	Salmon Reduced Form Price Model, Pooled	Regions touched by the oil spill	—	Table 7.1
Salmon	Processor	Fresh-Frozen Processor Price Model Based on Ex-Vessel Prices	Cook Inlet	—	Table 8.5
Pink	Processor	Canned Processor Price Model Based on BC Benchmark	Alaska	British Columbia	Table 8.7
Pink	Processor	Canned Processor Price Model Based on BC Benchmark	Regions touched by the oil spill	British Columbia	Table 8.7
Sac roe herring	Ex-Vessel Gill net	Benchmark Weighted least squares	Regions touched by the oil spill	Tomales, California	Table 9.2
Sac roe herring	Processor	Frozen Processor Price Model Based on Ex-Vessel Prices	Alaska	—	Table 9.7
Sac roe herring	Processor	Frozen Processor Price Model Based on Ex-Vessel Prices	Western (includes Kodiak)	—	Table 9.7
Sac roe herring	Processor	Frozen Processor Price Model Based on Ex-Vessel Prices	Bristol Bay	—	Table 9.7
Sac roe herring	Processor	Frozen Processor Price Model Based on Ex-Vessel Prices	Arctic/Yukon/Kuskokwim	—	Table 9.7

Note: Statistical significance is based on a 5 percent one-tailed test.

Table 12.2
Economic Evidence Consistent with 1989 Price Suppression from Oil Spill

- Findings from the survey by the Alaska Seafood Marketing Institute about consumer intent to avoid Alaskan seafood

- Labeling of origin for some canned salmon worldwide and some department store fresh and frozen salmon in Japan

- Some results for some specifications from the econometric reduced form price model for chum and coho

- The specific effect of Cook Inlet in 1989 on fresh and frozen salmon processor prices in the processor price model based on ex-vessel prices

- Benchmark comparison of canned pink processor prices in Alaska and British Columbia

- Isolated 1989 price effects for herring roe in the weighted least squares benchmark price models

- Significantly lower 1989 processor prices for sac roe herring in model based on ex-vessel prices

Evidence (Other than Forgone Harvests) Consistent with Price Elevation from the Oil Spill

Each statistical finding presented in Table 12.3 is consistent with an elevation of 1989 Alaskan seafood prices, but taken together the evidence does not display a consistent pattern across species.

Table 12.4 summarizes economic evidence consistent with 1989 Alaskan seafood price elevation as a result of the oil spill. Changes in the average quality of seafood as a result of fishery management decisions after the spill could have increased Alaskan seafood prices. Early season fears of reduced or uncertain supplies also could have enabled fishermen and processors to obtain higher prices for seafood. But like the evidence on price suppression, the evidence on price elevation, other than forgone harvests, is not compelling.

Evidence Consistent with the Absence of a Price Effect from the Oil Spill

The preponderance of the economic evidence that we have reviewed is consistent with the absence of price effects for Alaskan seafood in 1989 as a result of the oil spill (Table 12.5). Nearly every species and fishery that we examined is represented in this table, which shows a broader, more regular pattern of results than either Table 12.1 or Table 12.3. The weight of the evidence clearly indicates that there were no systematic price effects in 1989. The few instances of significant positive or negative effects in all likelihood reflect factors not taken into account in each model or random movement in the underlying data.

All of the economic evidence consistent with the absence of a 1989 price effect from the oil spill is summarized in Table 12.6. This evidence tends to cast doubt on any specific inferences of price effects that can be drawn from Tables 12.2 and 12.4. The repeated pattern of evidence in Table 12.6 leads us to the conclusion that 1989 price effects for Alaskan seafood from the oil spill were unlikely.

In addition, we have examined whether the oil spill in 1989 has affected Alaskan seafood prices in subsequent years. The Alaska Seafood Marketing Institute's recent effort to identify Alaskan salmon in its promotional campaign in Japan supports hypotheses of no long-term demand-side effects from the oil spill. Based on permit prices for commercial fishing licenses, we find no evidence to support the claims that prices for seafood since 1989 have been adversely affected by the oil spill or that prices of seafood in regions touched by the oil spill will be adversely affected relative to prices in other regions of Alaska.

Evidence from Supply-side Effects

In the models presented in Tables 12.1, 12.3, and 12.5, the supply of seafood coming onto the market in 1989 is taken as given, either directly (in the reduced form models) or indirectly (in the benchmark models). We see no basis for concluding that the oil spill affected prices, given the supply of seafood in 1989. That is not, however, the end of the story. The biologists retained by the Trans-Alaska Pipeline Liability Fund have estimated the additional quantity of fish that would have been caught in 1989 had the oil spill, and its attendant fishery closings, not occurred. Salmon harvests were lower in Chignik and Cook Inlet and particularly in Kodiak. The direction of the price effect from the forgone harvests is clear: other things equal, if more fish had been caught, prices would have been *lower* than they were. Our reduced form models estimate small but significant price effects from the forgone harvests.

Table 12.3
Statistical Evidence Consistent with Significantly Higher 1989 Alaskan Seafood Prices

Species	Price	Model	Region	Benchmark Area	Reference
Sockeye	Ex-Vessel	Benchmark	Regions touched by the oil spill	British Columbia	Table 6.1
Chinook	Ex-Vessel	Benchmark	Alaska	British Columbia	Table 6.1
Sockeye	Ex-Vessel	Benchmark	Regions touched by the oil spill	Bristol Bay	Table 6.2
Pink	Ex-Vessel	Benchmark	Regions touched by the oil spill	Bristol Bay	Table 6.2
Salmon	Ex-Vessel	Benchmark	Prince William Sound	Bristol Bay	Table 6.2
Sockeye	Processor	Canned Processor Price Model Based on Ex-Vessel Prices	Alaska	—	Table 8.4
Pink	Processor	Canned Processor Price Model Based on Ex-Vessel Prices	Alaska	—	Table 8.4
Chum	Processor	Canned Processor Price Model Based on Ex-Vessel Prices	Alaska	—	Table 8.4
Salmon	Processor	Canned Processor Price Model Based on Ex-Vessel Prices	Southeast	—	Table 8.5

Table 12.3 (cont.)
Statistical Evidence Consistent with Significantly Higher 1989 Alaskan Seafood Prices

Species	Price	Model	Region	Benchmark Area	Reference
Salmon	Processor	Canned Processor Price Model Based on Ex-Vessel Prices	Prince William Sound	—	Table 8.5
Salmon	Processor	Canned Processor Price Model Based on Ex-Vessel Prices	Bristol Bay	—	Table 8.5
Coho	Processor	Fresh-Frozen Processor Price Model Based on BC Benchmark	Alaska	British Columbia	Table 8.6
Salmon roe	Processor	Fresh-Frozen Processor Price Model Based on BC Benchmark	Regions touched by the oil spill	British Columbia	Chapter 8
Halibut	Ex-Vessel	Benchmark	Alaska	British Columbia	Table 9.4
Halibut	Ex-Vessel	Benchmark	Regions touched by the oil spill	British Columbia	Table 9.4
Sablefish	Ex-Vessel	Benchmark	Alaska	British Columbia	Table 9.6
Sablefish	Ex-Vessel	Benchmark	Regions touched by the oil spill	British Columbia	Table 9.6

Note: Statistical significance is based on a 5 percent one-tailed test.

Table 12.4
Economic Evidence Consistent with 1989 Price Elevation from Oil Spill

---

- The price-enhancing effect of reduced harvests caused by the oil spill

- Early season fears of reduced supply

- Isolated econometric results for Alaskan salmon ex-vessel prices benchmarked to British Columbia

- Econometric results for salmon ex-vessel prices in regions touched by the oil spill benchmarked to Bristol Bay

- Econometric results for Alaskan canned salmon processor prices estimated from ex-vessel prices

- Econometric results for Alaskan halibut ex-vessel prices benchmarked to British Columbia

- Econometric results for Alaskan sablefish ex-vessel prices benchmarked to British Columbia

---

ESTIMATES OF 1989 PRICES

Alaskan seafood prices in 1989 did not deviate significantly from those that would be expected given market conditions in that year. In all likelihood, the *Exxon Valdez* oil spill had no net effect on Alaskan seafood prices. We reach these conclusions primarily through analyses of average prices, but they apply with equal force to the prices received by individual fishermen and processors. Individuals are likely to have received the same prices as those they would have received if there had been no oil spill.

Claimants were prevented by the oil spill from catching or processing fish during portions of the 1989 season in certain regions. In order to compensate them, it is necessary to estimate a reasonable price for the forgone catch. We believe that the average prices received in actual market transactions are the most reasonable estimates of what individuals would have received for the forgone harvests.[1]

Table 12.7 presents average 1989 ex-vessel prices—inclusive of bonuses and post-season adjustments—for both salmon and non-salmon species in each region touched by the oil spill. These average prices reflect actual prices for fisheries that were open for at least part of the 1989 season and estimates for fisheries that were closed for the entire 1989 season. For fisheries that were closed, we use either a comparable price from a nearby fishery or a price based on a benchmark from an area not touched by the oil spill, whichever provided a better prediction based on historical data.

We have also found no consistent pattern of evidence that Alaskan salmon processor prices were significantly lower or higher in 1989 than market conditions would indicate. Table 12.8 presents our estimates of salmon processor prices in 1989 in regions of Alaska touched by the oil spill.

The prices in Tables 12.7 and 12.8 are simply averages of the actual prices received by individuals in 1989. They are intended for use as estimates of the average prices that would have been received for the forgone harvest. It would be incorrect to regard them as estimates of the prices that individuals would have received for fish actually harvested but for the oil spill. Thus the fact that an individual fisherman or processor received a lower price is likely attributable to reasons individual to the claimant, his gear type, or other individual circumstances, and would not mean that the individual is entitled to the higher but-for price.

The average ex-vessel prices for Prince William Sound reported in Table 12.7 are based on the entire Prince William Sound region rather than just those districts that were touched by the oil spill. Price data for separate districts are not available. Prices in two districts—Copper River and Bering River—historically have been the highest ex-vessel prices in Prince William Sound. Neither Copper River nor Bering River, which lie to the east of the Sound, was touched by the oil spill. Because these high-priced districts are included in the regional averages, the calculated regional average ex-vessel prices in Table 12.7 are likely to overstate the average ex-vessel prices that would have been received in those districts in the Sound where there were forgone harvests. This overstatement is likely to be most pronounced for chinook and sockeye salmon, because Copper River and Bering River account for a large proportion of the Prince William Sound harvests of these species.

NOTE

1. The prices that would have been received by individuals if the fish had been harvested would not, of course, have been uniform. We have no information upon which to base an estimate of prices for the forgone harvests on an individual-by-individual basis.

Table 12.5
Statistical Evidence Consistent with the Absence of a 1989 Effect on Alaskan Seafood Prices

Species	Price	Model	Region	Benchmark Area	Reference
"Fresh" Salmon	Retail	Analysis of Japanese consumer demand	Japanese households	—	Chapter 5
Salted salmon	Retail	Analysis of Japanese consumer demand	Japanese households	—	Chapter 5
Chinook	Ex-Vessel	Benchmark	Regions touched by the oil spill	British Columbia	Table 6.1
Coho	Ex-Vessel	Benchmark	Regions touched by the oil spill	British Columbia	Table 6.1
Pink	Ex-Vessel	Benchmark	Regions touched by the oil spill	British Columbia	Table 6.1
Chum	Ex-Vessel	Benchmark	Regions touched by the oil spill	British Columbia	Table 6.1
Sockeye	Ex-Vessel	Benchmark	Alaska	British Columbia	Table 6.1
Coho	Ex-Vessel	Benchmark	Alaska	British Columbia	Table 6.1
Pink	Ex-Vessel	Benchmark	Alaska	British Columbia	Table 6.1
Chum	Ex-Vessel	Benchmark	Alaska	British Columbia	Table 6.1
Chinook	Ex-Vessel	Benchmark	Regions touched by the oil spill	Bristol Bay	Table 6.2
Coho	Ex-Vessel	Benchmark	Regions touched by the oil spill	Bristol Bay	Table 6.2
Chum	Ex-Vessel	Benchmark	Regions touched by the oil spill	Bristol Bay	Table 6.2
Salmon	Ex-Vessel	Benchmark	Chignik Bay	Bristol Bay	Table 6.2
Salmon	Ex-Vessel	Benchmark	Cook Inlet	Bristol Bay	Table 6.2
Salmon	Ex-Vessel	Benchmark	Kodiak	Bristol Bay	Table 6.2
Salmon	Ex-Vessel	Salmon Reduced Form Model, Aggregate Price	Regions touched by the oil spill	—	Chapter 7

Table 12.5 (cont.)
Statistical Evidence Consistent with the Absence of a 1989 Effect on Alaskan Seafood Prices

Species	Price	Model	Region	Benchmark Area	Reference
Chinook	Ex-Vessel	Salmon Reduced Form Model, Pooled	Regions touched by the oil spill	—	Table 7.1
Pink	Ex-Vessel	Salmon Reduced Form Model, Pooled	Regions touched by the oil spill	—	Table 7.1
Sockeye	Ex-Vessel	Salmon Reduced Form Model, Pooled	Regions touched by the oil spill	—	Table 7.1
Chinook	Ex-Vessel	Salmon Reduced Form Model, Individual Species	Regions touched by the oil spill	—	Table 7.2
Chum	Ex-Vessel	Salmon Reduced Form Model, Individual Species	Regions touched by the oil spill	—	Table 7.2
Coho	Ex-Vessel	Salmon Reduced Form Model, Individual Species	Regions touched by the oil spill	—	Table 7.2
Pink	Ex-Vessel	Salmon Reduced Form Model, Individual Species	Regions touched by the oil spill	—	Table 7.2
Sockeye	Ex-Vessel	Salmon Reduced Form Model, Individual Species	Regions touched by the oil spill	—	Table 7.2
Chinook	Processor	Fresh-Frozen Processor Price Model Based on Ex-Vessel Prices	Alaska	—	Table 8.4
Sockeye	Processor	Fresh-Frozen Processor Price Model Based on Ex-Vessel Prices	Alaska	—	Table 8.4
Pink	Processor	Fresh-Frozen Processor Price Model Based on Ex-Vessel Prices	Alaska	—	Table 8.4
Coho	Processor	Fresh-Frozen Processor Price Model Based on Ex-Vessel Prices	Alaska	—	Table 8.4

Table 12.5 (cont.)
Statistical Evidence Consistent with the Absence of a 1989 Effect on Alaskan Seafood Prices

Species	Price	Model	Region	Benchmark Area	Reference
Chum	Processor	Fresh-Frozen Processor Price Model Based on Ex-Vessel Prices	Alaska	—	Table 8.4
Chinook	Processor	Canned Processor Price Model Based on Ex-Vessel Prices	Alaska	—	Table 8.4
Coho	Processor	Canned Processor Price Model Based on Ex-Vessel Prices	Alaska	—	Table 8.4
Salmon	Processor	Fresh-Frozen Processor Price Model Based on Ex-Vessel Prices	Southeast	—	Table 8.5
Salmon	Processor	Fresh-Frozen Processor Price Model Based on Ex-Vessel Prices	Prince William Sound	—	Table 8.5
Salmon	Processor	Fresh-Frozen Processor Price Model Based on Ex-Vessel Prices	Kodiak	—	Table 8.5
Salmon	Processor	Fresh-Frozen Processor Price Model Based on Ex-Vessel Prices	Peninsula/Aleutians	—	Table 8.5
Salmon	Processor	Fresh-Frozen Processor Price Model Based on Ex-Vessel Prices	Bristol Bay	—	Table 8.5
Salmon	Processor	Canned Processor Price Model Based on Ex-Vessel Prices	Cook Inlet	—	Table 8.5
Chinook	Processor	Fresh-Frozen Processor Price Model Based on BC Benchmark	Alaska	British Columbia	Table 8.6
Sockeye	Processor	Fresh-Frozen Processor Price Model Based on BC Benchmark	Alaska	British Columbia	Table 8.6

Table 12.5 (cont.)
Statistical Evidence Consistent with the Absence of a 1989 Effect on Alaskan Seafood Prices

Species	Price	Model	Region	Benchmark Area	Reference
Pink	Processor	Fresh-Frozen Processor Price Model Based on BC Benchmark	Alaska	British Columbia	Table 8.6
Chum	Processor	Fresh-Frozen Processor Price Model Based on BC Benchmark	Alaska	British Columbia	Table 8.6
Chinook	Processor	Fresh-Frozen Processor Price Model Based on BC Benchmark	Regions touched by the oil spill	British Columbia	Table 8.6
Sockeye	Processor	Fresh-Frozen Processor Price Model Based on BC Benchmark	Regions touched by the oil spill	British Columbia	Table 8.6
Coho	Processor	Fresh-Frozen Processor Price Model Based on BC Benchmark	Regions touched by the oil spill	British Columbia	Table 8.6
Pink	Processor	Fresh-Frozen Processor Price Model Based on BC Benchmark	Regions touched by the oil spill	British Columbia	Table 8.6
Chum	Processor	Fresh-Frozen Processor Price Model Based on BC Benchmark	Regions touched by the oil spill	British Columbia	Table 8.6
Chinook	Processor	Canned Processor Price Model Based on BC Benchmark	Alaska	British Columbia	Table 8.7
Sockeye	Processor	Canned Processor Price Model Based on BC Benchmark	Alaska	British Columbia	Table 8.7
Coho	Processor	Canned Processor Price Model Based on BC Benchmark	Alaska	British Columbia	Table 8.7
Chum	Processor	Canned Processor Price Model Based on BC Benchmark	Alaska	British Columbia	Table 8.7

Table 12.5 (cont.)
Statistical Evidence Consistent with the Absence of a 1989 Effect on Alaskan Seafood Prices

Species	Price	Model	Region	Benchmark Area	Reference
Chinook	Processor	Canned Processor Price Model Based on BC Benchmark	Regions touched by the oil spill	British Columbia	Table 8.7
Sockeye	Processor	Canned Processor Price Model Based on BC Benchmark	Regions touched by the oil spill	British Columbia	Table 8.7
Coho	Processor	Canned Processor Price Model Based on BC Benchmark	Regions touched by the oil spill	British Columbia	Table 8.7
Chum	Processor	Canned Processor Price Model Based on BC Benchmark	Regions touched by the oil spill	British Columbia	Table 8.7
Salmon roe	Processor	Fresh-Frozen Processor Price Model Based on BC Benchmark	Regions not touched by the oil spill	British Columbia	Chapter 8
Sac roe herring	Ex-Vessel Seine	Benchmark Weighted least squares	Regions touched by the oil spill	British Columbia	Table 9.2
Halibut	Ex-Vessel	Extension of Lin et al.	United States	—	Table 9.5
Halibut	Ex-Vessel	Revision of Lin et al.	United States	—	Table 9.5
Dungeness crab	Ex-Vessel	Benchmark	PrinceWilliam Sound	Kodiak	Chapter 9
Sac roe herring	Processor	Frozen Processor Price Model Based on Ex-vessel Prices	Southeast	—	Table 9.7
Sac roe herring	Processor	Frozen Processor Price Model Based on Ex-vessel Prices	Prince William Sound/ Cook Inlet	—	Table 9.7

Note: Statistical significance is based on a 10 percent two-tailed test.

Table 12.6
Economic Evidence Consistent with the Absence of 1989 Price Effects from Oil Spill

- Consistency of press reports in attributing low 1989 prices to large harvests, high inventories, competition from other sources of seafood, and reasons other than the oil spill

- Evidence of factors other than oil spill that explain price movements

- Absence of widespread labeling of source of seafood in retail trade

- Methodological problems and miscalculations in NRC study and sensitivity of its results to specification

- Econometric evidence that Japanese consumer demand for salmon did not change in 1989

- Econometric evidence that Alaskan ex-vessel salmon prices did not change relative to British Columbian ex-vessel prices in 1989 in benchmark model

- Econometric evidence that ex-vessel salmon prices in regions touched by the oil spill did not change relative to British Columbian ex-vessel prices in 1989 in benchmark model

- Absence of a consistent pattern of 1989 ex-vessel salmon price suppression in regions touched by the oil spill in reduced form price models

- Absence of a significant difference between 1989 price deviations in British Columbia and Alaskan regions touched by the oil spill in reduced form price models

- Econometric evidence for Alaskan fresh-frozen salmon processor prices based on ex-vessel prices

- Absence of a consistent pattern of 1989 salmon processor price effects in Alaska relative to British Columbia.

- Absence of a consistent pattern of 1989 ex-vessel price suppression for non - salmon species in econometric price and benchmark models

- The absence of a pattern of price effects from local and supply-related factors

- Findings of a survey by the Alaska Seafood Marketing Institute that traders and consumers did not actually change seafood purchase patterns as a result of the oil spill

- The absence of reports of actual contamination of Alaska seafood

- Absence of evidence to force labeling on Alaskan seafood

Table 12.7
Average Ex-Vessel Prices for Alaskan Seafood in 1989
(in 1989 dollars per pound)

Species and Region	Estimated Average Prices for All Gear Types
Sockeye Salmon	
Chignik*	$1.65
Cook Inlet	$1.72
Kodiak	$1.68
Prince William Sound	$2.08
Pink Salmon	
Chignik*	$0.33
Cook Inlet	$0.38
Kodiak	$0.53
Prince William Sound	$0.40
Coho Salmon	
Chignik*	$0.78
Cook Inlet	$0.69
Kodiak	$0.77
Prince William Sound	$0.62
Chum Salmon	
Chignik*	$0.40
Cook Inlet	$0.39
Kodiak	$0.37
Prince William Sound	$0.42
Chinook Salmon	
Chignik*	$1.05
Cook Inlet	$1.35
Kodiak	$1.17
Prince William Sound	$1.88
Sac Roe Herring†	
Cook Inlet	$0.32
Kodiak	$0.44
Prince William Sound	$0.19
Wild Roe on Kelp (Ribbon kelp)	
Prince William Sound	$2.00
Wild Roe on Kelp (Hair kelp)	
Prince William Sound	$0.89
Wild Roe on Kelp (Sieve kelp)	
Prince William Sound	$1.35

Table 12.7 (cont.)
Average Ex-Vessel Prices for Alaskan Seafood in 1989
(in 1989 dollars per pound)

Species and Region	Estimated Average Prices for All Gear Types
Roe on Kelp in Pounds	
Prince William Sound	$9.75
Halibut*	
Chignik	$1.46
Cook Inlet	$1.48
Kodiak	$1.51
Prince William Sound	$1.47
Sablefish*	
Cook Inlet	$1.40
Prince William Sound	$1.48
Spot Shrimp*	
Cook Inlet	$3.10
Kodiak	$6.19
Prince William Sound	$3.64
Pink Shrimp	
Prince William Sound**	$0.30
Statewide††	$4.14
Sidestripe Shrimp*	
Prince William Sound	$1.26
Coonstripe Shrimp*	
Prince William Sound	$1.76
Brown King Crab*	
Prince William Sound	$3.81
Dungeness Crab*	
Prince William Sound	$1.00

* Only one gear type used.
† Sac roe herring prices have been adjusted for 10 percent roe content.
** Trawl gear were used for pink shrimp in Prince William Sound.
†† Pot gear were used for pink shrimp statewide.

Table 12.8
Processor Prices for Salmon in 1989 in Regions Touched by the Oil Spill
(in 1989 dollars per pound)

Species and Region	Fresh/Frozen	Canned
Chinook Salmon		
Chignik-Peninsula†	$2.04	
Cook Inlet	$3.37	
Kodiak	$3.44	
Prince William Sound	$3.43	$3.05
Sockeye Salmon		
Chignik	$3.10	
Cook Inlet	$2.98	$4.07
Kodiak	$3.18	
Prince William Sound	$3.48	$4.68
Coho Salmon		
Chignik-Peninsula†	$1.81	
Cook Inlet	$1.78	$3.09
Kodiak	$1.86	
Prince William Sound	$1.78	$2.82
Pink Salmon		
Chignik-Peninsula†	$0.69	
Cook Inlet	$0.91	$2.23
Kodiak	$0.89	
Prince William Sound	$0.97	$1.99
Chum Salmon		
Chignik-Peninsula†	$1.10	
Cook Inlet	$1.44	$1.95
Kodiak	$1.80	
Prince William Sound	$1.34	$1.79
Salmon Roe		
Chignik-Peninsula†	$5.02	
Cook Inlet	$5.69	
Kodiak	$4.00	
Prince William Sound	$3.16	

Source: CFEC processor data.

† CFEC processor data do not provide Chignik prices for chinook, coho, pink, and chum in 1989. We provide CFEC's Chignik-Peninsula prices for those species instead.

Note: Because of the absence of claims of price suppression for non-salmon species, only processor prices for salmon are shown.

13

Conclusion

The economic effects of disasters include changes in prices of goods or in the amount of goods traded. A disaster may make some individuals worse off and perhaps some better off. The U.S. liability system provides individuals with incentives to account for the costs of a disaster. If the liability system ignores or underestimates a significant component of those costs, individuals do not have incentives to take adequate steps to avoid disasters. If, on the other hand, the liability system exaggerates or overestimates the costs, individuals are induced to invest more than is optimal in accident avoidance.

The effects of disasters tend to be both varied and widespread, making it difficult for the liability system to account for all the costs. Nevertheless, society may choose to invest the resources in determining the costs. Without knowing the costs, the liability system would be unable to provide the proper incentives for precautions, and the costs to society of improper levels of accident avoidance could be very high for disasters.

In most circumstances, an individual takes precautions against accidents based on his or her assessment of the likelihood of an accident occurring and that portion of probable injuries to the victims and their property that will be felt directly (or through liability) by that individual. Victims may claim commercial losses if they or their property were injured as a result of an accident. To induce individuals to make the optimal investment in accident avoidance, commercial and other losses must be properly calculated.

Small accidents are not likely to affect prices, although they may cause commercial losses. Great disasters, however, can so affect the trade of goods that prices change. Measurement of those price effects is central to the task of implementing the liability system. We propose a useful framework for describing the price effects of disaster. Disasters may primarily affect the demand for a product, the supply of the product, or both. The *Exxon Valdez* disaster has provided a case study for this approach.

Under most aspects of tort law, individuals not physically touched by an oil spill would not have standing to sue for damages. The liability system, however, exempts fishermen from that rule. Thus, the *Exxon Valdez* case falls into a unique legal niche.

To measure price effects resulting from the oil spill, we postulated different sources of change in demand and supply of Alaskan seafood. Several quantitative models were used to test our hypotheses. One of our quantitative models tested for changes in Japanese demand for salmon. Another utilized econometric techniques that tested simultaneously for changes in demand and supply of Alaskan seafood. The third quantitative model used a benchmark approach to compare seafood prices in Alaska with those in British Columbia. We also examined the prices of a related commodity, commercial fishing permits, for reflections of changes in the expected profitability of commercial fishing in Alaska.

In addition to our quantitative models, we considered several sources of qualitative evidence. These included consumer surveys, press reports, and, in this case, the conditions necessary for the existence of a price effect (seafood labeling).

We found that a precise measurement of price effects was difficult to achieve. Any model could provide results that contradicted any other model. For this reason we employed a series of quantitative and qualitative approaches for testing our hypotheses about the impact of the disaster on prices. The preponderance of the evidence was consistent with the absence of a price change caused by the *Exxon Valdez* oil spill.

There is little in these methods that is unique to Alaskan seafood. They can be used to determine price effects in other maritime disasters and to evaluate whether to change the standing rule to permit recovery of commercial losses in nonmaritime disaster cases. Our models could be adapted easily to measure price effects of product disasters (e.g., Tylenol, Ford's Pinto, or Rely tampons) or natural disasters (e.g., drought or fire). Careful measurement of price effects in such disasters enables the liability system to provide the incentive for optimal accident avoidance.

Appendix 1

A Brief Description of Statistical Terminology

Statistical data analysis has three components: model specification, estimation, and statistical assessment. This appendix provides a brief description of these components for readers who may be unfamiliar with statistical terms. Further details can be found in statistics textbooks. One textbook written for lawyers is D. W. Barnes and J. M. Conley, *Statistical Evidence in Litigation: Methodology, Procedure, and Practice*, Boston: Little, Brown and Company, 1986.

MODEL SPECIFICATION

The first step is the specification of the mathematical relationship between the quantitative variables of interest. This specification is referred to as the **model**. Our models relate some **dependent variable** (in our case typically some Alaskan seafood price) to a set of **explanatory variables** (variables that we suppose influence, or can help predict, the Alaskan price). Associated with every explanatory variable is its **coefficient**, which indicates the quantitative relationship of this variable to the Alaskan price.

Our study makes frequent use of a particular type of explanatory variable called a **dummy variable**. A dummy variable has a value of either zero or one. We often use dummy variables that have a value of one for 1989 observations and a value of zero for other years. The coefficient of a 1989 dummy variable can be used to help determine the presence of a 1989 price effect.

A simple benchmark price model could be written:

$$\text{Alaska Price} = a + b \times \text{British Columbia Price} + c \times \text{1989 Dummy Variable}$$

The numbers b and c are the coefficients of the indicated explanatory variables. The coefficient c indicates how the Alaska price was different in 1989, taking into account the British Columbia price of that year.

ESTIMATION

The values of the coefficients in our models are estimated using **linear regression,** a standard statistical technique. The estimated coefficients are often referred to as the **estimates**. We do not presume that these estimates are fixed values or known with exact certainty. Rather they represent our best determinations of what the true coefficients are, given our sample of actual market data.

Our explanatory variables will not be able to completely predict the Alaska price. In other words, the model will not perfectly fit the data. The discrepancies between the actual values of a price series and the values predicted by the model are called the **residuals**. Ideally, the residuals will be small and will show no predictable pattern. The residuals represent the effects of factors that influence price but were not explicitly included in the model plus errors in the measurement of price.

To learn how well an estimated model has fit the data, we use a common measure called the **R-squared.** The R-squared of a regression is a number between zero and one. One indicates a perfect fit; zero indicates no fit. The R-squared can be viewed as a measure of the ability of the explanatory variables to account for the fluctuations in the dependent variable. The R-squared is only a measure of the closeness of fit of the linear relationship. A high R-squared does not establish the existence of a causal connection. An **adjusted R-squared** is simply an R-squared that takes into account the number of explanatory variables. There is usually a small quantitative difference between an adjusted and a non-adjusted R-squared. Many statisticians feel that the adjusted R-squared is preferable when the sample size is very small.

STATISTICAL EVALUATION

As important as estimating the coefficients of the model is estimating their accuracy. The primary factor determining the accuracy of statistical estimates is the **sample size**, the number of observations used to generate the estimates. Some of the regressions in our study have unavoidably small sample sizes.

The accuracy of the estimate can be evaluated by the use of **confidence intervals**. The confidence interval is set so there is some prespecified probability that the interval contains the true value of the coefficient. For example, we might estimate a 1989 price effect with a 90 percent confidence interval between -$0.20 and $0.05, meaning that there is a 90 percent probability that the true size of the effect is contained in this interval. Wide confidence intervals are often not useful. Nevertheless, they accurately summarize the uncertainty arising due to sample size limitations.

Another measure of an estimate's accuracy is its **standard error**. The standard error is a measure of the average or typical error of the estimate. There is a very close relationship between the width of an estimate's confidence interval and its standard error.

In our study we frequently ask whether the coefficient of the 1989 dummy variable is **statistically significant**. To answer this question, we put forward the **null hypothesis** that the true value of the coefficient is zero. If the true value of a coefficient is zero, the associated explanatory variable has no effect on price. We then "test" this hypothesis against some alternative by seeing how well it conforms with our data.

Even when the true value of a coefficient is zero, we will never in practice obtain an estimate of exactly zero. We should, however, obtain a small value of the coefficient. Exactly how big an estimate can be while remaining statistically indistinguishable from zero is determined with the help of the standard error. The ratio of the estimated coefficient to its standard error is called the ***t*-statistic**. Values of the *t*-statistic that are large in magnitude (absolute values) lead to skepticism about the null hypothesis. Estimates that have *t*-statistics larger than a certain "critical value" are statistically significant. Statistically significant estimates enable us to reject the null hypothesis that the coefficient of the variable in question is zero.

It is possible that the true value of the coefficient is non-zero, but because the standard error of the estimate is high, the *t*-statistic falls below the critical value. Then the estimated coefficient would not be judged statistically significant and the evidence against the null hypothesis would be too weak for it to be rejected. We say that we "fail to reject" the null hypothesis rather than that we "accept" the null hypothesis. Statistical testing operates very much like the U.S. legal system: a person (hypothesis) is innocent (true) until proven guilty (false). Insufficient evidence leads to the conclusion of innocence (or failure to reject the null hypothesis).

The critical value of a hypothesis test is based on the **significance level** of the test. Significance levels are usually between 10 percent and 1 percent. The data analyst must chose the significance level; it is not estimated. If the chosen significance level is 10 percent, the probability of having a *t*-statistic different from the critical value, *when the null hypothesis is true*, is 10 percent. Estimating a large *t*-statistic suggests discord between the data and the hypothesis.

Statistical theory provides the mathematical relationship between the chosen significance level and the corresponding critical value. An estimate needs to be 1.65 times the magnitude of its standard error (i.e., have a *t*-statistic of 1.65) to be deemed significant at the 10 percent level.

It is not always clear what the significance level should be. The lower the significance level, the more difficult it is for an estimate to be deemed statistically significant. A test with a lower significance level is more stringent. In the tables of results in our study, we provide ***p*-values** that allow the reader some flexibility in determining statistical significance. The *p*-value is a rescaling of the *t*-statistic that allows it to be directly compared with the significance level. For example, a *p*-value of .08 means that the coefficient is significant at the 10 percent level, but not at the 5 percent level. A *p*-value of .03 implies significance at the 5 percent level but not at the 1 percent level. The lower the *p*-value, the lower the significance level at which the null hypothesis can be rejected.

The issue of statistical significance is related to confidence intervals. If the confidence interval of an estimate contains zero, then the estimate is not statistically significant.

When testing the null hypothesis that the true value of a certain coefficient is zero, one could consider three **alternative hypotheses**: the true value is *greater* than zero, the true value is *less* than zero, or the true value is simply *different* from zero. The choice of alternative has bearing on interpretation of the *t*-statistic. If one is interested in the possibility that the coefficient is different from zero, then only the magnitude of the *t*-statistic matters. On the other hand, if one is only interested in, say, the possibility that the coefficient is less than zero, then large *negative* values of the *t*-statistic lead to rejection of the null hypothesis. Large positive values of the *t*-statistic would not lead to rejection of the null hypothesis in this case.

Tests to see if the coefficient is different from zero are often referred to as **two-tailed tests**. Tests to see if the coefficient is less than or greater than zero are called **one-tailed tests**. In this book, we conduct both types of tests, depending on the context. Unless otherwise noted, the significance level of two-tailed tests is 10 percent, and the significance level of one-tailed tests is 5 percent. When *p*-values are provided in the report, they pertain to two-tailed tests.

Appendix 2

Modeling Japanese Consumer Demand

This appendix presents the economic theory and econometric assumptions underlying our model of Japanese consumer demand for seafood.

ECONOMIC THEORY

In order to conduct an informative examination of Japanese consumption data, we develop and estimate a statistical model of purchasing behavior. The two most important determinants of purchasing behavior are income levels and relative prices. The relationship between the share of a budget w_i devoted to a particular commodity i and a consumer's income level x—the so-called Engel relationship—was analyzed in 1943 by H. Working.[1] A particularly successful statistical form is

$$w_i = a_i + b_i \ln(x) \tag{1}$$

where w_i is the budget share of the ith commodity, $\ln()$ is the natural logarithmic function, and a_i and b_i are parameters to be estimated. The b_i parameter indicates whether the commodity is a luxury or an ordinary good.

A natural extension of this specification accounts for the effects of changes in relative prices between commodities that would be expected to occur over time. The so-called Almost Ideal Demand System (AIDS) does this in a manner that retains considerable flexibility in the estimation process.[2] The basis of the AIDS specification is the assumption that consumers are minimizing the cost associated with achieving some level of utility. The cost function is given by

$$\ln c(u,p) = a(p) + ub(p) \tag{2}$$

where $a(p)$ and $b(p)$ are functions of prices.

It is further assumed that

$$a(p) = a_0 + \sum_k a_k + 1/2 \sum_k \sum_l g^*_{kl} \ln p_k \ln p_l \tag{3}$$

and

$$b(p) = b_0 \pi p_k^{b_k} \tag{4}$$

where a, b, and g are parameters. If these two equations are substituted into the original cost function, the budget shares for the AIDS model can be specified as

$$w_i = a_i + \sum_j g_{ij} \ln p_j + b_i \ln(x/P) \tag{5}$$

where P is a price index defined by

$$\ln(P) = a_0 + \sum_k a_k \ln p_k + 1/2 \sum_k \sum_l g_{kl} \ln p_k \ln p_l \tag{6}$$

and the parameters g are defined by

$$g_{ij} = 1/2 (g^*_{ij} + g^*_{ji}) = g_{ji} \tag{7}$$

The AIDS model can be considered a first-order approximation of the general relationship among the shares, the logarithm of income, and the logarithms of the prices. To be consistent with economic theory of optimizing behavior, three restrictions must be satisfied. The first is the adding up restriction, or

$$\sum_k a_k = 1, \ \sum_k b_k = 0, \ \sum_k g_{kj} = 0 \tag{8}$$

The second restriction is homogeneity, or

$$\sum_k g_{jk} = 0 \tag{9}$$

The final restriction, that of symmetry, is satisfied if

$$g_{ij} = g_{ji} \tag{10}$$

The unrestricted estimation of (5) will automatically satisfy the adding up restriction. The homogeneity and symmetry restrictions can be statistically tested by estimating the model in both an unrestricted and restricted form. In practice, the exact price index (6) is approximated with Stone's Price Index, which is

$$\log P = \sum_k w_k \ln p_k \tag{11}$$

Stone's Price Index avoids the nonlinearities inherent if (6) is used. The b parameters in the system indicate whether the commodity in question is a luxury (b>0) or an ordinary good. The g parameters measure the changes in budget shares associated with a ceteris paribus change in relative prices.

The AIDS model has been widely applied in studies of consumption behavior, particularly food consumption behavior. Its advantages are that it is flexible and relatively easy to estimate. The model allows computation of familiar own-price and cross-price elasticities as well as expenditure elasticities. A disadvantage is that it is not easy to estimate confidence intervals for these elasticities since the model is estimated in share form and does not produce elasticity estimates directly.

Expenditure elasticities are computed as

$$e_{i,x} = 1 + b_i/w_i \tag{12}$$

Own-price elasticities are computed as

$$e_{i,pi} = -1 + g_{ii}/w_i - b_i \tag{13}$$

Note that both expenditure elasticities and own-price elasticities are calculated from basic parameters estimated in the full AIDS system.[3] Variance estimates for the elasticities could be estimated using a bootstrapping or Taylor-series approximation method, although we have not done so.

ECONOMETRIC ASSUMPTIONS

We assume that the typical household is minimizing the cost function in equation (2), subject to an expenditure constraint on a sub-budget for fish and shellfish. The budget shares devoted to any fish commodity i is given by the budget share equation (5).

An underlying assumption is that fish expenditures are "separable" from other categories of major food purchases. This means that households have separate sub-budgets for different expenditure groups, such as food, clothing, and household items. Then within the food group there are further sub-budgets allocated to fish, meat, fruits and vegetables, and so on. This allows us to separate the fish and shellfish into an independent group within which budget shares are determined only by relative prices within the group and the group expenditure allocation. Without these assumptions, the system would have to be enlarged to include cross-effects between meat and fish, clothing and food, and so on.

The complete model was estimated using the Stone's Price Index approximation in equation (11). The system was estimated as a seemingly unrelated regression, corrected for first-order autocorrelation, and with the restrictions for homogeneity and symmetry in equations (9) and (10) imposed. Also included were shift dummies for each month in the intercept term to allow for seasonal patterns of consumption. The system was estimated by dropping one equation whose choice did not affect results. Estimating as a seemingly unrelated equation improves efficiency by accounting for any covariance between share equations.

The correction for first-order autocorrelation follows a procedure suggested by Berndt and Savin.[4] This technique estimates a single autocorrelation coefficient for the whole system. First, an uncorrected system is estimated, and the errors are saved and stacked. Care should be taken not to overlap errors from different share equations. Next, the errors are regressed on lagged errors to get an estimate of the system first-order autocorrelation coefficient. Finally, the estimate of the coefficient is used to transform lagged right-hand side variables. The regression is rerun including these transformed variables. In the system reported here, the system auto correlation coefficient estimate is 0.476.

NOTES

1. *Cf.* H. Working, *Statistical Laws of Family Expenditures*, 38 JOURNAL OF THE AMERICAN STATISTICAL ASSOCIATION at 43–56 (March 1943).

2. A.S. Deaton & J. Muellbauer, *An Almost Ideal Demand System*, 70 AMERICAN ECONOMIC REVIEW No. 3 at 312–336 (June 1980).

3. There is some confusion in the literature regarding how to compute price elasticities in the AIDS model. The problems arise in part because the typical estimation formulation uses the Stone's Index as an approximation to the true price index. These issues are addressed in R. Green & J. Alston, *Elasticities in AIDS Models*, 72 AMERICAN JOURNAL OF AGRICULTURAL ECONOMICS, No. 2 at 442–5 (May 1990).

4. E. Berndt and E. Savin, *Estimation and Hypothesis Testing in Singular Equaton Systems with Autoregressive Disturbances*, 43 ECONOMETRICA at 937–957 (1975).

Appendix 3

Reduced Form Model for Alaskan Salmon

The reduced form econometric model for Alaskan salmon contains cross-sectional and time-series dimensions. For each of the 13 years covered in the data, there are more than 100 ex-vessel prices. These prices correspond to the five species and to multiple combinations of region and gear type. Thus, we have a large data set of 1,373 observations.

The primary issues in this study pertain to the time dimension. We are most interested in the possible shift in prices in 1989, as viewed in light of the economic environment that prevailed that year. Therefore, the cross-sectional information in the data is not especially useful.

Although our original data set contains prices from the entire state of Alaska, we focus on the four oil-touched regions: Prince William Sound, Cook Inlet, Kodiak Island, and Chignik. Annual average prices from these regions are the basic variable used in our analysis. We average prices over gear types, regions, and species. To explain the variation in this average price, we regress it on the price-determining factors discussed in chapter 7. We are left with 13 annual price observations and at least five or six corresponding explanatory variables. The smallness of this sample size limits the strength of any conclusions that can be drawn from the analysis.

Ordinarily in a model with cross-sectional and time-series dimensions, the Generalized Least Squares (GLS) estimator is used. This estimator seeks to extract information from the cross-sectional and time-series dimensions and then optimally combine it. In technical jargon, one takes a weighted average of the "within" and the "between" estimates to find the GLS estimate. In our case, the regressors of interest have no cross-sectional variation, hence the "within" estimators do not exist. The estimator we use is essentially the "between" estimator.[1]

Price data are not always available for a given gear-species-region cell for all 13 years. Simple averages could be subject to spurious variation due to the presence or absence of data from high-price or low-price cells. To alleviate this problem, we construct price indexes by regressing the log of real price on gear, species, region, and year dummy variables. We also include as a regressor a variable measuring capacity utilization (the poundage for all salmon caught in a region divided by the 1978–1990 average poundage for that area). We include in the poundage the harvest sold by hatcheries in Prince William Sound and Kodiak Island generally referred to as the "cost recovery harvest." This harvest is not used in the calculation of the ex-vessel price received by commercial fishermen. We use the logarithm of the capacity utilization ratio in the regression.

The coefficients on the year dummy variables are then taken as the average price indexes. This method is an application of the well-known hedonic index technique, and the coefficients of the annual dummy variables could be interpreted as hedonic indexes.[2]

The Commercial Fisheries Entry Commission of the state of Alaska aggregates data geographically. In this aggregation, there is a wide disparity in the poundages and permits associated with the various regions, gear types, and species. Therefore, we weight each observation by its share of the total annual harvest poundage for all regions and gear types. As a result of this weighting scheme, all years are equally weighted. Another possible weighting variable is revenue. The analysis was replicated using revenue weights, and we found the results to be virtually unchanged. In using our hedonic regression technique, we incorporate the weights by estimating the regression using weighted least squares.

We estimate average price indexes for a five-species average as well as for individual species. To obtain indexes for an individual species, only prices for that species were used in the regression.

Ex-vessel prices are available for British Columbia for the years 1984 to 1989. For these data, like the Alaskan data, we construct annual indexes of the log of real prices. A reduced form regression can be estimated by pooling the Alaskan and British Columbian price indexes.

NOTES

1. For details *see* JUDGE G. G., W. E. GRIFFITHS, R. C. HILL, H. LUTKEPOHL & T-C. LEE, THE THEORY AND PRACTICE OF ECONOMETRICS 522–24(2nd ed. 1985); G.S. MADDALA, ECONOMETRICS 326–31 (1977).

2. *See entry Hedonic Functions and Hedonic Indexes* in J. EATWELL, M. MILGATE & P. NEWMAN, THE NEW PALGRAVE: A DICTIONARY OF ECONOMICS 630–33 (1987).

Appendix 4

Supply Effects

The oil spill reduced the Alaskan seafood harvest in 1989. All other things constant, a smaller harvest would have raised the price of seafood. This appendix describes how we estimate the volume of salmon harvest that did not reach the market in 1989.

Although the 1989 salmon harvest for some gear types was lower due to the oil spill, the 1989 harvest for other gears and for certain hatcheries was higher. Consequently, using just the forgone harvest for closed fisheries would overestimate the volume of salmon harvest that did not reach the market in 1989. To compute the net volume of harvest (in pounds) that did not reach market in 1989, we subtract the actual total harvest for each species in each oil-touched area (the sum of all gears for commercial fishermen and the hatchery cost recovery harvest) from estimates of the harvest that would have occurred in 1989 in the absence of the oil spill (*see* Table A4.1). The harvest from the Copper and Bering rivers is entirely excluded from the analysis.

The estimates of the salmon harvest that would have occurred in 1989 in the absence of the oil spill came from biologists.[1] They provided catch estimates (in numbers of fish) and corresponding mean fish weight estimates (in pounds). The actual harvest for commercial fishermen (in pounds) came from the Commecial Fisheries Entry Commission.[2] The actual hatchery cost recovery harvest (in numbers of fish) came from the biologists.[3] We applied the same mean estimate of fish weight as provided above to the actual hatchery cost recovery harvest.

NOTES

1. *Fax* from Alan N. Braverman, Wilmer, Cutler & Pickering, Dec. 9, 1991.
2. CFEC 1980–90 MMT Reports by Fishery, Year, & Species, Project 91166, August 20, 1991.
3. *Fax* from Karl English, LGL Limited, Oct. 18, 1991.

Table A4.1
Forgone Salmon Catch, 1989

Species	Prince William Sound[a]	Cook Inlet[b] Lower	Upper	Kodiak	Chignik
Predicted Total Catch (Number of Fish)					
Chinook	1,183	1,893	28,442	4,500	3,900
Chum	1,120,000	47,779	967,355	1,007,800	56,700
Coho	223,150	18,360	700,458	208,100	160,600
Pink	21,374,000	1,542,014	109,429	18,880,566	710,400
Sockeye	161,000	163,923	5,633,171	2,749,580	1,353,720
Average Weight (Lbs.)					
Chinook	25.58	14.10	24.04	13.00	21.65
Chum	8.71	8.60	7.25	8.35	7.81
Coho	7.75	7.00	6.58	8.45	8.19
Pink	3.44	3.10	3.19	3.45	3.61
Sockeye	6.77	4.60	6.60	5.63	6.87
Predicted Total Catch (Lbs.)					
Chinook	30,260	26,691	683,746	58,500	84,435
Chum	9,759,417	410,899	7,013,324	8,415,130	442,827
Coho	1,728,932	128,520	4,609,014	1,758,445	1,315,314
Pink	73,460,436	4,780,243	349,079	65,158,598	2,564,544
Sockeye	1,089,565	754,046	37,178,929	15,488,841	9,300,056
Actual Total Catch (Lbs.)					
Chinook	17,111		669,119	2,037	76,698
Chum	8,802,447		981,579	174,158	11,888
Coho	1,419,944		2,277,566	14,139	559,140
Pink	74,197,267		4,213,584	20,113,981	94,269
Sockeye	987,933		33,654,724	7,098,034	7,922,748
Forgone Catch (Lbs.)					
Chinook	13,149		41,318	56,463	7,737
Chum	956,970		6,442,644	8,240,972	430,939
Coho	308,988		2,459,968	1,744,306	756,174
Pink	(736,831)		915,738	45,044,617	2,470,275
Sockeye	101,632		4,278,250	8,390,944	1,377,308

a Catch data exclude the Copper and Bering rivers.

b CFEC did not provide separate catch statistics for Lower and Upper Cook Inlet. Upper Cook Inlet predicted catch (in numbers) overestimates the catch because it sums actual set net catch and predicted drift catch.

Selected Bibliography

Alaska Seafood Marketing Institute, Salmon 2000 (undated).

Alley, A., *Speculation, Risk and Consumer Demand in Japanese Markets for Herring Roe*, Proceedings of the International Seafood Trade Conference 123 (September 1982).

Anderson, J. L., J. T. Gledhill, and Y. Kusakabe, The Japanese Seafood Market. Herring Roe 25–28 (February 1989) (prepared for the Canadian Department of Fisheries and Oceans).

ANDERSON, J. L. AND KUSAKABE, Y. THE JAPANESE SEAFOOD MARKET: SALMON, Market Analysis Group, Canadian Department of Fisheries and Oceans, Economic and Commercial Analysis Report No. 21, April 1989.

B.C. SALMON FARMERS ASSOCIATION, CURRENT DEVELOPMENTS IN WORLD SALMON MARKETS: IMPLICATIONS FOR THE CANADIAN SALMON FARMING INDUSTRY, Canadian Department of Fisheries and Oceans, Economic and Commercial Analysis Report No. 46, January 1990.

CANADIAN DEPARTMENT OF FISHERIES AND OCEANS, ANNUAL SUMMARY OF BRITISH COLUMBIA COMMERCIAL CATCH STATISTICS, PACIFIC REGION (1989).

Commercial Fisheries Entry Commission, State of Alaska, Annual Report (1990).

Doll, J., *An Econometric Analysis of Shrimp Ex-Vessel Prices: 1950–1968*, 54 AMERICAN JOURNAL OF AGRICULTURAL ECONOMICS No. 3 (1972).

Economists Incorporated, An Economic Analysis of the Effect of the *Exxon Valdez* Oil Spill on Alaskan Seafood Prices, report submitted to the Trans-Alaska Pipeline Liability Fund (December 1991).

FOOD AND AGRICULTURE ORGANIZATION, FISHERY STATISTICS YEARBOOK, CATCHES AND LANDINGS, Vol. 68 (1989).

HASTIE, J., AN ECONOMIC ANALYSIS OF MARKETS FOR U.S. SABLEFISH, National Marine Fisheries Service, NOAA Technical Memorandum F/NWC-171, September 1989.

INTERNATIONAL PACIFIC HALIBUT COMMISSION, SCIENTIFIC REPORT NO. 72. METHODS OF POPULATION ASSESSMENT OF PACIFIC HALIBUT.

KARPOFF, J. M., LIMITED ENTRY PERMIT PRICES (State of Alaska, Commercial Fisheries Entry Commission Report No. 83-6, 1983).

Knapp, G., and T. Smith, The Alaska Seafood Industry (1991) (report prepared at the Institute of Social and Economic Research, University of Alaska, Anchorage, for Alaska Department of Commerce and Economic Development & the Alaska Industrial Development and Export Authority).

Lin, Biing-Hwan, H. Richards, and J. Terry. *An Analysis of the Ex-Vessel Demand for Pacific Halibut*, 4 MARINE RESOURCE ECONOMICS 305-314 (1988).

MARKET ANALYSIS GROUP, CANADIAN DEPARTMENT OF FISHERIES AND OCEANS, ECONOMIC AND COMMERCIAL ANALYSIS REPORT 81, SALMON MARKET OUTLOOK (JANUARY 1991).

Mittelhammer, Herrmann, and B. Lin, An Economic Analysis of the Pacific Salmon Industry: Effects of Salmon Farming (1990) (prepared for the National Marine Fisheries Service).

Mittelhammer, Herrmann, and B. Lin, U.S. Salmon Markets: A Survey of Seafood Wholesalers (1990).

MORRISON, R., AND N. DUDIAK, CENTRAL REGION GROUNDFISH REPORT TO THE ALASKA BOARD OF FISHERIES (Division of Commercial Fisheries, Central Region, Alaska Department of Fish and Game, Regional Information Report No. 2H88-6, November 1988).

MUSE, B., PERMIT VALUES AND FISH STOCKS (STATE OF ALASKA, COMMERCIAL FISHERIES ENTRY COMMISSION, Report No. 90-9, 1990).

NATIONAL MARINE FISHERIES SERVICE, NATIONAL OCEANIC AND ATMOSPHERIC ADMINISTRATION, U.S. DEPARTMENT OF COMMERCE, FISHERIES OF THE U.S. (1990).

POSNER, R. A., ECONOMIC ANALYSIS OF LAW, 3rd ed., Little, Brown and Company, Boston (1986).

Shavell, S., *On Liability and Insurance*, 13 BELL JOURNAL OF ECONOMICS (1982), 120–132.

UNITED STATES INTERNATIONAL TRADE COMMISSION, PUBLICATION NO. 2371, FRESH AND CHILLED ATLANTIC SALMON FROM NORWAY (April 1991).

U.S. General Accounting Office, Factors Affecting the Price of Alaskan Bristol Bay Sockeye Salmon (September 1991).

Wellman, K., Chicken of the Sea? The U.S. Consumer Retail Demand for Fish Products (1990) (unpublished Ph.D. dissertation, Dept. of Economics, University of Washington).

Wessells, C., An Economic Analysis of the Japanese Salmon Market: Consumption Patterns, the Role of Inventories and Trade Implications (1990) (unpublished Ph.D. dissertation, Dept. of Agricultural Economics, University of California, Davis).

Index

ADF&G (Alaska Department of Fish and Game), 20, 22, 35, 142 n.16
Alley, A., 63 nn.93, 94
Americanization, 46, 55
Anchorage, 55, 138
Anderson, J.L., 62 n.56, 63 n.92, 72, 81 n.33, 89 n.1, 141 n.8
Aquaculture, 102
Arctic, 140
Atkinson, Bill, 63 n.91, 66, 73, 75, 77–78, 79 n.5, 81 nn.40, 43, 82 nn.53–54, 58, 61, 64, 68, 72, 74, 83 n.83
Atlantic, 38, 41–43, 52–55, 72, 77, 104

Bering, 134, 137, 171, 193
Bernton, H., 61 n.44, 142 n.22
Bonuses, 58–59, 103, 170
Botulism, 70
Brannian, L., and K. Rowell, 141 n.7
Brealy, R.A. & S.C. Meyers, 161 n.1
Bristol Bay: benchmark, 92–99, 126, 133, 149; herring, 66, 77; sockeye, 75; strike, 38, 57. *See also* Regions
British Columbia, 38, 41, 43, 51–54; benchmark for ex-vessel salmon prices, 92–94, 96–97, 98 nn.2, 3, 6, 7, 99 nn.9, 11; benchmark for non-salmon processor prices, 126, 129, 132–133, 138, 140, 148–149; benchmark for salmon processor prices, 115–122; herring, 73, 76; salmon prices, 101, 103–109. *See also* Regions
Burson-Marsteller, 66, 79 n.3

California, 10, 14; roe benchmark, 126, 130, 149
Canada, 35, 38; crab, 46–47; halibut, 133–136; herring, 43, 77; salmon, 41, 51, 53, 55, 72
Canadian Department of Fisheries and Oceans, 61 nn.30, 31, 62 nn.56, 63–65, 67
Canning, 30, 57, 71, 112, 115
CFEC (Commercial Fisheries Entry Commission), 59 n.3, 60 n.22, 63 n.100, 64 n.103, 98 n.5, 103, 114–115, 121, 122 n.1, 132–133, 142 n.16, 148, 150, 152 nn.2, 3, 155
Chignik. *See* Regions
Chile, 22, 53, 75
Chinook. *See* Salmon species
Chum. *See* Salmon species
Clean-up, 16, 71, 73, 78, 151

Coho. *See* Salmon species

Compensation, 26, 103

Contamination, 15, 65–66, 68, 70–71, 78–79

Cook Inlet, 77, 164. *See also* Glacier Bay; Regions

Copper River, 66, 171, 193

Crab: background, 30–31, 35, 46–47, 55–56, 59; closed fisheries, 146, 149; ex-vessel prices, 125–126, 138; permits, 155; processor prices, 140

Cyanide, 9

Derbies, 34

DeVoretz, D. & K. Salvanes, 63 n.80

Dinneford, Elaine, 142 n.27

Dog (chum), 31. *See also* Salmon species

Doll, J., 63 n.101

Dore, I., 81 n.38

Earthquake, 14

Egan, D. & G. Gislason, 80 n.9

Emperor, 75, 77

Europe, 50–51, 54, 75

FAO (Food and Agriculture Organization), 61 nn.42, 48, 50, 62 n.54

Farm-bred, -raised, 22, 53

France, 47, 51–53, 66

Frost, G., 81 n.46

Gazey, Bill, 63 n.99

Gill net, 95, 98 n.7, 126, 129–131, 140, 148–149, 155

Glacier Bay, 64 nn.112, 114, 71, 94, 118, 120

Gledhill, J.T., 63 n.92, 141 n.8

Goldberg, Victor P., 5 n.5

Haddock, 136

Hastie, J., 61 n.46, 63 n.98

Hatcheries, 41, 53, 75, 145, 192–193

Herring: background, 4, 30–31, 34–35, 43, 49, 54–55, 59; closed fisheries, 146, 149; ex-vessel prices, 125–132; permits, 155; press reports, 70–71, 73, 76–78; processor prices, 139–141. *See also* Roe

Hillenbrand, Barry, 17 n.5

Humpy (pink), 31. *See also* Salmon species

Imports, 41, 47, 55–56, 77–78, 85

Inspections, 68, 78

Inventories: halibut, 78; Japan, 4, 22, 41, 52–53, 72, 76, 131; and processor margins, 113; roe-on-kelp, 77–78; supply factor, 13–16, 20, 29, 47, 59, 92; United States, 22, 53; used in model, 101, 103–104, 127, 135; world, 38, 70, 74–75, 79

IPHC (International Pacific Halibut Commission), 46, 61 nn.43, 44, 78, 142 n.23

ITC (U.S. International Trade Commission), 60 n.34, 62 nn.72, 74, 75

Japan: consumption, 49, 52, 54, 85–89, 187; harvest, 38–39, 41, 43, 45–46, 50, 52–53, 55; herring, 54–55, 76–78, 129; imports, 41, 44, 47–52, 54–56; labeling, 72–73, 167; press reports, 70, 75–79; processors, 57–59; survey, 66-69; yen, 74–75, 102. *See also* Emperor; Inventories

Karpoff, J.M., 161 nn.4, 5

Kazunoko, 76–77

Kelp: Ribbon, 131–133, 149; Rockweed, 131–133; Roe-on-kelp, 34, 77–78, 126, 131–133, 148–149

Kenai Peninsula, 129
Ketchikan, 134, 137
King (chinook), 31. *See also* Salmon
    species
Kleeschulte, C., 82 n.50
Knapp, G., 82 n.55
Knapp, G. & T. Smith, 59 n.1, 60
    nn.4, 6, 8, 14, 24, 26, 28, 61
    nn.40, 41, 45, 47, 49, 62 nn.53,
    55, 59, 61, 63 nn.90, 96, 64
    nn.102, 104, 83 n.80, 122 n.3
Kodiak, 70–71, 75, 77. *See also*
    Regions
Korea, 51, 54, 77
Kusakabe, Y., 62 n.56, 63 n.92, 72, 81
    n.33, 89 n.1, 141 n.8

Labeling, 25, 47, 65, 71–73, 79, 182
Landes, William M., 5 n.6
Lee, C., 80 n.13
Lin, Biing-Hwan, H. Richards & J.
    Terry, 142 n.21

Macey, J., G. Miller, M. Mitchell & J.
    Netter, 161 n.2
Magnuson Act, 46
McDowell Group, 61 n.44, 62 n.62,
    64 n.105, 142 n.22
Mittelhammer, Herrman & Lin, 63
    nn.76, 78
Morrison, R. and N. Dudiak, 80 n.7
Morrow, T., 80 n.14
Muse, B., 161 nn.4, 6, 7

Natural Resource Consultants, 64
    nn.107, 109
Nelson, Kristi, 141 n.6, 155
NOAA (National Oceanic and
    Atmospheric Administration), 60
    n.27, 61 n.33, 62 nn.60, 70
Northwest, 53, 99
Norway, 22, 42, 53, 74–75
Noviseau, Chuck, 81 n.37
Nunivak Island, 155

Oakland, 14–15
Ocean-farm, 76
Open-to-entry, 29
Oregon, 38, 42

Pagano, Rosanne, 5 n.11
Peltonen, Gordon, 61 n.43
Pen-reared, 53–54, 75
Permits: number, 29, 34–35, 46;
    value, 35, 153–162
Pesticide, 65
Petersburg/Wrangell, 134, 137
Peyton, Paul, 80 n.15, 81 nn.42, 47
Phillips, Natalie, 5 nn.9, 10, 12–14
Pink. *See* Salmon species
Pintos, 9–10
Posner, Richard A., 5 nn.3, 4, 6
Prince William Sound. *See* Regions

Quotas, 35, 46, 78

Ranching, 50, 85
Reconditioning, 42
Red (sockeye). *See* Salmon species
Regions: background, 30–31, 34, 57;
    canned salmon, 115–117, 120–
    121; closed fisheries, 4, 26, 66,
    71, 77, 108, 125, 129, 136, 137,
    146–149, 170; crab prices, 138–
    139; ex-vessel prices, 96–98,
    104–108, 151, 167; halibut
    prices, 134–135; herring prices,
    121, 129–130, 139–140; per-
    mits, 155-160; processor prices,
    119–121, 139–140; sablefish
    prices, 136–137
Roe: background, 60 nn.13, 14, 164;
    Japanese market, 86, 88; salmon
    roe, 121–122. *See also* Herring
Romeo, Jean B., 17 n.1

Salmon, 4, 20–22, 164, 167, 170–
    171, 182; closed fisheries, 145–
    48; Japanese market, 85–89;

labeling, 72–74; model, 191–93; permits, 155; press reports, 70–71, 75–76; reduced harvests, 150–151; survey of spill effects, 65–67

Salmon species: background, 30–31, 34–35, 38, 41, 47, 49–53, 55, 59; ex-vessel prices, 92, 95–98, 102, 105–106, 108; labeling, 72; processor prices, 111–113, 115, 119, 121

Seine, 98, 129–131, 140, 149, 155

Seward, 55, 138

Shavell, Steven, 5 n.4

Shrimp: background, 31, 35, 46, 55, 59; closed fisheries, 146; ex-vessel prices, 137–138; Japanese market, 86, 88

Sieve, 131, 133, 149

Silver (coho), 31. *See also* Salmon species

Sitka, 129

Skeins, 129

Smith, Hillary H., 17 n.5

Sockeye: Japanese market, 85, 88; press reports, 76, 79. *See also* Salmon species

Southeast. *See* Regions

Surimi, 30

Swordfish, 135–136

Tampons, 9, 11, 182

Tingley, Al, 162 n.9

Togiak, 34, 77, 133

Tokyo, 66, 70, 75

Tylenol, 9, 11–12, 182

Wahpepah, W., 60 n.25, 64 n.108

Washington, 38, 42, 138

Weinberger, Marc G., 17 n.1

Wellman, K., 61 n.52

Wessells, C., 60 n.7, 62 nn.57, 66, 71, 72, 81 nn.32, 35, 36, 89 n.2

Yoachum, Susan, 17 n.6

About the Authors

BRUCE M. OWEN is President of Economists Incorporated, a Washington, D.C., consulting firm specializing in antitrust and regulatory issues. He also teaches a seminar on law and economics at Stanford University's Washington campus. Owen has been an expert witness in a number of antitrust and regulatory proceedings, including *United States vs. AT&T*. In 1992, he headed a World Bank task force that advised the government of Argentina in drafting a new antitrust law. He was also chief economist of the Antitrust Division of the U.S. Department of Justice in the Carter administration, and of the White House Office of Telecommunications Policy in the Nixon administration. Owen is the coauthor of *Electric Utility Mergers: Principles of Antitrust Analysis* (1994).

DAVID A. ARGUE is a senior economist at Economists Incorporated in Washington, D.C. While at Economists Incorporated, he has researched many issues in environmental economics. Previously, he was an economist at the Center for Public Service in Charlottesville, Virginia, and taught undergraduate economics.

HAROLD W. FURCHTGOTT-ROTH is a senior economist at Economists Incorporated in Washington, D.C. He was formerly a research fellow at the Brookings Institution and a member of the research staff at the Center for Naval Analyses. His publications include *International Trade in Computer Software* (Quorum, 1993).

GLORIA J. HURDLE, prior to joining Economists Incorporated in Washington, D.C., spent over 13 years as an economist in the Antitrust Division of the U.S. Department of Justice on the Antitrust Subcommittee of the U.S. Senate, and taught at the Colorado College, the Eastern Michigan University, and the University of Michigan. She has authored or coauthored a number of articles related to industry structure. She has also testified before the U.S. District Court, the Department of Transportation and the Canadian Competition Tribunal. Her work primarily involves transportation, agriculture, and energy.

GALE MOSTELLER, during her years at Economists Incorporated in Washington, D.C., has provided economic analysis and litigation support to law firms, corporations, and government agencies concerning antitrust issues, transfer pricing, FIFRA data compensation and economic damages from false advertising, securities fraud, and contract breach.

ISBN 0-89930-987-9

HARDCOVER BAR CODE